D1526851

THE ABSOLUTE
JOY
OF WORK

ALSO BY CARLETON CARPENTER

THE ABSOLUTE JOY OF WORK

From Vermont to Broadway, Hollywood, and Damn Near 'Round the World

by

Carleton Carpenter

BearManor Media

2016

*The Absolute Joy of Work: From Vermont to Broadway, Hollywood,
and Damn Near 'Round the World*

© 2016 Carleton Carpenter

All Rights Reserved.
Reproduction in whole or in part without the author's permission
is strictly forbidden.

For information, address:

BearManor Media
P. O. Box 71426
Albany, GA 31708

bearmanormedia.com

Typesetting and layout by John Teehan

Published in the USA by BearManor Media

ISBN—978-1-62933-082-2

TO PHILIP ROTH, a marvelous writer who, in his memoir *The Facts: A Novelist's Autobiography*, decided that I was the perfect young guy to represent youth of a certain bygone era. Describing the blonde, blue-eyed apple of his eye, Roth wrote that "her speech and dress and manner made her a virtual ringer for the solid, energetic girl in the cheery movies about America's heartland, a friend of Andy Hardy's, a classmate of June Allyson's, off to the prom in his jalopy with Carleton Carpenter." I read it and thought, why me? But I was pleased, flattered, and gratified that he'd spelled my name right.

Mr. Roth is seven years younger than I. I've never met the man.

TO ALAN GURGANUS, author of my favorite book, *Oldest Living Confederate Widow Tells All*, a masterwork I've read countless times. By page fifteen, I'm in tears. Then, as with Dickens, I'm laughing so hard I have to set the book down. I've bought several copies for friends, who are still thanking me.

A friend of mine, Martin Tahse, turned the book into a one-person play, bound for Broadway. For the first and only time, I was an investor. I flew out to California for the opening night at the Old Globe in San Diego. It was terrific. The star was marvelous. There was a party after the show. A man came running toward me, smiling and introducing himself. Alan Gurganus was a movie fan! I asked if he'd sign my program. He said, "Happily, if you'll sign mine!" We gabbed together for the rest of the party.

Later I saw the play's opening night on Broadway. I was shocked. Scenes had been switched all through the piece by someone other than Tahse. It made no sense. After nineteen previews and one performance, the show went to Cain's warehouse.

I'd go see Alan at the 92nd Street Y in New York whenever he presented a new book there, so we kept in touch.

Mr. Gurganus is young enough to be my son.

Foreword
by Debbie Reynolds

My dear friend Carleton Carpenter has been in my life for more than sixty-five years. We met at the MGM studios when we were both starry-eyed kids who were fortunate enough to have front-row seats in the Golden Age of Hollywood.

Our first movie together was *Three Little Words*. I wore a dark brunette wig and played Helen Kane, who had a big musical hit with the song "I Wanna Be Loved by You." It had the memorable phrase, "Boop-boop-a-doop." Carleton and I stood together while I lipsynched Helen Kane's voice.

In our next film, *Two Weeks with Love*, Carleton and I sang and danced together. Our big number was a lively duet about monkeys and chimps called "Aba Daba Honeymoon." It became a top-ten hit. It was so popular that MGM sent us to perform our song on the Loew's Theater circuit. It was my first time on the road. Carleton had performed onstage since he was a kid. Now there we were doing the vaudeville circuit together. Carleton and I did several shows a day. We sang our hit and another number from the movie, "Row, Row, Row." It was a lot of fun.

Because I was only eighteen years old at the time, my mother, Maxene, went along with us on the tour. During the trip, Carleton got a cold. He curled up in bed next to my mother, who laughed and said, "Carleton is the only other man I've slept with besides your father." I guess curling up with Mother made Carleton feel better!

When I look at my photo albums from those days, Carleton is always in the picture. He came to my house with other friends for pool parties. We laughed and joked. His nickname for me was "Little Creature."

Carleton and I share decades of wonderful memories. I'm sure you'll enjoy reading his accounts of making movies and performing onstage. He worked with many great stars. Those were magical days!

Prologue

I n 1930, as a four-year-old in Bennington, Vermont, I sang a duet with a gal who was a couple of years older at some huge "do" in the great hall of the State Armory. The song: "When You and I Were Young, Maggie." We were paid a dollar, which we split. Fifty cents was a huge deal in 1930. In my precocious mind, it made me a pro. Those who earned money for performing were professionals. From then on, I considered any performance without remuneration a "benefit."

Even better than making such a ton of loot was the applause. I was hooked. By age nine, using the moniker Professor Upham (Upham was my grandmother's maiden name), I was traipsing all over Southern New England—for pay—with my own magic act. Our school's singing teacher, Grace Barr, a wild character, arranged for me to participate in the annual Boar's Head Ceremony at Hoosac School, just over the border into New York State. Hoosac was an exclusive private school for the very rich: It cost one thousand dollars per year! I was Head Candlebearer in the elaborate Christmas Procession. I was blond, beautiful and (looked) innocent.

A new magazine called *Life* was covering the event and I was chosen and photographed for the cover. Never made it. I was bumped by someone called Adolf Hitler. (Later I would be photographed four more times for the cover. I was always bumped. The last shot was to have gone with an article about an actor who had been shot and bumped from the cover four times. His fifth chance was bumped as well. That's life.)

At seventeen, three months into my senior year—and with enough credits to graduate by Christmas break—I landed my first Broadway play and got my union card. Actors Equity. Then I was a *certified* professional.

Chapter 1

Long before I was born there on July 10, 1926, my hometown of Bennington, Vermont had three memorable female residents: Gussie Bingham, Bessie Upham and Alta Bugbee. Gussie lived at the entrance of a place called Lyons District; Alta lived not far up the road where it ended and where Brooklyn, Vermont began. Bessie lived about halfway between. When she married she became Bessie Carpenter and gave birth to one girl and three boys. The middle son was named Carleton Upham Carpenter, who became a Sr. I was the Jr.

Gramma Bess was a funny, feisty character, her emotions sleeve-worn, tumbling and cascading into one another at nanosecond pace. Her attractive, round little face sported chipmunk cheeks, each one decorated with a little circle of rouge. She called it "roogee" and claimed, "I don't feel dressed without my roogee."

Lyons District was named after the family who ran the kaolin mill, across a small creek from the no-name lane we lived on. The lane branched off a no-name road and had three houses: a big one matriarched by Flora Lyons on the left, Gram and Grampa's on the right and ours, up a small rise at the dead end. Carpus (my dad, Cart to most) built the house.

Ages later, when roads became streets with names, they wanted a name for the lane. My mom (whose maiden name was Marjorie Main, although she wasn't the actress—more about that later) was always called Dar. No one, including mom, had any idea where that came from. It was Dar and Cart for over sixty years of marriage. Sometimes Dar became Darcie, so my older sister Betty-Jim, dad and I all agreed that the lane should be called Darcie's Dead End. Of course it wasn't; it remained nameless for years. After Gram and Grampa had died and I had done several films, the town finally settled on Carpenter Lane. Although I'd like to think I had something to do with the eventual appellation, I'm sure I didn't.

We lived almost exactly one mile from the Big Town—that's what I considered it then—and its main drag. Bennington was a quiet, tiny village in the southwestern bottom of Vermont. Starting in 1932 it was home to Bennington College, which Dad had helped build. This was one of many, many assorted jobs he had, when he had any job at all. It was Depression time, although Betty-Jim and I weren't aware of it. Maybe Dar and Cart were. We never knew we were poor and almost surely in debt. Across the no-name road we had a barn with a cow (which I milked) and sometimes a few chickens.

We never said we were going into town. It was always "going over-street." Main Street held all sorts of wonders: Woolworths; Fishman's 5¢ to $1.00 Store; the Bookshop; and best of all, catty-corner from the Hotel Putnam, the General Stark Theater and the wagon outside, with the very best buttered popcorn in the world. Five cents a bag. A big night out for us (after Dad got a Model A) was going overstreet, parking, popcorning, sitting in the car and watching everyone going up and down, in and out of the stores. Bliss.

On my *Saturday Evening Post* route I earned points for magazines delivered, and soon I had enough to win a free bike. I also had a rock-garden business; I sold rocks and moss and wild strawberries and ferns filched from the woods. Whenever I'd saved enough money, I went to the movies. Later, when Pocket Books (which produced those twenty-five-cent paperbacks) first started, I'd buy books. I think the first I got was Dorothy Parker's *After Such Pleasures*. I read all the time. The library up Main, nearly as far away as the high school I much later attended, was a magnet. I went through all the Oz books; *The Marvelous Land of Oz* is still my favorite (the one with Jack Pumpkinhead, not the Wizard).

I loved them all. I read everything and anything. My mom found a wonderful book of fairy tales called *My Book House*. (I think there were several volumes.) I've always wondered if it's in print somewhere. It was sensational. She read to us until we could read for ourselves, which happened soon. She was a fanatic about education, bless her. She had been unable to go beyond third grade, I think, since she was the eldest of eleven children and was needed at home; but she read constantly and became the brightest, best-informed, funniest uneducated lady I've ever known. She had my sister and I reading long before kindergarten.

I always loved school and, with a couple of exceptions, the teachers. They worked for salaries that barely paid enough for food and board, and they paid for their own summer sabbaticals. But they loved what they did; it wasn't a job to them, it was their calling. They fired our imaginations. They made us think. Wow, how lucky we were.

Usually I walked (or ran) to grade school. It was shorter than the mile by road because I went crosslots past our barn and through some woods, finally joining the road just past Barnhardt Construction, where the bridge over the Roaring Branch River began. I can't remember many times that the river actually roared. Most of the time there was little water in the huge boulder-crammed thing, except in the warmish early springs when the snows from Woodford Mountain melted too quickly. Well, maybe there was more than just a little water, to be honest. But hardly enough to cause a roar; maybe a whimper or maybe it really did roar at one time. Don't want to knock the poor old thing.

Up the no-name main road, about halfway between Bessie and Alta, was another lady named Laura Shelby. She lived in a huge white house with a long veranda and well-tended flowers and shrubs. I think she employed a gardener. She had two daughters: Marge (married) and Jeanne (unmarried). Jeanne Shelby. Actress. For me, it was love at first sight. I believe I was not quite three. She was up for one of her infrequent visits from New York City, where she lived and worked—*on Broadway*. Well, I was an absolute goner. Jeanne was so beautiful, gentle-natured and sweetly theatrical. She had to have known I was completely smitten. The two of us basked in each other's company—my forever favorite stage star and her newest and youngest fan. Her voice was as deep and rich as spice cake. My God, that voice. When she said the word "theater," it sounded like something I'd never heard before. Sort of *the-ah-tah*. Three lovely syllables. I knew then and there that this was what I was destined for: The Stage.

She called me Buz. The family called me Brud or Bub. Carp came when I started school. Then I was Stretch when I sprouted up, but I loved Buz. Only Jeanne called me that. (Years later I learned it had been a nickname for Burgess Meredith. Anyway, the name had an instant effect on me. "Affect" might be more accurate, since I had begun dramatizing everything at home, causing wonderment and dismay in Cart and tolerantly subdued delight in Dar. B-J and I, for some reason, always called our parents by their nicknames—rarely Mom (that was for Dar's mother, Gramma Main) or Dad, and almost never Mother or Father, except for frustrated emphasis.

I'm not exactly sure what B-J thought of my blossoming personality. Probably, from the three years of worldly experience she had on me, she considered me a spoiled brat. If so, Jim was right.

Then came my "professional" debut at four, when the older girl, Constance Wagner (she was five) sang a duet with me of "When You and I

Were Young, Maggie." (Twenty years later I recorded an updated version, "Maggie Blues," with Debbie Reynolds as one of the follow-up discs to "Aba Daba Honeymoon," which had risen to number one on the Hit Parade.)

The only really disappointing thing about that terrific night with Constance was that my beloved Jeanne wasn't there. She was back on Broadway with the great actress Mary Boland, doing a show whose name I can't remember. Jeanne had become a great phone friend of my Gramma Bess. She got a big kick out of the way Gramma would end every call. Whichever party was talking, when Bess had heard enough or had said all she wanted to say, it was, "Well, be good, goodbye!" That was it. Sometimes she'd interrupt herself in mid-sentence. "Be good, goodbye!" Click. Gramma was a hoot.

I spent so much of my young life down the small hill in Cart's parent's house. Gramp was a caution as well. One of the things that fascinated me was a small miniature chest of drawers Bess had, maybe a bit over a foot wide and a bit less in height. It had row after row of small drawers, twenty or thirty all totaled, with small knobs to pull out. All were carefully labeled: "NEEDLES," "RUBBER BANDS," "PAPER CLIPS," "UNMATCHED BUTTONS," etc. One label really caught my young and somewhat confused attention. "PIECES OF STRING, TOO SMALL TO SAVE." Why was she saving pieces of string if they were too small to save?

Only once did I ever consider another field of lifetime endeavor. It was in second grade. We did a playlet called "Dr. Health." All the other kids played vegetables and fruits. I played Dr. Health himself, and decided I wanted to be a doctor when I grew up. The notion lingered for about three days. Then it hit me that, of course, I liked the idea of *pretending* to be a doctor. Aha! Playing a doc was just acting, and it was going to be terrific spending the rest of my life earning my living pretending to be all kinds of people instead of just me. I probably got all goosepimply. I goosepimple easily.

It was around that time that I ran away from home. Well, as far as the cellar. I wanted to be on my own. I moved a cot down there where I could ponder the future, work on my magic act (I'd received a small magic set the Christmas before) and write more plays. Of course I went upstairs to get the peanut-butter sandwiches and milk I mostly subsisted on, but I took them back down to my cubbyhole near the cellar to eat.

Since the washtubs, ringer, furnace and scrubbing board were down there, I was constantly invaded, and after maybe three days I moved back up to my own bedroom. A few years later, I built a "cabin" in the woods, really a tiny shack, and spent a lot of time there. This was much better. A school buddy, Jack Root—a guy who lived overstreet and built wonderful model planes—made a cabin too. His was much better. Jack was a meticulous guy who, at home overstreet, built wonderful model planes.

So I had a neighbor, but still had privacy. Jack and I smiled a lot. We smoked grapevine, pine-needle cigars rolled in newspaper, or anything else you could draw smoke through. Cornsilk was the "Acapulco Gold" of that era. Thank God we never inhaled anything. Just puffed away, like big shots. The first pack of real cigarettes I bought was called Paul Jones. Ten cents. Big popular brands like Avalon and Herbert Tarryton were fifteen cents. I still didn't know about inhaling them. The first time I did inhale—big decision—came later. (I'll get to that.)

When I began performing at home, I started under the card table, with a big tablecloth covering three sides and curtained on one end like a stage. I loved curtains. Years later, in New York, I adored revues with lots of curtains and scrims and moving panels coming from the wings. I still do. Under the card table, I did shows with marionettes I'd made myself and little sketches I'd written. I'd cribbed some from the Bookhouse, I'm sure. Dar and Cart—even B.J.—pretended to enjoy everything and would, just as they were supposed to, applaud and cheer afterward. My bows were no doubt better than my shows.

Later, I moved from the card table to the end of living room. There were colonnades on either side, a couple of feet from where the staircase started. With a line stretched high between, I could hang actual curtains. Well, old sheets. And I had my own stage at last. The shows became a bit longer and, wonders of wonders, I was able to cajole B-J into performing with me from time to time. Since I seemed to write better parts for the ladies, I usually played them myself and left poor, patient B-J to play the male roles. Actually, she was pretty good at it.

As the play grew, so did the audience. Gramma Bess, Grampa Charlie, Aunt Elizabeth (I always thought she was a dead ringer for Jeanette MacDonald) and sometimes Uncle Lewie. (I never knew Cart's older brother, Ken. He died when I was two, I think, but I knew he was a fairly well-recognized commercial artist who had done several *Saturday Evening Post* covers.) If any of the assorted group wound up with stunned expressions, I wasn't aware of it—then. Now, pausing to reflect, I think there must have been a few New England jaws slightly agape. Who knew? I loved the applause and the bowing and I never noticed. Maybe they thought that gender-switching was what theater was all about, and they dutifully showed up for everything.

I had a circus act (called *Jolly Time*) most summers, and impromptu magic shows. Jeanne encouraged me as a magician, even giving me a subscription to a magazine called *The Linking Ring*, the prestidigitator's bible. She also helped me with my diction, explaining I should learn to speak with golf balls in my mouth. I never figured that one out. I'm sure she must have meant pebbles. No matter. I practiced with two golf balls swelling my cheeks out for quite awhile.

Dar only once asked what I was doing.

I said, "Ooommbblloaohho."

"I see," she said, and never questioned me again.

The magic act was getting better. I made my own flip-over box, painted it bright glossy red and added black, fairly authentic-looking Chinese characters. It really looked nice. The special silk handkerchiefs that crushed up so tight were too expensive at the shop I had a catalog for, Max Holden's on 42nd Street in New York City, so I got the cheapest, flimsiest material I could find overstreet and made my own. I stitched the tiniest hems so that they wouldn't unravel as they "magically" appeared. It took forever, but it was worth it. A couple of years later I did order some stuff from Holden. Disappearing wands, I remember, and some larger linking rings. (I traded in the small ones that came with the original set for a nice discount.)

By the time I was nine I had started getting bookings. I played all the animal clubs—Lions, Elks, Masons—plus the boys' and girls' Rotary Clubs. I had given up another of my projects, a weekly home-typed and carbon-copied newspaper I called *The Pine Needle Press*. (It was mostly gossip and ads for the films at the General Stark Theater.) I continued selling whatever I could create a market for, but for the next two years I was mostly just selling myself: Professor Upham, magician.

I really wasn't very good, but I was young and had a pretty good line of gab, so I got away with murder, and built up my bankbook. I found another way to fill my pockets. Does anyone remember candlepin bowling? It was very popular then. There were ten nearly cylindrical pins, each about a foot high and two inches in diameter (a bit wider in the middle), and played with a small ball about the size of a grapefruit. Back when I was nine or ten, I used to set pins in an alley on weekends, when I wasn't being Upham, the Magician.

The alley was on Union Street in Bennington. I loved the job, but it was difficult, and also dangerous. This was long before pin-setting equipment was invented, so after setting the pins on the marks you had to jump up to a corner of a shelf-like place to protect yourself against flying pins. Then you'd get back down and gather them up and replace them as fast as you could. The quicker you were, the better the tip. If you pleased the bowler you could get a quarter or half-dollar slid down the gutter.

Candlepin stayed very popular in the area for a few more years. Then an alley with duck pins and a big ball with a thumbhole opened just around the corner.

By that time I had long since moved on to other sports. I was a fearless skier and jumper and a good swimmer and hiker. I had many secret places to hike where there were wonderful Lady Slippers—mostly pink, but sometimes the rare yellow—as well as swamp pinks and trailing arbutus. Later in junior high I took to basketball, but it didn't take much to me. Coach Williams might put me in for a couple of minutes a game. I was really lousy, but I loved it. I played in the band, so at half-time I'd run, change into street wear and race out to the gym to play. Then I'd change back into shorts for the second half.

It must have been a terrible disappointment for Coach that I was tall and getting taller, but not getting any better. I was good at sax and drums, though, and also played the cello and violin, thanks to free lessons from the Bennington County Music Society. But my real love was the piano. B-J got the lessons, since she was older. There was a long triple-folded chart that came with her instruction book, and when you unfolded it and put it behind the keys, the written notes showed where you should hit. That's how I learned to read music. I played by ear from the time I could climb up on the stool, thinking I was the first ever to discover a C seventh chord by adding a B flat. Ah, the wonderful egotism of the very young.

Anyway, I started writing music back then and never stopped. (Eventually in New York City, I learned to play well enough to pass the exam. I got my musician's union card from local 802 by playing "How High the Moon".)

Summers were extra-special whenever Jeanne was home and "at liberty." There was a long, long Willys-Knight convertible in the Shelby garage; I think it belonged to Jeanne's sister Marge and her well-to-do husband. Jeanne was masterful, though cautious, behind the wheel, and she'd pack a gang of us in the back and head for North Bennington and Lake Paran, the closest swimming hole. Spring fed an icy cold all season long. A steep bank sloped down to the water, so our blanket and spread towels were at a hazardous angle. An orange or apple would roll down the hill unless you secured it in the fold of some clothes. There was a diving board, and a raft was always out. B-J was a terrific diver, but a bit flat-footed when she hit the water. She never pointed her toes.

Butterfingers (a nickel each) were the treat of choice. Jeanne always paid for everyone. She wore a sort of squashed-down baker's hat, more floppy bonnet than swim cap. It looked to me like something from the 1800s, but it suited her and made me love her even more because she was so unique. I showed off shamelessly for her in the water.

Brief addendum: I once asked my mother how I learned to swim. Dar said that when I was little more than a baby at an outing at Shaftsbury Lake, which had a very shallow swimming area, she just carried me out and tossed me in, then backed up a bit and kept yelling, "KICK, HONEY, KICK!" I must have kicked pretty well. She said she was laughing all the time so I wouldn't be scared. She hauled me out, tossed me in the air, hugged me and said, "Now you can swim." And I did. Good quick lesson, and I was never frightened of water. I wish she had had such a quick cure for my acrophobia. I still don't like being higher than a bar stool.

Jeanne and I would have long talks about everything. Well, mostly she'd want to hear of all the various exploits of her Buz, and I was more than happy to oblige. She was ever-enthusiastic, complimenting me and telling how it was *all* good experience for *the-ah-tah*. Of course Dar was just as supportive, but less theatrical. Cart, I'm not so sure. I had to prove myself to him. Happily I was able to, several years before he died. Those years were precious to me. Before and during his struggle with Alzheimer's we became very close. Real friends. I wish it could have happened earlier.

I learned hardly anything about Jeanne's personal life, although there were rumors of various lovers. I did learn that she had lived for years and years in Lincoln Square at 2020 Broadway between 69th and 70th Streets—so she really *did* work and live on the Great White Way. A bit north, but still Broadway.

Dar and Cart managed to see her on Broadway (at the Center Theater on Sixth Avenue) before I did, in 1939. The play was George S. Kaufman and Moss Hart's *The American Way*. The Center was a few blocks north of the Hippodrome; both showplaces are long gone. The three of us had recently made a wondrous excursion on a train from North Adams, Massachusetts to Manhattan then and out to Flushing for the 1939 World's Fair. Trylon and Perisphere time. I won't even try to describe the adventure of that one-day excursion. I was in complete awe. I could have stayed a year. Dar, Cart and I made the most of it, rushing from one line to the next. We even saw *Billy Rose's Aquacade*. I pushed for *The Hot Mikado*, a sexy Michael Todd musical, but Father and Mother would have none of that. I lugged two huge sacks of free whatevers—brochures, samples, anything they were giving away—back to Bennington. There were too many incredible memories to carry except in my happy heart. I was twelve.

I wished that B-J could have been along, but she was at the age when more important things were happening for her. Probably something amorous. Or maybe it was purely a financial matter and I had just gotten lucky. As for our family finances, they were built on strict rules: Scrimp, save, don't waste and don't throw anything away that can be mended or repaired. "Remember the starving Armenians" meant, don't leave anything on your plate at meal times—breakfast, dinner and supper. ("Lunch" for the midday meal didn't loom on the horizon until much later.) Most important, don't get big eyes for something you can't pay for, even if it only cost pennies. When you've saved enough and *really* need it, then you can splurge. Don't borrow. Scrape it together, then buy. This was so ingrained in me that for many, many years I never had a credit rating. I've paid cash for every car I've ever bought.

One of the jobs my father had was at a place in Williamstown, Massachusetts called Sand Springs, where some family-owned company produced ginger ale. They used a special formula, and the product was incredible—very peppery, with some kind of natural carbonation from spring water that made it the most delicious soft drink I've ever tasted. No other ginger ale has ever matched it. Unfortunately, the secret recipe died with the old owner. When Sand Springs Ginger Ale became King's Ginger Ale, something extra-special was lost to the world—at least to the small local family market they delivered to. Cart's first job with the company was to drive the delivery truck; then he got promoted to the office at the plant. His Albany business schooling had paid off.

He also went into several solo ventures, none getting farther off the ground than his head. One of his enterprises, called Betty-Buddy Horseradish (named for B-J and me), did get as far as printing labels. Boxes of them eventually wound up in my folks' bedroom closet. Dad never threw anything away. I'm not sure he ever did make a batch. He was thankful to take a job with F.D.R.'s Civilian Conservation Corps somewhere up over Woodford Mountain, almost to New Hampshire, as a chef or mess-hall cook. We didn't see much of him during that period.

The four of us were great "greens" eaters. Milkweed, cowslip, beet, turnip and the favorite, dandelions. Dug in early spring, the brown stuff peeled back by knife and root cut clean, the tasty green leaves (before they started to bud) soaked in our spring water to get the dirt out. We never got it all, but as Dar would say, "Got to eat a peck of dirt before you die." She had a ton of her own truisms, including, "You'll never be able to earn your own living until you can cut your own toenails." In lush times we'd have a bit of streak-of-lean salt pork, boiled with the dandelions.

Grampa Charlie would say, "If I can make it through the winter 'til my first mess of dandelions, I can live another year." We all said: "Always a mess of greens." Was that saying southern, or just from southern Vermont? Gramp, along with his brother Theodore, had a lumber mill overstreet, as well as a paint and hardware store on the corner of Main and Stafford, a few blocks up from the High School. I figured Gramp and Gramma Bessie were very rich. Charlie always seemed to have a new Chrysler, but maybe it was just that the automobile always sparkled from constant polishing. He never drove over twenty-five miles an hour when he and Gramma went for their Sunday tours—maybe even as far as North Bennington!

Uncle Lewie worked at the paint store and later lived in the apartment upstairs. Gramp retired very early and spent most of his time sitting by the radio.

I remember so clearly Gramp sitting there in that chair, his hands crossed on opposite knees and his feet toeing in, tips of shoes almost touching. I toed in, too. He'd look up at me and say, "I'll give you a nickel if I see you going all day without toeing in." My feet would suddenly splay outward as far as I could make them go. I'd grin and say I would. Then I'd really try to walk toeing out, but it would last for probably less than an hour, when I got involved in something else. I'd never collect the nickel because I hadn't earned it. (One time he gave me the nickel beforehand and I kept at it probably fifteen minutes longer. But since I gave it my best shot, I kept the cash.) I think my piqued toes helped me be such a good fence-rail walker.

Finally I got to see Jeanne on Broadway in 1941, when I was fourteen. I took the bus to Albany and the train into Grand Central Station. I really loved traveling by myself. What a thrill! Jeanne knew I was arriving and had booked me into the Shelton Hotel, close to where she was now sharing a small apartment with her close friend Minette Barrett. The show was *Lady in the Dark*, a musical by Moss Hart with music by Kurt Weill and lyrics by Ira Gershwin.

Wow, what a first show to see! Two revolving stages, spectacular scenery and costumes, and dances by Albertina Rashe. It was very innovative for its time. It's about psychoanalysis—this was just before therapy became the next chic-growth business—and it starred the truly fabulous Gertrude Lawrence as Liza, a fashion editor who undergoes psychoanalysis. I looked up at the blazing marquee. It read MISS G. LAWRENCE in huge letters. I realized her name was too long for the size of the billing. I counted the letters in my name: one letter longer. Oh, well, I'd be more than happy to be C. Carpenter in order to accommodate a theater sign. *Lady in the Dark* played at the Alvin (now the Neil Simon) and the show featured the debut performance of a guy named Danny Kaye. Jeanne played the secretary to Dr. Brooks (the shrink treating Miss G.). She also played, in a flashback scene, Liza's mother.

Although her roles were small, I thought she was absolutely radiant. I never left my seat during the interval and could barely contain myself until the curtain rose once more. Then, natch, I didn't want it to ever end. But end it did. Backstage I went to greet my beloved, who introduced me to everyone in sight. I felt like the Pauper suddenly turned into the Prince. Then, after the audience had left, Jeanne, along with a couple of the gals in the cast, took me out front and told me to jump down into the orchestra pit, sit at the piano and play them all my new songs. The three ladies sat on the edge of the stage and I played and sang my inspired heart out. I was too dumb to be scared and too much of a ham not to love every second of it.

The next evening, back to the Alvin I went. Jeanne put me into the care of an assistant stage manager and I watched the entire show from the wings, except for one unforgettable moment. When one of the two revolving stages went dark and the audience watched the other, I got to ride the circling set around. There were the entire audience, orchestra, loge and balconies right there in front of me. If I thought I'd been stage-struck before, forget it. This was it, the real deal. I was positively hooked for life. I'm still at it. God knows less often—not by my choice—but plugging away. Too dumb and to hooked to quit. Go figure.

One summer I worked with a traveling carnival called, appropriately enough, Chautauqua, which is another name for carnival. But perhaps it was called that because it was based in Chautauqua, New York. I worked with an old gal who ran the pitch penny concession. There was a big, low, square table-like thing covered with dots (circles, really), each a tiny bit larger than a dime or nickel or penny, and a few (for the high-rollers) that were a fraction bigger than a quarter. If the coins landed within the labeled spots, you doubled your investment.

My job was to make sure folks didn't lean too far over the three-sided fence, and to bark out, "Pitch 'em in. See what you win." The old gal checked every coin tossed to make sure it was clearly within the black circles; then she quickly raked all the losing coins into an eave-like catcher that ran around the board. There were very few winners, but it seemed to be a tremendously popular (and profitable) game. I guess that's why the rubes kept coming back to it.

I was no rube. I was "with it." I had discovered *Billboard*, which then focused on circuses, carnivals, and burlesque shows. (Now *Billboard* is all about music.) I had a great gig. My wages were a buck a night and a buck and a half on Saturday, because we were open all afternoon. The fringe benefits were terrific. I got to ride the rides free during breaks. I liked the Tilt-a-Whirl and the swings. I even tried to cure my acrophobia with a jaunt up and around on the Ferris wheel. Once was enough. I thought the damned ride would never end. I knew the guy who ran the thing. First revolution around he said, "Stretch, you can stay on as long as you like. Just let me know when you want to get off." Trying to seem calm in my near-hysterical state, I quickly said, "Now. Gotta get back to the booth."

That summer was an exotic adventure. And in a spooky way, erotic. Everything about carnival life seemed sexy. All the hustling concession-aires flirting with their prospective marks, luring innocents to the games they hawked. Promising, with seductively sly smiles, all sorts of forbidden awards. It was fascinating to watch the interplay between crowds and the cons.

When my stint was over, I left with a bit of cash, tons of experience and the happy thought that I'd had a chance to play one hell of a part. Curtain.

Chapter 2

Years earlier, just when I was ready for third grade, a new two-room schoolhouse was built just a bit up the East Road from the Shelby place. It was very close to our house, crosslots, so my sister and I had to go there instead of overstreet. Brooklyn School. Grades 1-4 in one room, 5-8 in the other. B-J hated the place. Some of the guys in her room were nearly twenty. She missed her former, smarter classmates. She lasted about half the school year there. Cart caved in and spent the stipend required to let her return to the old school, overstreet.

But while she was still there we acted together again in a short *Alice in Wonderland* playlet. We were Tweedle Dum and Tweedle Dee. Neither one of us can remember who played which.

I stuck it out for the year. Instead of bounding crosslots home (about a three-minute bound) I usually trekked the long way, down the hill and to the right on the no-name road, but never on the road itself; on the fence-rails. I imagined I was the best fence-rail walker ever. I felt like King of the World. Of course I envisioned myself as a circus tightrope walker with invisible masses cheering me on. (In fact, I *was* pretty good.) I returned to the old school the following semester. Brooklyn School closed shortly after. There had been dropouts galore. I have a feeling the school never had a graduation. Maybe the whole idea of building a school there had come from a W.P.A. project. After the place had stood empty for several years, a couple of businesses failed there as well.

Shortly after B-J had been born, my folks found she was dragging one leg in her crib. One doctor put her leg in a cast, but after months and months there was no improvement. Another doctor discovered she had no left hip socket. One more cast went on. A long time passed. She didn't improve. Another doctor. Same result. Finally, Doctor Hatt operated on her at the Shriners Hospital in Springfield, Massachusetts. I think he put in a steel socket. It worked. B-J thrived: She became a super dancer of the jitterbug variety, and later had five kids. She had a barely noticeable limp.

Before B-J's successful operation, my mother had discovered she was pregnant again—with me. She told me the following when I was eighteen and home on boot leave from Sampson, New York, after I'd enlisted in the Navy and was all grown up. Understandably, she was positive that I'd be born with "something askew," as she put it. "I went all over up here, honey, trying to get you scraped off. But what do they know about abortion in Vermont? I don't think anyone knew what the word meant." Neither did I.

She continued. "Well, when you were born at Putnam Memorial Hospital, the nurse came into my room and said, 'You have a beautiful baby boy, Mrs. Carpenter.' I knew she was lying. She knew I was crazy. I threw her a dangerous look, then I threw an ashtray at her. A couple of days later I calmed down and let them bring you in. Wrapped up like a gift from the devil, I thought. I held you in your little blanket in front of me with my knees propping you up. Then I started at the top of your head and checked and counted everything on you. When I got to your feet, I passed out." (My feet, although pigeon-toed, were big and the butt of many jokes later in my life.)

She had me rolling on the floor with laughter. When I could catch my breath I jumped up from the floor and gave her the biggest, longest kiss I ever did. We were not, I repeat, *not* a big kissing family. A bit of hugging and a peck now and then but that was about it. Maybe that accounts for me turning out to be the almost constant kisser I am. All friends, old and brand new, male as well as female, bartenders—everybody. Charlotte, an old lady-friend of mine from Louisville who often came to New York City to see the shows, once told me: "I don't believe you. You talk to everyone, in restaurants, bars, strangers walking down the street. It's a wonder you don't get killed. You jabber away at them as if they were good old friends and by the time you get to the end of the block, you're kissing them goodbye."

Well, I like people. No excuses.

Dar was a caution. And poor Cart usually got the full brunt. When B-J and I were little kids, our family became the proud owners of a Ford Model A. It was late fall and the trees were bare; you could see clear to the bridge crossing the Roaring Branch and the road that turned on to the no-name road passing Gussie Bingham's. Dar spotted the car, heading home from wherever the family provider was working then, and suddenly yelled out, "Quick. Come here." We hurried to her. She was standing on the piano stool, motioning, "C'mon, get up here with me." She held out her arms and helped us up. "Don't say a word," she whispered conspiratorially, "and no giggling."

Cart came in. There the three of us sat on top of the old upright. "What the hell are you doing up there?" he said. Dar stared into space. After a very long, theatrical pause, she said, "It's the only warm spot in the house." Cart smirked and grumbled his way down to the furnace in the cellar. The three of us cracked up and climbed down. We could hear him quietly cussing, which tickled us even more.

The heating system was very basic—a grate in the living-room floor, a bit bigger than a yard square, and a small grate in the ceiling that heated the bathroom above. On really cold mornings we'd dress on the grate.

We had finally replaced our old icebox with a Fridge, which is what we still called the icebox, and a butter churn plus the aforementioned set-tubs and roller wringer. Whenever something around the house got upgraded Dar would grumble, "More of these modern inconveniences!"

I loved it whenever Gramma Main came to stay with us. She was calm and unflappable and so beautiful, with glorious, long white-gray hair. I'd sometimes brush it for her and she'd allow me to give her a wild new do. She could play a mean "Rock of Ages" on the piano and was a terrific story-teller. Since three of my mother's youngest sisters (first Pat, then Nan, then Bobby, who was only a few years older than B-J) lived with us before they married and all of them called Gramma Main "Mom," B-J and I did, too.

Mom was a constant reader. I guess those genes traveled down the whole line of Mains right into the Carpenters. She had been married first to a man named DePeyster, who died very young. She bore him two children. Then she met and fell hopelessly in love with James Garfield Main. He was handsome, very funny and a real charmer. He was also "given to the drink" and would disappear at intervals, leaving Mom with her ever-growing brood of kids. Grampa Jim was always forgiven whenever he returned, usually broke. He and Mom would move from farm to farm, running the places for the owners. The pay was a place to live and food to eat, with maybe a buck or two extra. We'd visit them, and they always seemed madly in love no matter how primitive their circumstances.

I never had much of a chance to spend time with Grampa Jim, but the moments with him were always sunny and fun. He died very young. Mom never had anything bad to say about him. She cherished their love for the rest of her life, which she spent staying with one child after another. We had all became family. Each of her two sons had a half-dozen kids of his own. The Main family get-togethers could fill a small baseball park. The ever-changing aunts in and out of the Carpenter household were like extra older sisters.

Poor Cart must have been swamped by all the very talkative, very competitive Main gals constantly playing games like Parcheesi, Chinese checkers, pick-up sticks, pinochle and bridge. Sometimes they competed at holding a pencil between their toes and trying to write the most legibly. Don't think for a moment that these gals played polite, proper, ladylike games. They made a blood sport of bridge, the card game once described as the "greatest way for couples to spend an evening with their clothes on."

My father played a good game of bridge, but would get bored after a bit. He was a dominoes and cribbage man at heart—especially since the card games went on rubber after rubber after rubber till the wee hours. You'd make yourself a quick bite to eat when you were dummy.

Dar taught me to play early on, in case they ever needed a fourth. She had rigid rules. Defending, *always* second hand low, except sometimes. *Always* third hand high, except sometimes. Against no-trump, *always* lead fourth from your longest and strongest suit, except sometimes. You get the idea. She liked sitting in a rocking chair while playing. When doubling a bid, it was *always* on the backswing of the rocker. B-J was a good bridger and so was I, after a bit. From Culberson to Goren to Sheinwold to whomever, all the experts who had written books on bridge. I pretty much stuck with Goren. I haven't played for a spell.

The entire Main clan was a freewheeling vocal gang and always great fun. The Carpenters, a few yards down the slope, were more contained. I don't mean prim or proper (anything but); just smaller and, well, more contained. Of course I saw more of them than the multitudes of Mains, so when Dar's relatives showed up it seemed extra-special.

My mother had a whistle. It was the store-bought police kind, and when she lowered the kitchen window and blew, you could hear the thing damn near a mile away. It signaled a wide variety of things: Get your tardy butts in here, it's mealtime! There's a telephone call. (We had a party line.) Help, I've nearly cut my finger off! I need one of you two for a fourth (at bridge). And so on. Instant communication, with a whistle. Try a few bars of this (as old sheet music used to say on the back cover) on your computer. Have you guessed I'm a wee bit low-tech? Whatever happened to tin cans and strings? I'm not sure they really worked, just helped develop your lung power.

As for me, I developed certain powers of my own, easily and very early. June, the granddaughter of Flora Lyons, a nubile gal two years older than I, eagerly encouraged my maturation even before kindergarten. Bless her happy, horny heart. We explored the wonders of each other's tender

June, the "older woman" who taught me the ways of the flesh in Bennington.

bodies. It usually happened in a playhouse directly across from Gram and Grampa's parlor room. For added excitement, we would meet in the tall weeds and grass outside. We really thought we were doing "the deed" just like the old folks. We believed we were practically inventing sex. We had a ball together on and off for quite a few years. Then she and her mother, Hope, moved away. I never told Jeanne about my "affair."

Flora Lyons made root beer from scratch. I say scratch since I have no idea what ingredients go into the making of that soft drink. It was a cause for delicious celebration whenever she made a batch of the stuff. (It rivaled the superb Sand Springs ginger ale.) Mrs. Lyons had another daughter, younger than June's mom, named Barbara. She had one of those faces in which all the rather ordinary-looking features fuse into a very handsome whole. She was serene and extremely bright, and more or less replaced the blank in my life left when June and her mother vanished. (No, not in that way!) Her extensive vocabulary, carriage, and beautiful speaking voice made Barbara a real role-model for me. Without letting me know at the time, she was teaching me to become more of a gentle-man, more caring about others' feelings and less of an obvious show-off. It would be ages before I recognized how much this lady had influenced me. Years later when we reconnected, I told her. She smiled and said, "Nonsense."

Somewhere around seventh grade, we rented our house and moved overstreet. It was partly for diminished financial reasons, but mainly (this was explained to me) so that Betty-Jim could become more datable. First we went to the corner of Union and Silver Streets, right next door to the library—what joy—then a couple of blocks up Union where we settled in until school days were finished. The house was sort of on a curve and had a garage with a Tydol gas pump on the property. That was a plus and a new career for Cart. (Actually, we sold very little gasoline, and less Veedol—the motor oil—and we stopped pumping and lubing fairly soon.)

The terrific thing about this house was that it was just about a block or so to the school. I remember it, too, as the place where we were living when I made my first solo trip to New York City for *Lady in the Dark*. After that trip, I spent all my spare time away from school making money for more forays to the Big Town. Lots of gigs: a stint as a bell-hop at the Putnam Hotel, another as a teletype operator at Western Union, magic shows whenever, and a fairly steady job at the Bennington Bookshop. I made many trips and saw as many shows as I could squeeze in during school breaks and vacations, piling up Playbills.

Jeanne's mother, Laura Shelby, had started, several years back, to spend winters with us so she wouldn't have to heat her big house. By the time we were renting on Union Street she was living with us year round. She had become "Auntie Shelby" some time ago, and the four of us grew accustomed to her softly poop, poop, pooping around the house with almost every step she took. Kind of like an older horse. She ate a lot of vegetables and always finished off what she called "pot liquor": juice that the veggies were cooked in. (She also, from time to time, would finish off a bit of the real stuff, John Henry, from her ever-hidden pint in her room.)

I remember the Sunday in December when we were listening to the radio and heard F.D.R. telling us about infamy because of Pearl Harbor, half a world away. It seemed so unreal. All too soon it would be all too real and certainly not all that far away for me.

A couple of brief scenes from 259 Union Street. One day B.J. came out of the bathroom, blue clouds of smoke sneaking out after her. No one said a word except B-J herself, who cried out defiantly, "I haven't been smoking, I haven't!" Then she ran upstairs. Dar, Cart and I looked at each other but said nothing. Auntie Shelby, whose room was beside the john, opened her door, stuck her head out and said, "Is there a fire?" The three of us burst out laughing, shaking heads no for reassurance.

Then there was the time I came downstairs late at night (well, after ten, anyway) stark naked to use the john. I passed by sleepily and didn't see Jim and a boyfriend necking on the living room couch. (B.J. swears this is true. I still don't believe it.) I do know that Cart once made the same trip, in pajamas, past my sister and her kissing partner. He headed for the kitchen, rattled a few somethings together and calmly walked back past the by-now-disentangled couple. He never spoke or looked at the two as he slowly ambled by, holding a large box of Kellogg's breakfast cereal. B-J's Romeo took the hint and quickly took to his heels. My father said later that he heard the front door slam before he had finished the climb up the stairs.

The teachers were a wildly assorted bunch of characters. Mr. Edmunds, a very odd duck, could be seen on his front lawn in the rain—umbrella in one hand, watering can in the other—tending to his flowers. He was a super teacher, and kept us reading *Time* magazine to learn what was going on outside our peaceful New England town. He even made us cut out articles as proof that we'd read it. Unfortunately, he had a rather pronounced stuttering problem. During one of his sudden quizzes—his way of catching us off guard—kids began raising their hands to ask permission to go to the johns, located on the floor below. He would have no more of it.

"Th-th-there will be no more r-r-raising of hands t-to leave the room," he said. "Th-there's been a s-s-steady stream in the b-basement all day." That's what the lav was called. The basement. Of course the poor guy meant "to the basement," but it was too late. The class erupted. Stifling ourselves, even with handkerchiefs to mouths, was impossible. Eventually we calmed down and went on with the quiz. He never knew why we had found something funny. Before class was over he even said, "Next time s-someone tells a d-d-dirty joke in my c-class, sh-share it with me." A really dedicated, nice man. But odd.

By this time I'd augmented my acting in all the school plays—from something called *Big Hearted Herbert* to Gilbert & Sullivan's *Iolanthe*—by writing short stories. Brazenly I sent them off to the *New Yorker*, the *Saturday Evening Post*, the *Delineator*, and others, piling up (then adorning the bedroom wall with) form-letter rejection slips. Still, I was thrilled that they arrived. Finally, a short piece I'd written called "The First Day" was accepted and published in *Liberty* magazine. Success, wow! And fifteen bucks. I couldn't wait to cash the check and add the money to my bank account. (Now I wished I hadn't cashed it. It would be fun to have. People don't even remember *Liberty*.)

I started a novel for the first time in a peculiar way. I had a dream one night with a complicated but coherent plot line. The next morning I wrote everything down. That night in bed I somehow willed myself to pick up where it had left off. I promptly recorded everything again in the morning. This continued for five nights in a row (with a title, "The Madonna Murders") and then the next night I couldn't conjure the darn thing back. Thus ended the novel. No matter how often I reread the five nights' worth of plot, in the daylight my imagination failed and I never was able to add even one additional sentence to the thing. Is there such a thing as subconscious writer's block?

I loved working part-time at the bookshop. It was a great gig. The boss, Ronald Sinclair, and the regular lady clerk were wonderful to me. I guess they recognized my deep love and supreme awe of books. Even today, I can read a paperback and no one would be able to tell it'd been touched. That respect was firmly planted in me by my second-grade teacher, Mary Carver, who told us to never break the back of a book and how to prepare a new one before reading it. This became an obsession. It kills me when I see a reader turn down a page corner to mark the place instead of sticking in a piece of paper. Maybe that's why some bookstores advertise "Books - New and Hurt" instead of "New and Used." I like that; it's tender.

The first floor of the Bookshop was mainly books. On the second floor, open only at Christmastime, we had toys and trimmings and such. One late summer afternoon I was alone in the place. Suddenly the front door banged open and a little kid came running past me toward the rear with Olympic speed.

"Where're you going?" I called to the boy. Hurdling midway up the staircase he yelled, "I'm going to the basement!" The bathroom was up there. There was that "basement" again. Sometimes it takes ages to grow out of things.

A truly magical thing happened, even surprising me, Professor Upham.

A thick envelope arrived in the mail from, of all places, Northwestern University in Evanston, Illinois. There was a letter about some summer program called "Cherubs." It seems that one of the gals whom Jeanne had brought out at *Lady in the Dark* to listen to my songs and watch me cavort in the pit was Ann Lee. She had been a cherub at the college a few years earlier and had given them my name and address. Enclosed were all kinds of tests to be done, lists to make about what you were planning to do with your life, pages and pages of stuff to fill out and a biography to write. It took me days to do it all. I finally finished, stuck it in the mailbox and promptly forgot about it—mainly because I was then working on the score and sketches for a revue I wanted to do at school the following year when I'd be a junior. They always had a senior revue, but I intended to break a tradition and do a junior show—*and* an original one. (To be perfectly honest, some of the sketches were cribbed from shows I saw in New York, like *Hellzapoppin'.*) But the music and lyrics and most of the other material were mine. I had a title, *Up and Up: A New Revue,* followed by a slogan: "Brings Broadway to Bennington." I had a ball working on it, drumming on the old upright (brought with us overstreet, at my pleading) and writing out lead sheets. The orchestra would be an odd assortment of whomever I could talk into playing. We ended up with two fiddles, a cello, an E-flat French horn, a trombone, a trumpet, a sax and drums, I think. And a piano, which someone else would play because I'd be conducting. I wrote out parts for all the instruments—my first orchestrations.

The first read-through was a complete fiasco. I was so dumb. You never heard such a discordant racket. I didn't realize that some instruments play in different keys. Only the strings and the drums didn't have to be rewritten. How I wished the sax had been a C-melody instead of a B-flat tenor. That would have saved one rewrite. But I learned and finally got all the enlistees playing in the same key. Thank God none of them knew any better, either, and it worked out without excess humiliation, except for the heap I dumped on myself.

Up and Up turned out to be a smash, heavily hyped by *The Bennington Evening Banner*, the local paper, which I called the *Bennington Evening Astonisher*, since most folks read it to see if what they'd heard a couple of days ago had made the *Banner*. It had incredibly fascinating space fillers, such as: "Lincoln was a great man." I shouldn't knock the dear old rag, because the review for the revue was so glowing that we played two nights instead of the advertised ONE NIGHT ONLY TO SEE THE SHOW THAT BRINGS BROADWAY TO BENNINGTON.

There was one little hitch in the whole affair. Among those classic hits of mine—"Damn the Torpedos," "Can We Forget?," "Boogie Woogie Stomach Ache"—was a number called "I Lost My Sweetie at the Beach," which featured a lot of class beauties in bathing suits. I'm not talking bikini, mind you; not even two-piece. These were regular Esther Williams-type, full one-piece jobs. Some even had those little skirts. Even so, the public exposure of so much female flesh was too much for Walter C. Wood, the principal, who saw the second-night performance and promptly barred me from classes for a week. It was more than worth it just to hear a talented young violinist named Viola Keeler playing a beautiful obbligato above the chorus as it sang "Can We Forget?" The lyrics for that number were written by a girlfriend named Caroline Philips; the rest by me. My favorite words were for a tune called "Midsummer Madness."

Looking back, it probably didn't help my cause that I was onstage only for one skit: the old vaudeville bit about an emcee having to stall because the next act behind the curtain wasn't ready. (Oh, yes, I had two sets of curtains.) I had to jump onstage to ad lib while the (planned) delay was taking place. The gag is to start telling a joke, and every few seconds to stage-whisper to the curtain behind me, "Are you ready yet?" "No, not yet," is heard. The joke is about a traveling salesman who visits a farmhouse and meets the farmer's v-e-r-y attractive daughter. Nothing is prurient—just the tiniest bit suggestive. The emcee doesn't really want to tell the story, but he gets further and further along, and still they're not ready backstage. Finally he takes a long breath, gives in, and is about to get to the punchline when he hears a loud "Ready!" Blackout.

A gag with whiskers, but it always works. It got the biggest laugh and applause in the show.

I still think my short expulsion was a result of the bathing beauties. Most summers our family and a bunch of Main cousins, mainly Uncle Chet and Aunt Max's large brood, called the Jeggedon gang (don't ask), would spend a week at either Lake Lauderdale or Hedges Lake, usually under a huge tent we got from somewhere. It was cheaper by far than a cabin, and with bunk beds closely stacked and an *It Happened One Night* curtain down the middle, we could cram in a ton of us. Both resorts (if you wanted to use that tony name) had a big lake, lots of cabins, floats with a regular diving board and a high dive, which I avoided like the plague. When threatened with overwhelming jeers I'd screw my courage to the sticking post, climb up, and with eyes closed and nose held tightly, jump in. I don't remember *ever* diving off.

Best of all, there were huge pavilions with giant jukeboxes—a nickel a tune, six for a quarter—and a bandstand. Saturday nights they had bands for round and square dancing. One favorite band was "Bessie Worms and The Night Crawlers," consisting of a fiddle, drum, sax and Bessie herself at the eighty-eights. Hot stuff.

There were canoes and rowboats available, but they cost extra and thus weren't very popular with any of us. But every night, at sunset, we kids, at least, would head for the wonderful dance floor. (The frozen Powerhouse candy bars were a big draw for the youngest, too.)

Betty-Jim taught me the double lindy, first sitting side-beside in chairs and just bouncing the feet to the beat. Gents' part: left-right-left, right-left-right, left-right. And repeat over and over. Keep the beat going in your head and whatever happens on the dance floor with turns, jumps, splits, whatever, you and your partner will always be in sync. By the age of five I was doing the basic step, step, step-step. But by now the Lindy Hop was hot. B.J. had her reasons for liking it. I quickly learned that with me as a partner she could wiggle and twirl and catch the eye of all the older studs. I could show her off well and she'd be set for the evening with dance requests like Glenn Miller's "Little Brown Jug" and "Pennsylvania 6-5000." Great jitterbug music.

I stretched and practiced till I could do an all-the-way-down split like Ray Bolger. I later worked with him on Broadway in *Three to Make Ready*. Me and Ginny Clark, one of my sister's best friends, hit it off pretty great together on the floor; we sometimes ended a number with her picking me up while I threw my legs around her waist. She was a healthy, big, wonderfully funny gal.

One sunny and very hot day under the canvas, a male cousin and I sort of fooled around with each other. That was the first time that had happened to me. No big deal. The really big deal had happened a few years before that. There's a sad old joke about a family so poor they couldn't afford toys for their son to play with so they cut the bottom of his pants pockets off. Anyway, I'll never forget the day when that frightening big deal had arrived. I nearly wrote "came." Maybe I should have. That's exactly what happened.

I was scared to death. What was that stuff? Was I really going to go blind now? I'd been warned, but I never believed. Maybe it was true. It had always felt so good, but it had never erupted like this. I promised myself I'd never do it again. I was too ashamed to tell anyone about the terrible thing that happened to me. Certainly not Cart. He'd get out the razor strap for sure.

Shortly after the disaster, thank God, I was sitting in Raleigh's restaurant on Main Street having a coffee frappe and listening to the older guys (maybe by a year or two) talking in the booth next to mine. I thought they were talking about "pepper tracks" that one guy's mother had found on the sheet. Well, it was "pecker tracks." I kept my ear to the booth and by the time I left I realized they were talking about the same thing that had popped out of me. So the old saw about learning all the good stuff from the street, not from your folks, was true.

That's when I turned into a living, breathing, walking hormone.

On one of those summer outings, this one at Lake Lauterdale (where eventually the folks and B.J. and her husband bought a cabin-cottage), I met a gal I immediately hit it off with. She was a couple of years older, a farm gal who lived about a mile or so down the road from the lake. She didn't swim much, but looked terrifically sexy in her bathing suit. I rarely took me eyes off her and had to stay in the water for long stretches at a time, for a reason that would have been all too obvious had I stood up in the shallow water.

After a full day of exquisite agony, I was madly in love.

At one point, when she disappeared for a minute, I scrambled out, grabbed my towel, held it in front of me and made my way to our cabin. (My immediate family had one this year.) Then I changed into clothes that were a bit more concealing of my impatient ardor.

I raced back to where I'd seen her last, and there she was. By the lake's edge, leaning against a tree, we made a date to meet in that same spot later, after supper, at five forty-five. She kissed me goodbye full on the lips; hers were slightly parted, with a tip of a tongue edged into mine. I must have blushed because she laughed, wheeled around, and took off down the lane toward the main road, waving without looking back. I couldn't move. I was frozen with love.

I don't remember what Dar dished up for supper, but I'm sure I didn't eat much of it. My mouth was full of heart. I must have checked my wristwatch a hundred times. My head was racing. Would she really show up? What would we do? Did she like dancing? What if she didn't show up?

But at a quarter of six, there by the tree was my inamorata (a word I'd learned from a lyric by Ira Gershwin, "The World's Inamorata").

I asked her what she wanted to do and she said, "Let's go for a walk." I was thrilled she didn't want to go to the pavilion. I didn't want to share her.

The walk she suggested was back to her farmhouse. She didn't talk very much and I found myself rattling on about everything, my tongue racing faster than my head, which was going at warp speed. It was almost dark when we reached her house, which was quite close to the main road. I could see there were some kerosene lamps burning upstairs. She must have been really poor. Plopping down on an old frayed couch on the porch, she told me that her folks were home, but everything would be all right. I looked at the road. She said not to worry; there wasn't much traffic along here, and nobody could see, anyway, because of the porch railing. She said, "C'mere," and began pulling down her shorts. I sort of scrunched down a little and began to unbutton my trousers. She was stretched out there in front of me. My first time. Heaven awaited.

But I couldn't. Before I got the kajolliker (family euphemism) out of my shorts, it was over. I had never been so deeply embarrassed in my entire life. Pre-premature. I hauled up my pants and fled off the porch and back up the road, running furiously, tears streaking down my cheeks, leaving the love of my life, whom I could never face again, lying there half-naked. It left me with a feeling of shame so strong I was sure I'd never be able to shake it. A true friggin' fiasco.

At home we augmented the *Evening Astonisher* with the Sunday *New York Herald Tribune*. Sometimes Cart would buy the *Springfield* (Massachusetts) *Republican*, too. He claimed it was for the Sunday comics but I had a sneaking suspicion it was because of the paper's name. I would grab the theatre section of the *Trib* and read everything. I had the habit of counting the number of shows playing from the ABC listing. I loved the reviews and ads for all the plays and musicals. One Sunday I spotted an ad for a place called the American Academy of Dramatic Arts and sent away for a brochure. When it came, I read it very carefully. One part explained what you would need to bring if you happened to be allowed to enroll. Among the items was "exercise rompers." Exercise *rompers*? That put me off the whole thing. I wouldn't be caught dead in rompers. So much for the AADA.

All that was forgotten when I received another letter from Evanston, Illinois. I had been selected for a summer scholarship at Northwestern University at the end of my junior year (only six weeks away) at Bennington High. The letter said that eighty-three out of 15,000 applicants from all over America had been chosen to be cherubs that summer. I hadn't realized I was applying for anything. I was just following instructions and filling out forms when that initial package had arrived months ago. Now I was going to be a cherub, like that dear Ann Lee. Wow. All expenses paid. I just had to show up in the last week in June.

It was summer 1943. I was sixteen years old—I turned seventeen while I was there—and suddenly I was no longer the oddball I'd been considered at high school. Instead I was one of eighty-three kids fanatically interested in all the same things as I. Wonderful young men and women crazy to learn everything about the theater. And what more-than-wonderful teachers we had to guide us, including the fabulous Alvina Krause, whose students included Patricia Neal, Charlton Heston, and Jennifer Jones.

I quickly morphed from walking hormone into theater-study sponge. There was so much to learn, with classes in practically everything: acting techniques, speech and diction, physical carriage, radio, make-up, set construction, vocal coaching, theater history and on and on. We had non-stop practice and study almost around the clock. I loved it, and I loved all the projects we got involved with. They included a version of Koessler's *Darkness at Noon* (which had been published about five years before) and a stage adaptation of *The Devil and Daniel Webster* that starred Robert Wright, who became a singer in Broadway choruses and later a producer for Carol Burnett. I wrote the background music and played a harpsichord. There were many radio scripts and poetry-reading contests; I won with "High Flight," the famous poem by the American aviator John Gillespie Magee, Jr. (If you don't know it, find it and read it. Glorious.) We even had a trip to Soldier's Field in Chicago, where I had the chance to see and hear my first opera, *Carmen*.

Some of my fellow cherubs were Claude Akins, who became a very well-known character actor in Hollywood; Phyllis (P.J.) Love, who did several Broadway shows; and a crazy guy from Indiana named Michael Barr, who was such a Fred Astaire fan that he danced, very Fred-like, all around the campus and in and out of Annie May Swift Hall, a sort-of headquarters for most of the classes. Mike wrote music, like me, so we hit it off and have remained friends ever since. We even collaborated on a couple of unproduced musicals with Dion McGregor, the songwriter who became known for an album in which he talked in his sleep.

Former cherubs like Jennifer Jones (*Song of Bernadette* was in release then) were held up as inspirations. (Years later, at MGM, I met Patricia Neal and was happily surprised to find she was an ex-cherub; a bond was born between us. This has happened over the years with many others.)

Our days at Northwestern were so jammed-full, and so much was salted away for (one hoped) our future use, that it seemed as if we'd been there for a complete college career. Actually I think we were only there for four or six weeks. It's hard to believe. I do know that the "graduating" party before heading home was the saddest moment of my life. I didn't want it to be over. Somehow I knew this had been the most exciting and educational hunk of my life. I felt nothing would ever top it, or even come close. When we all sang a parody of "Hit the Road to Dreamland" from the movie *Star Spangled Rhythm*, all eighty-three kids were in tears. But in true show-must-go-on tradition, we braved our way through it, then hugged and kissed everyone in sight, including those incredible teachers, and "hit the road" to home. It was indeed a dream time, and the curtain had finally fallen. But what memories!

Chapter 3 _____

When I reached home, I couldn't wait to tell Dar about everything. I had to wait for her to come from work; she had a day-job at Bennington College. First I asked her what she was doing there.

She told me she'd been sewing for days, on acres and acres of red jersey. The only jersey I knew was a breed of cow. She explained it was a type of material, sort of stretchy-like, and bright red. It turned out she'd been stitching the costume for Martha Graham's most famous dance piece, *A Letter to the World*. Fun, huh?

When I started recounting my Illinois adventures, it was difficult to stop. I must have rattled on a week's worth, nonstop. The family pretended more interest, I'm sure, than they had. The only thing Dar and Cart didn't really appreciate was the cat I'd adopted on campus and lugged back on the train with me. My mother named it (her) Nuisance and I eventually forget what I'd called her before. It was Nuisance now.

So, unfortunately, I was returning to school for my senior year. And keep in mind that I loved school. But while I was back with kids I'd known forever and truly liked, we were picking up where we were before summer vacation, and it wasn't the same for me. They didn't have a prayer of stacking up against the eager, dedicated and creative group I'd just been with. And I guess I had changed. Try as I might, I couldn't help comparing my old buddies with the cherubs. Of course I didn't even talk about my summer. They wouldn't understand; and worse, they wouldn't have cared.

I plodded ahead, trying to be the oddball of old. It was difficult. I got impatient with things that would never have bothered me before Northwestern. And I grew impatient with my classmates, who to my mind weren't really interested in anything except extracurricular activities. I was impossibly eager to get finished with school, get my diploma and get to work. Nothing else seemed to matter.

One day I blew my top over something as stupid and inconsequential as Mary Sue Young, or somebody, not showing up with the Victrola for an afternoon tea-dance. I thought, okay, that's it. The last straw. I stormed out of the assembly hall, went home, packed, left a note for the folks under their pillow (Dar was domestic-nursing somewhere and wouldn't be home till late), and caught the bus for Albany and the train that would take me to New York City for good.

I knew my mother had a cousin (maybe a second cousin) named Stafford Howard who lived in Brooklyn, and in Grand Central I found his address in the phone book. I asked the guy in the subway change booth how to get to 4th Street and whatever the avenue was; dropped in my nickel train fare; and was off to meet somebody I'd never met. I hoped to be taken in, like Little Orphan Andy.

The place was a big brownstone. When he came to the door he said, "Why, you're Carleton. Marjorie's son. Come in, come in." I did.

"What in the world are you doing here?"

I told him very matter-of-factly that I had come to New York to go on the stage. He seemed very calm about everything. He managed to say, "That's nice." Then he assured me he had an empty bed for me. Actually it was a whole floor, with my own bathroom. I found out the next morning that he'd called my mother as soon as he'd stowed me away for the night. Stafford worked on Governor's Island (a ferry ride away) for the military, I think in the payroll department. He shared this big old building with a German man named Leslie Ludwig. I'm not sure what Ludwig did—I think something on Wall Street. He rented out space to my, what, great uncle? I don't know. Mr. Ludwig made me feel right at home, not as though I were imposing on him at all. And he was a great cook. I had really stepped into something lucky.

The next morning I headed back into Manhattan by subway, truly thinking the world was my oyster. I felt I'd learned absolutely everything there was to know about the theater. I was prepared. Let me at 'em. I'll show 'em. I figured if you want a job in the theater, you'd just go to the theater and try out. What else? Seemed simple enough. (How dumb can you be? Simple, indeed: That was me then.)

So I went to the Great White Way and started knocking on stage doors—during the day. Even dumber. Who knew? The doormen who even opened the door gave me really strange looks before slamming it in my face. A couple gaped at me long enough for me to ask cheerfully, "Is there a part in the show?" They really looked at me as if I were an alien from Pluto. (The shows in these theaters had been up and running—some for a very long time, mind you.) One nice, old, partially deaf doorman at least smiled at me before shutting the door.

I kept at it for two days. In the evening I'd buy a fifty-five-cent balcony seat and see some show, then head back to Brooklyn.

It's important here to note that, in all the dozens of classes and lectures I'd taken during my cherub-learning period, nothing had ever been said about agents, casting folk, producers' offices or anything that told you how to *get* the job. We were just taught how to *do* the job. So on I plowed with dumb naïveté, thinking a terrific break was a-waiting.

As it turned out, something did happen, on day three—a matinee day, when the curtain was at two-forty. I showed up at the Winter Garden Theatre stage door at a little before two. *Ziegfeld Follies* with Milton Berle was playing, and there was lots of activity backstage. They must have been having auditions for a chorus replacement because the guy with a clipboard, of whom I asked my usual question—"Is there a part in the show?"—said to me, "Kid, you just missed it. We filled it five minutes ago." I was all smiles. Wow, I thought, only five minutes late. I thanked him, grinning, and shook his hand. Probably amazed that I seemed happy rather than disappointed, he said, "Listen, they're taking *Chocolate Soldier* on the road. Go on up to the Broadway Theatre and see the stage manager."

I thanked him again and raced off, running all the way to that stage door, where I asked for the guy. He said, "That's me. You'll have to audition for Mr. Simmons at the Shubert office." I was smiling so hard my lips hurt. "I'll give him a call if you like," he said. I couldn't speak but I nodded like hell. He talked a minute, hung up and said, "Tomorrow. Ten a.m. Shubert office, top of the theater." I wrung the bejesus out of his hand.

I arrived at the Shubert the following morning, shiny, scrubbed and fifteen minutes early. The guy in the box office told me where the elevator was and buzzed me through into the theater. It was the tiniest little cage I'd ever seen. At best it might have held the three Andrews Sisters; the five Marx Brothers would never have fit in. It was a do-it-yourself type of elevator: Open the door, pull aside the folding grate, then push a button for the floor.

I believe there were maybe three offices on the top floor. When I ungrated myself and stepped out, a door to the right said, "Casting." I checked my watch. Still a bit early, and too dumb to be nervous, I knocked. A voice said, "Come in."

Mr. Simmons turned out to be a grandfatherly type who couldn't have been nicer. Pink cheeks and friendly smile. The room was fairly small, with windows that looked out on the back of the Astor Hotel. There were ferns in pots by the windows and a baby grand piano at one end of the room. He asked me what I was going to sing, and did I have my music with me? I told him I didn't know I was supposed to bring any.

He sat behind the piano and studied me for a bit. "What are you?" he asked.

I told him I was a Vermonter. For some reason unbeknownst to me, he laughed. He said, "Let's find out," and started playing rippling chords. "Just sing the scales for me," he said. I belted out do-re-mi-scales in several keys.

"You're a high baritone," he said. I probably laughed.

He wanted to know how old the Vermonter was. I told him seventeen, and when he asked if I could read music, I said yes, and that I wrote it as well. He didn't seem to be impressed with that, so I didn't go on about what a success *Up and Up* had been. He told me I had a good voice, clear, loud and on pitch.

He said I looked very young, and wanted to know if I was out of school. I explained I was in my senior year and had enough credits to graduate, except for the required senior English, but (I was racing on a bit by now) that I was sure I could send in my essays, stories and other homework to Miss Bonham by mail and still earn my diploma next June.

He studied me a long time, then said, "Well, Carleton, you're very tall. We probably could find a spot for you somewhere in the back row. The show has two more weeks at the Broadway. Replacements will be put in, and the tour opens in three weeks in New Haven."

My eyes bulged out. "You mean I got the job?"

"You'll have to join Equity, but first you have to have a contract. That, my boy, will be ready for you in the morning. Meantime, take care of your school mail-in problems." And that was it. Almost as easy as I had imagined. We shook hands and I told him I'd see him in the morning.

I sailed from his office on suddenly acquired professional wings. I danced my way across town to the F subway train at lucky ole Grand Central, and arrived back in Brooklyn before noon. On the train I stared plotting how I could talk my school principal into my scheme to secure my diploma from high school. I knew how important it was to my parents, especially my mother.

Soon I was on the phone with the man who just a few weeks ago had tossed me out of school for public indecency. I was in desperate need of his assistance. It wouldn't help matters that I'd been a truant for the last few days. I was so polite it nearly sickened me. I explained how this job was the most important thing in the world to me and the very beginning of what I'd been working for all my life: a life in the theater. And how sure I was that Miss Bonham would agree to let me mail in whatever I had to since we'd be traveling from town to town and I would have no chance to go to night school, and how much I wanted that diploma, and how he had to let me know as soon as possible because I had to go in the next day *to sign my contract*.

He hemmed and hawed like mad and said he'd never had a problem like this arise, and would have to confer with the school board and some trustees. With a close-to-tears trembling voice, I pleaded for him to be quick, for my life depended on it. Please, I begged, send a wire later today because I had to *sign my contract tomorrow*.

He promised to do his best. I put the phone down, rather pleased with my performance: part Uriah Heep, part Twist, and part Little Eva.

The telegram arrived the next morning, sixty-three cents collect. Three words. PROPOSITION NOT GOOD. (signed) Walter C. Wood, Principal.

Heartbroken, I headed back into Manhattan, promising myself I would hold on and not cry, and made that dreaded trip back to Mr. Simmons's office. There on his small desk was a contract. Pink (for chorus), fifty dollars per eight-show week. My name was spelled correctly, with the 'e' in Carleton. Oh, how I longed to pick it up, sign it and put it into my jacket pocket next to my heart.

This was no scene. No acting. Just incredible bravery that I pulled up from somewhere. I told him that the school had turned me down and that I had to return in order to get my diploma, and was sorry I couldn't go on the road with the show. I kept my back as straight as I could and held in, I hoped, all the disappointment that was on the verge of breaking loose. He must have seen my crushed heart, anyway. I thanked him profusely and he smiled and said that, of course, I should finish high school.

As I headed for the door he said, "Carleton, when you finish school, come by and let me know. Maybe we'll be able to find a place for you in one of our shows."

That did it. I couldn't respond. I just dashed out the door and the tears began before I could get into the elevator. I think I must have bawled myself all the way back to Stafford's brownstone. I sat there in the big living room all alone. Both men were at work. When the heavy grief had subsided enough, I lit one of their cigarettes, a Herbert Tareyton, and in-haled for the first time. I didn't even cough. It felt good and I felt better. I decided, the heck with it, I'd stay on a couple more days, probably just to "show them."

That night the men took me out for dinner at a place called Asti. The waiters all sang opera or show tunes and the guys let me have a rye and ginger. The black world became much rosier, and I knew I'd survive to come back and give it another shot.

I saw two more shows before heading home to Bennington: Rodgers and Hart's *A Connecticut Yankee* (starring Vivienne Segal and Vera-Ellen) and, I think, John Steinbeck's play *The Moon Is Down*. I missed seeing my real love, Jeanne Shelby, on this trip. She was on the road with *Lady in the Dark* and Miss G.

Back in Vermont, a funny (well, peculiar) thing happened to me. In school once more—no explanations to anyone about my week-or-more absence—I stopped talking to everyone except my teachers. I quit as edi-tor of the Catamount (our school paper), as president of the dramatic society, president of the band. I left the stamp club; I stopped basket-ball and whatever extra things I had been involved with. Now it was just classes. Just study. No tea dances. No anything else.

My folks knew what had happened in New York (thanks or no-thanks to phone calls from Stafford), and were never anything but posi-tive about the whole thing, just as they been with all the touring I'd done with the magic shows. Those too, of course, had stopped. I took a job at Western Union in the old Putnam Hotel building and worked after school and into the evening until eight. I wanted to salt away as much money as possible. My funds (the ol' bank account), fairly well padded before this recent trip, had been nearly tapped. A good hunk had been added earlier that fall, because we got off afternoons from school to help local farmers gather their apple crops. Ten cents a bushel, and I picked like mad. Now Western Union was my main source of income. It was fun working the telephone machine. (Eight years earlier I'd gotten my Social Security card when I worked as a bagger at A&P.)

I found a new girlfriend, too. Joan. The younger sister of a classmate. A good Catholic gal, a bit of a tomboy, and great fun. I was really in love. More than puppy. On Sundays I'd go to early mass with her then on to the Second Congregational Church, where I sang in the choir. My folks were Baptists, so that's where I was baptized. Right behind the pulpit, panels would open to reveal a good-sized tank of water. (When I saw the Harold Rome musical *Wish You Were Here* years later on Broadway I kept thinking about that tank, because the show had a real swimming pool onstage.) My sister B.J. had joined friends and moved to the Episcopal Church. Some years later, so did I. They paid a nickel to choir members. The lure was too great. I really admired the minister who preached at the Second Congregational Church. So I switched to his flock. I found it terrific. His sermons were useful, funny, to-the-point and actually inspiring. I had always found everything about church really boring, except the singing. Now I could hardly wait for the sermon. That minister was so good, the town eventually got rid of him. I guess his brand of honesty was too much for them. They tore the church down and, it figures, put up a bank.

Joan and I went everywhere together. For me, at least, it had grown pretty intense. I remember that Thanksgiving she was in, I think, Wallingford, almost up to Manchester, having dinner with relatives. I missed her so much, I walked all the way there, singing "It's Always You" (a big Crosby hit) the whole trek. I got a kiss and hiked most of the way back. I finally bummed a ride. What a great day.

It was a wonder to me that Joanie even liked me because I talked her ears off most of the time. Since my silent phase had begun in school, poor Joan got the brunt of my babbling. I wrote a love song for her, "Alone with Joan." It ended with a plea:

> *I can't do it on my own*
> *Maybe one day they'll decide to let me be alone with Joan*

A seventeen-year-old sentimental sop to quasi-unrequited love.

Joanie and I never "did it." Close, but no White Owl. And no worry about premature anything.

By winter break, I'd more than finished everything I needed to earn my diploma the coming June. I had also eased off out of my vow of silence by spending time with the kids who'd moved into high school from the parochial (church) grade school. I still more or less—I don't know why—shunned the kids I'd hung out with since kindergarten. I gave my love to Cart and Dar and headed back to the city.

Three of the guys were going up to Rutland to enlist in the Navy, because they would turn eighteen before graduation and didn't want to be drafted into the Army. I got a letter from my folks, giving me permission to enlist as well; so one Saturday morning the four of us bused up to Rutland to be interviewed and take the physical. If the three guys passed, they'd be put on inactive duty until the end of school. If I passed, I could get in immediately. (I wouldn't turn eighteen until July, when I'd be finished with high school.) The others all passed. I didn't. The Doc said my pulse was too fast. I think it had to be between sixty and eighty. Mine was 120.

He told me to come back the following Saturday. What a week that was. Talk about playing a part! I didn't drink coffee, smoke or dance. I moved through the entire six days in slow motion. A clam at high tide couldn't have been calmer. On Saturday I returned to Rutland, sitting on the bus with my hands folded in my lap like an old crone. I edged slowly into the doc's office for the recheck.

My pulse was 127.

On my bus trip back down to Bennington I made my decision. Easy. I'd head back to New York at Christmas break.

And I did.

Chapter 4

It was January 3, 1944. Once again I checked my two suitcases at Grand Central and headed to the St. James Hotel on 4th Street. Not for a room; there was a place near the entrance where, for a nickel, you could purchase *Actor's Cues*. The *Cues* was a single mimeographed sheet, published daily, with casting tips. I spent the five cents and headed for Horn & Hardart for lunch. Munching the macaroni and cheese (a fave), I read that a play called *Bright Boy*, set in a prep school, was seeing young men between sixteen and twenty. The address was Penthouse, Mansfield Hotel, 12 West 44th Street. I thought, well, after lunch, I'll go over and get that play. Dumb doesn't go away easily.

Over I went, bundled up in my best Wooltex overcoat. It was a cold January. I entered the penthouse, where one room had been turned into a waiting area. Twenty-some guys were crowded in, waiting. An older man with the proverbial clipboard approached before I had gotten myself fully into the mob. "You're too old," he said, and disappeared into another room with an anxious actor in tow. I started to leave. Some kid grabbed my arm.

"He told me that six months ago," he said, "and I'm still reading for it." That was enough to hear. I quickly slipped out of my heavy coat, sat on it in a corner, where I was partially hidden in the mob, and smoked a couple of cigarettes. Forty or so more minutes later, the clipboard guy came over and said, "Okay, you're next." He led me into the inner office and left. There I stood like a big stupe in front of three people behind a desk. Two men and a woman. One of the gentlemen asked my name and slowly wrote it down.

They asked me to read, and handed me a script with the page open to the part. The lady read from her chair, throwing the lines in between my character.

Then the two men whispered while I shifted from one foot to the other. They gave a page number and asked me to read another part, then another. In all, I read five different characters.

The questions began: Where was I from, what was my experience? I told them about Wills's *Iolanthe*, *Big Hearted Herbert*, *Twelfth Night* (in which I'd played Aguecheek) and my other credits. (I didn't mention *Up and Up*, doubting that the word of mouth for the thing had reached this far from Vermont.) When asked my age I said seventeen, and quickly added that I wouldn't be eighteen for six months. All three perked up a bit. Then I told them I'd just tried to enlist in the Navy and had been turned down. (I didn't mention the word pulse.) Their friendly collective smiles seemed suddenly a mite broader. They all conferred, and after what seemed like ages, the older man said, "Take the script into the bedroom there and read it. We have others waiting to try out." I sort of bowed and headed to the door he'd pointed at.

It took an hour or maybe more to read the entire play. It was half-serious and half-funny, but I was fascinated with it all; and when I knocked gently on the door to reenter, the three all told me together, like a chorus, to come in. When I placed the script on the desk, the old head gent asked me how I liked the play. From the depths of my soul I said, "It's the most wonderful thing I've ever read."

The trio told me they had decided they wanted me in the play, but didn't know in which role, and asked if I could come back at ten the following morning. I assured them I could, thanked them all (especially the lady for reading with me), picked up my coat from the outside office, went to the locker in Grand Central, retrieved my bags and caught the old D train to Brooklyn.

Stafford was just coming home from work. We met on the steps of the brownstone.

"You back again?" he said, unfazed as usual.

"Yes sir," I answered, adding, "Think I just got my first Broadway show."

"That's nice," he said, opening the door. I carried my bags in after him, wondering how on earth he could keep himself from jumping up and down with joy. God knows I was—inside, of course.

That night in bed, going back over my first day in the city and thinking that everything had gone the way I was certain it would, I slept soundly, like the naïve babe in the woods who had no idea forests were supposed to be frightening.

I arrived—always a touch early—at the Mansfield Hotel at 9:50 a.m. The outer office was empty and the door to the room where I'd read was open. The same three people were in deep conversation so I hung back by the door until the older gent saw me and waved me in. After good mornings all around, the very first thing he said was, "What part did you see yourself in?" I thought this was standard procedure.

I didn't hesitate.

"Tittman." This character was called "Shake," for Shakespeare, and was described in the script as a tall, lanky, seventeen-year-old blond who wants to be an actor. (I'd never heard of typecasting.) Shake was also the second comedy lead.

"So did we," the man said. He produced a contract, which he and I signed. So did the two other men, who were coproducing. One of them was Arthur Beckhard, the director. The other guy—a young lawyer from St. Louis, I learned later—was David Merrick. The lady was an actress named Helen Shields, wife of the playwright John Boruff, who was currently on duty in the U.S. Navy.

That was it. Simple as all get out. Rehearsals were to begin the very next Monday in the ballroom of some hotel farther west on 44th. I gave Mr. Beckhard my Brooklyn phone number and he gave me directions to the Actors Equity Association office, as well as my "sides." These were small pages containing the last few words (cues) before an actor's complete lines. They haven't been used for eons, since they're very confusing. The character giving the cue isn't identified, so it's just: "... out of the water." Then you speak. But you get used to it, and the "sides" were handy to carry while learning lines.

I headed to the union, contract in hand. $57.50 per week, Equity minimum—the last time I ever worked for so little. I made a deal to pay off my initiation fee, and got my membership card. I'd pay part of my salary every week until my debt was met. This was the first time I didn't pay cash on the barrelhead. But this was so special and important, it wasn't exactly like starting off my theater life in debt. At least, that's what I told myself.

Today it amazes me that after a little more than twenty-four hours in New York City, I'd landed a good role in a Broadway play. Thank heavens I had no idea how difficult it was to do that. I'm sure that being dumb and just expecting it to happen like that helped. As some mystery writers are prone to write at the end of a chapter: "Had I but known."

That night I celebrated with a dinner at Sardi's. They had an actor's menu with cut-rate price; you just had to show your Equity card. (They still have one, and you still have to.) I loved the cannelloni. It cost about a buck. Not exactly Horn & Hardart or Childs penny-pinching prices, but what the hell. I splurged. Naturally I was anxious to exhibit my brand-new union card.

At the first rehearsal, I met the rest of the cast—thirteen actors including me. Several kids were making their debuts like I was; but our star, Ivan Simpson, was an English character actor who had appeared in many motion pictures. He was playing the headmaster. Also starring was Don-

Prep Schools Again

Carleton Carpenter and Michael Dreyfus in "Bright Boy."

From the Sunday *New York Times*, Feb. 26, 1944.

ald Buka, who'd worked in several plays with the Lunts and had made a movie with Bette Davis called *Watch on the Rhine*. Buka was the villain of the piece. Frank Jacoby had been on the road with *Junior Miss* and Michael Dreyfuss had been on Broadway in *Life with Father*.

After studying my sides for days, I made an important discovery. When we got on our feet and started blocking, I found it easier to memorize the lines when I tied them to movement. Forever after, I could never really learn lines until I knew where I was going. Even if they changed that blocking later, by then the words were locked in with movement, and the new blocking never bothered me.

I learned how simple acting was. All you had to do was be whomever you were playing, and listen—not to the other actors, to the other *characters*. If you're listening, you'll react as your character, not as yourself.

Sidenote: I've always adored rehearsing. I'd rather rehearse for six months and play a week than the other way around. That's where the fun and the creating happens. The character you originally think you're playing will most times evolve into somebody more complex, maybe even totally different. It takes time to discover who you are. Most plays don't have enough rehearsal time.

With *Bright Boy* we had about three and a half weeks, which included a week of previews with paid audiences—very unusual in those days. Most shows played out of town for at least a couple of weeks of tryouts before opening on Broadway. Critics' night was March 2, 1944. Dar, Cart and B-J were there. She was studying to be a nurse at St. Luke's Hospital in Pittsfield, Massachusetts.

Afterward we celebrated at some club where, I think, the flamenco gypsy dancer Carmen Amaya was headlining. Later, at the Edison Hotel where they were staying, we waited for the newspapers—there were ten or eleven then—until dawn. Who could sleep? The reviews were, as they say, mixed. Some very good, a couple very bad and the rest sort of so-so. Who cared? I was on the Great White Way, and the critics were very kind to "Shake."

One of the best writeups was a "puff piece" that had run in the Sunday *New York Times* theater section before we opened. They used a picture of Michael Dreyfuss and me, three columns wide, on the front page. If I had a chest—I don't; it's concave just like my father's—I'd have really puffed it up. What a shock to open the paper and see that. I tried to be nonchalant about it with the rest of the company, but I'm sure some of my excitement oozed out.

The boyish cast members of *Bright Boy*, 1944. Standing, L-R: Eugene Ryan, John Cushman, Donald Buka, Charles Bowlby, William "Biff" McGuire, Beman Lord. Crouching: Jeff Brown, Frank Jacoby, Michael Dreyfuss, me, Joyce Franklin.

I got an agent, a great gal named Jane Deacy, who worked at the Lester Shurr Agency. Her office was in the old Paramount Building on Broadway. During the first week of *Bright Boy*, she set me up for a reading with Don Appell, the director of a play called *Career Angel*, which was due to start rehearsals in a couple of weeks. They liked me and offered me the role for sixty-five dollars a week. I told them I'd have to let them know. I met with Mr. Beckhard that evening before the show and told him I had another offer but that I really wanted to keep playing Shake, and would he consider giving me a raise to sixty-five dollars.

He patted me on the back and said, "Well, Carleton, we're closing a week from Saturday, I'm sorry to say. But perhaps you'll be able to do that other show then."

The week and a half after the closing notice went up was a sad time, but a lot of things happened in those remaining days. I was offered a movie contract with Paramount, probably thanks to Miss Deacy. I received several phone calls on the backstage phone from some old guy who wanted to put me through college or some weird thing. All the guys would listen in and giggle. They said the old fruit was hot for my body. They said that's what I got for opening the show half-naked. In the first scene I entered in boxer shorts with a towel around my neck, fresh from the shower, stepping over the twin beds—they were narrow—and going to the window to gaze out at the tennis court where the headmaster's daughter, played by Joyce Franklin (the only girl in the show), was practicing her serves. Shake's first line was: "Isn't that something? Isn't that beautiful?" And John Boruff's play was off and running, for a total of sixteen performances, not counting the eight previews.

Every night, during a rather fast costume change, I'd have to dump thumbtacks out of my loafers before going back on stage. The general understudy, I guess, had a particular dislike for me. Or maybe he just wanted to have his own crack at Shake. He was short and would never have been able to step over the beds for the first laugh, poor kid. I felt sorry for him. It must be terrible to hang around watching everyone else get to go on but you.

I promised myself I'd never understudy. I was able to hold out on that promise for years before giving in to a standby job. I wasn't required to show up at the theater unless the star didn't.

Ivan Simpson, our ancient star, was a caution. I think he hated the show. I know he hated the sets Watson Barrett had designed. During the first runthrough on the set, Simmie (always with walking stick) came lumbering up from the house where he'd been watching and walked around the second-act outdoor set, kicking things and flailing his cane at everything. He shouted in Shakespearean tones: "This whole damn thing should be cast into the sea." But the set remained and he calmed down. This same set was used at the end of act three, when the headmaster enters and sort of ties all the loose ends of the play together. Simmie made a rather long speech that ended with: "Well, the jury is in and the verdict is up to you." Then he tossed his scarf around his neck with a grand gesture and exited.

Now, it must be said the old guy liked his scotch, and was partial to a bar almost directly across the street from the theater. Some nights he'd hurry the speech or cut parts of it out, or go up (forget his lines). On one such occasion, his fellow actor Beman Lord, trying to save the show, edged close to Simmie and whispered into his ear. The old actor rose from the log, where he sat nightly to wrap up things; and with great dignity and in a voice that carried to the last row of the second balcony he roared, "Goddamn it, that's not it!" He delivered his last line, tossed the scarf and departed. We went on to finish the play for what was surely a very puzzled audience.

Simmie departed not only from the stage but from the theater as well, and headed straight across for his beloved scotch. He didn't appear for curtain call.

Liam Dunn (years later, the minister in *Blazing Saddles*) played a professor. He once cornered Mr. Simpson and said that he should be ashamed of himself for having lived so long. "You must be at least a hundred and three. Think of all the actors you're keeping unemployed by constantly working. What with all your countless ladies, and your boozing, Simmie, don't you think that's burning the candle at both ends?" Simmie replied, "Dear boy, I've discovered that's the only way one can make ends meet."

Blackout.

The very best thing that happened during those last few days in *Bright Boy* was receiving a note at the theater from my darling Jeanne. She had seen the picture in the *Times*. I thought she was still on tour, but she had returned to New York to open at the Winter Garden in the Cole Porter musical *Mexican Hayride*. This was in the last week in January, while I was in rehearsal. Now, for at least sixteen performances, we were working on Broadway at the same time, on the same schedule. I couldn't see it until we closed, which we did on Saturday, March 15.

I didn't take the Paramount movie contract. It was hard to refuse since it would pay me one-hundred-and-fifty dollars a week for forty out of fifty-two weeks a year. I loved the movies. But I thought that being a movie star wasn't really acting. Acting, to me, was the theater. I was much too stagestruck to ever go to Hollywood, much less for seven years, the term of the deal. I would be an old man by then. At the moment I was doing exactly what I'd always planned on. I didn't want anything to rock the blessed boat I was sailing along on. And I never met the guy who wanted to give me a college education.

I missed my girlfriend Joan, who had taken over my stint at Western Union. I wrote to her about every other day. She wasn't much of a correspondent, but I kept on sending letters. I also started getting a weekly letter from Dar, who hoped I was having fun and doing well. She always ended with, "When are you coming home to get a real job?" I guess she was sure I'd never earn a living acting. No matter how much I explained things to her, the weekly query arrived. At one point I even wrote, "C'mon, mother, I can cut my own toenails."

Those letters eventually stopped. I'll tell you about that later.

I had signed for *Career Angel*, and rehearsals began the following Monday morning. That night I headed for *Mexican Hayride*. It was a lavish Mike Todd production that starred Bobby Clark, June Havoc and Wilbur Evans. Jeanne played an American tourist. Backstage we hugged and kissed. It seemed like ages since we'd seen each other. She told me I was all grown up. I guess I was. We went somewhere to eat (probably Childs down the street) and talked and talked. I rattled on, bringing her up to date, and she said how proud she was of me. But there was a hint of sweet sadness about it. Years later I realized she must've felt cheated in a way, because I'd landed on Broadway on my own when she'd so wanted to have helped me in some fashion.

I felt guilty that I'd deprived her, unwittingly, of the opportunity—just as I felt about never having stopped by Mr. Simmons's office to thank him for the encouragement and the parting offer he'd made.

Michael Dreyfuss had secured a role in *Career Angel* as well. Not wanting to overstay my welcome at Stafford's, I moved to another part of Brooklyn to stay with Michael and his parents while *Career Angel* was in rehearsal. They lived in Bay Ridge—Senator Street between 68th and 69th. It was great. I subwayed into Manhattan every day. There was another gang of guys in this play, too; we were all in an orphanage which, with help from a guardian angel, gets national attention that saves it from closing.

We had a short out-of-town run in Boston at the Wilbur Theatre, across from the Shubert. Because our final curtain fell early, most nights I'd run over to the Shubert to see the last forty minutes or so of the huge musical playing there, *Dream With Music*, starring Vera Zorina. In a number toward the end of the show, eight ladies stood at the back in big vase-like things, playing statues. They were naked from the waist up, but there was nothing lewd about it; they didn't move. Still, the Boston Bluenoses banned the show and they finally had to gauze up the statues. It broke my heart.

Once we were in New York, I rented a tiny room on the top floor of a brownstone on West 52nd Street, known as Swing Street. It cost twenty bucks a month. A bit below street level was the Swing Club. The Latin Quarter was a couple of doors east, Tony's a couple of doors west, and right across the street was a place where Billie Holiday sang. I was in neon and music heaven. Then there was Nedick's on the corner of Sixth Avenue, where you could get breakfast—a small orange juice, a donut and coffee—for eleven cents. Maybe they thought ten cents sounded too cheap.

Anyway, life was great, *and* I was on my own for the first time. The cast of *Career Angel* had three or four days off while they moved in the sets and lights. I got to see *Dream* from the top (instead of the topless) and loved it. I remember someone singing, "When you're marching to the altar, better shoot square with Thompson, J. Walter." (J. Walter Thompson was the ad agency for Lever Brothers.) In another number, showgirls stood around with giant cakes of Lux Soap. It was, as far as I know, the first show to go truly commercial.

Another musical I saw before the New York opening of *Career Angel* was *Follow the Girls*, starring Gertrude Niesen. A young, much-slimmer Jackie Gleason played a sailor named Goofy. The show was the first leg of a double-date night out on the town. The other guy was Tony Miller from the cast. Our dates were two of my classmates from school, Mary Sue Young and Eleanor Thompson. Ferd (that was Eleanor's nickname) had a crush on me.

Anyway, she was mine, and Tony was happy with Mary Sue. After the show, we sported the gals to the Astor Roof. Tony and the girls were eighteen and I was underage, but in those days nobody ever checked as long as you looked old enough, and we were dressed to the nines. So, cocktails all around. Just one for each of us, however. Budget restrictions. The girls had their hearts set on a carriage ride through Central Park, so that's where we headed. It was now a little after midnight and no horse-hacks were lined up. Besides, during the war, the park closed at midnight.

We were out of cigarettes, and Tony said there was a place on Central Park West that would still be open; he suggested we cut through the park. We were at the Seventh Avenue and Central Park South entrance, where a sign clearly stated the wartime hours. Tony, a native New Yorker, assured us nothing would happen; he'd done it hundreds of times, he claimed, and it would be a fun adventure. He said he knew how to avoid any cops on patrol, and that he knew the park like the back of his hand. The thrill of it all swept us along, and into the woods we went. There were fewer lights in the park then, but we were avoiding them anyway. Our faithful Indian guide, Tonto Tony, led the novices. The four of us stuck pretty close together.

Suddenly Tony stopped. "Car patrol," he stage-whispered. "Quick, up that hill." I grabbed Ferd's hand and we flew up the hill. I urged her on. Looking back, I saw Tony and Mary Sue running the other way. Headlights were approaching, and came to a stop only a few yards above us. That's when poor Ferd slipped and fell. I was helping her up when the flashlight beam hit us.

"Come up here," a voice demanded.

"Oh, Carleton," Ferd moaned softly, scared.

Up we went. There were two policemen. One wanted to know what we're doing in the park. Just walking, I told him.

"You weren't walking when we spotted you."

Was I going to be charged with rape? My mind boggled.

"You're too young to be prowling around the park this time of night."

Then he asked how old I was. Dumbness reared its head. "Eighteen," I lied. Somehow I thought it would be all right if I were legal. Everything was okay if you were of age. "Got any I.D.?"

"Sure do, officer."

I reached into my wallet and dug out half of my castmate Allen Rich's draft card. I'd used it to get into some Boston burlesque theater, and to buy beer at Jacob Worth's. I felt fairly smug and was on the verge of congratulating myself for my quick thinking. I handed him the card, and gave Eleanor a comforting wink. She stood frozen beside me.

"Aren't you a little more than five foot, seven inches tall?" I broke down and told them the truth. I was seventeen, nearly eighteen, and the card belonged to this guy who was in a show with me in Boston that was about to open on Broadway, and I had it 'cause I told some other guy in the show I was married and he said I wasn't old enough even to be drafted, so Allen loaned me half of his draft card so I could prove a point and …

I was wound up and ready to go on and on, when they interrupted me.

"This card says it belongs to a Benjamin Norman Schultz."

"Well, Allen Rich is his stage name," I said, running on empty.

"You have a draft card?"

No, I said; I was only seventeen.

"Can you prove it?" I just shook my head.

"You look old enough for the service. You dodging?"

"No, sir," I mumbled.

"I think you'd better come along with us." He turned to Ferd and told her to get herself home and to be more careful of the company she kept. She stood there, teary-eyed, looking at me; then she turned and moved away a little while the two piled me into the police car. She was waving as if she were never going to see me again.

I was carted off to that precinct station smack in the middle of Central Park, off the cross street between Central Park West and Fifth Avenue. They didn't handcuff me, so I was, in a perverse way, kind of enjoying this whole adventure—a real bad-guy role. I was fingerprinted, and the officers who brought me in told the booking guy behind the counter that

I was being held for F.B.I. investigation on the charge of draft-dodging. That impressed the hell out of me. They took off, and a guard took me to a cell and locked me in. That wasn't quite so impressive. But the old guard was a real character. All the time he was locking me up, he mumbled to me about how unfair the law was. How stupid the legal system was. Locking up young kids for walking in the park, while there were murderers running around loose all over the city. How dumb could that be? I half-expected him to quote the Dickens line from *Great Expectations*: "The law is a ass." He was really a sweet old guy.

Two cells away, a drunk was singing, badly off-key and off-tempo, "As Time Goes By." (*Casablanca* was a big hit then.) I settled, almost happily, down on my slab, knowing Tony and Mary Sue must have been watching the entire scene hidden safely behind some trees and would have taken Ferd back to the Taft Hotel where the girls were staying. I fell innocently asleep, in spite of the crocked crooner.

Suddenly, I don't know how long later, the old guard was back, tapping gently on the bars and apologizing for waking me up. He unlocked the cell door and handed me a package. "A friend of yours named Tony came by and said you'd need this right away," he whispered urgently. He relocked my cage, apologizing again, and shuffled away. The urgent parcel turned out to be a carton of Chesterfields. Tony somehow had found out where the patrol car had taken me and, no doubt, pictured me pacing back and forth in a jail cell with no cigarettes, worried and nervous as a cat. It made me laugh. I didn't even open one pack; I simply went back to sleep with a smile on my face.

At seven-thirty the next morning, a different guard took me from my cell and brought me back to the booking counter. There, a tall man around thirty asked me if I could prove my age. I told him I had my birth certificate in my room on 52nd Street. He was very nice. He said, "Fine, let's go have a look at it," and we left the precinct. He drove us there and double-parked, which really impressed me. We climbed the four flights to my room and I showed him my proof of birth, signed by the Bennington Town Clerk, and also my contract for *Career Angel*.

I told him we were opening tomorrow night. Very knowledgeably for a non-Equity member, he said, "Well, son, break a leg."

He was gone and I was free. It was about eight o'clock. My criminal career was cut short and the curtain closed on my bad-guy part. The guy never even said a word about my having been in the park after hours.

On Broadway (for a hot minute) in *Career Angel*, 1944. L-R: David Kelly, unknown, Allen Rich, Gerald Matthews (kneeling), Michael Dreyfuss (looking over Rich's shoulder), me, Bobby Lee.

We had a tech-through that night at the theater. I quickly returned the Benjamin Norman Schultz half-a-card to Allen Rich, read out and finally thanked Tony, and feasted on my tale of the night before. The girls saw the opening the following night, then made a beeline for the train and away from the wicked city.

Career Angel starred Whitford Kane and Glenn Anders in adult roles. Among the other grown-ups in the cast were Donald Foster and Mason Adams, who played the lead on radio's *Pepper Young's Family* for years. Then there was the gang of us orphans. Both our show and *Dream with Music* opened around the same time. I remember *Dream with Music* had an electrical failure on opening night and it took a cash investment from Lever Brothers to get the set-heavy spectacle (which included flying carpets) on its feet. *Dream* was at the Majestic; we opened at the National (now called the Nederlander). We ran twenty-two performances; they ran twenty-eight. Both shows closed the same night, Saturday, June 10.

On the Sunday morning following our last performance, I headed home to Bennington. Talk about spectacular timing: That very evening was the baccalaureate service, which kicked off senior week for the class of '44. As if I'd never been away, I joined in the whole nine yards: senior picnic, senior ball, everything leading up to graduation night. I even played in the orchestra concert. It was the first time I'd touched a fiddle since years before, when I was second violinist with the Vermont State Children's Symphony and played at a benefit for the opening of Adams Hall in Williamstown, Massachusetts. Jose Iturbi was the guest artist. (That building is now home to the prestigious Williamstown Summer Festival Theater.)

I donned the cap and gown and was handed the Big D. I gave it to my folks, kissed them both—Cart was embarrassed as hell by my public show of affection—and told them, "Well, I got it. Now it's yours." They were both a little moist around the eyes. That made me happy.

The following week, the three guys with whom I'd tried to join the Navy in December were on their way to Springfield, Massachusetts to be sworn in. I went along with them. Dar said, "I'll see you tomorrow." She didn't know I'd visited a physician, Dr. Richling, the day before, and that he had checked me over and said my health was fine. When I asked about my pulse, he told me that a "double-pulse" was normal and that nothing was wrong with my heart. I'd grown too tall too fast, he said, but that would sort itself out in time. I asked what I could do to pass the physical for the Navy. He gave me a digitalis pill and told me to break it in half, and explained when I should take it.

So armed with my folks' letter of consent and my birth certificate *and* the pill, I joined the trio on the bus to Massachusetts.

At the Naval station in Springfield, a CPO collected the papers from the four of us. They of course had a copy of their physical. "Where's your fitness report?" demanded the Chief. I didn't lie, exactly. I just said that those were the only papers I had, and that we all had enlisted together. They backed me up. I looked eager and innocent. After they cussed out the recruiting station, he told me I'd have to have another exam. I said that was jake with me, and he showed me a room to head for.

I had swallowed the prescribed dose of digitalis as we approached Springfield. Now, to make sure I'd pass, I swallowed the other half before I went into the doc's office. I really felt mellow. Everything was fine—except that my pulse was just barely fast enough to pass. The doc stamped a paper of some sort, passed it over to me and said, "Welcome aboard, sailor."

The three guys and I joined a larger group, and shortly we were all standing with our arms in the air saying "I do," like we were getting married. Herded onto a bus, we rolled away to Sampson, New York, where the boot camp was. I was in the Navy at last. What a few days! Diploma'd and Navy'd.

Then the adjustments began. To begin with, the worst thing for me was getting used to sharing the head with others. I was pee-shy as hell. But there was no privacy about anything in boot training. In the barracks we were double-bunked only a couple of feet from double-bunks on both sides. So you heard everything. The crying from some, the snoring from many and gastronomical noises from practically everybody. After lights-out, there was a sea of motion in the place, almost as if we were already on board a ship. Everyone knew what everyone was doing—including, apparently, the CPO in charge of the barracks, who would greet us in the early morning with a loudspeakered, "Drop your cocks and grab your socks." A profound way to start the day. Right off, I wrote three letters: one home, one to my agent Jane Deacy and the third to Joan.

Miss Deacy was the first to reply. She wrote that she was glad I was so patriotic, but that there was a deal for me to test for two Warner Bros. pictures, *Janie* and *Junior Miss*. Since she'd underlined the word "patriotic," it was clear she wasn't too happy about my enlistment. I wrote a quick note back, full of apologies and promises about how I'd make up for everything as soon as the war was over. I tried not to seem to gung-ho, and thanked her for understanding. I'm sure she must have. World War II was, although it sounds awful to say, the "good" war.

We were raced through boot training. It was usually twelve weeks; we got six. I should say, most of the kids did. After four days, because I was an actor and had done some radio shows during my four months in New York City—not a heck of a lot, but enough to have become a member of AFRA (American Federation of Radio Artists), I was culled from my company to work at the radio studio on base. We did multiple editions of *Bluejacket Time* and *Serviceman's Diary* every week. These were transcribed and sent to ships on active duty. It was fun. And I had turned eighteen. Legal at last.

But except for the morning sprints around the track and the exercises before breakfast mess, I learned nothing about the service I'd been so anxious to join. Nothing except port and starboard, fore and aft (stem to stern), mess, head, and innumerable ways to inject the word fuck into practically every sentence. Sometimes even between syllables, like Hono-fucking-lulu. It seemed to be the required adjective. And it became a habit hard to break. I had to watch myself like a hawk when I got boot leave at home. I slipped a couple of times.

After the first three weeks we were named "Rooster Company." It was a fake award, I'm sure, that every company in camp at one point received because it allowed us an evening off to relax and play and take a needed break. We were stuffed into buses and deposited in the nearby "big town" (Geneva, New York, population about seven), whereupon we piled out, ate too much spaghetti and meat balls, drank way too much beer, threw up, and were retrieved by the buses at eleven p.m., happy as idiots could be. We were the fucking Rooster Company.

After our weeklong boot leave, we all talked about which field in the Navy we wanted to specialize in. For some reason I decided I wanted to go to the Rangefinders School. I had no real idea what that was. It made no difference. Every morning a sea-duty list appeared. I hit it the third day. It was alphabetical, so I was near the top. There were three C's: Carpenter, Castanza, Costello. We lined up as a medic passed from one boot to the next, saying, "Skin it back and milk it forward." The pecker-checker. Several guys were pulled out and sent to sick bay for treatment. They'd been lucky enough to have picked up a dose of clap. We envied them. Not for the clap, just the getting of it.

The three C's passed. The following day, we and a couple of dozen others found ourselves aboard the oldest train I had ever seen, except in movies. I guess because of the war, the rolling stock was really squeezed. Old, once elaborate but now frayed and shaky Pullman cars became bunks at night. The C's were billeted together and we became fast friends. At night Costello and I would sing across the aisle to each other. Our big favorite was "Time Waits for No One" from the movie *Shine on Harvest Moon* with Ann Sheridan. The mess car was really a bare cattle car. Hints of manure hung in the air. But we scarfed down the aptly named "shit-on-a-shingle" (chipped beef gravy on toast) while standing up.

After several days—the old choo-choo crawled—we ended up in California.

We had no idea where we were headed, or for what. It turned out to be a place in Oakland call Camp Parks. Still, no one told us what was going on until two days later. We were scrunched into a small theater and an officer up on stage proudly announced: "Men, you are now Sea-bees."

We turned to each other and practically chorused in whispers, "What the Fuck's a Seabee?" None of us had ever heard the word. Well, we learned we were now part of the 38th Naval Construction Battalion. We received one night of liberty before departure for god knows where. The three C's spent that night in San Francisco at a burlesque house, and the whole trio fell madly in lust with a stripper named Virginia Ballentine. We promptly nicknamed her "The Wet-Dream Girl of the 38th."

The next morning, ditty bags stuffed and hearts pounding, we board-ed a huge troop ship that was so crammed with men I was sure the thing would sink. I was billeted in the bowels of the monster in the second up in the stack of four hammocks swinging in the dim, stifling place, where the smell of fuel oil was intense. There were about twelve stacks of four. I stowed my gear and joined the throng on deck as we shoved off from the pier in San Francisco. The ship glided gently under the Golden Gate Bridge. What a spectacular sight.

But the wonder of it all didn't last long. Everyone agreed later that the roughest the entire Pacific got was just outside that gilded bridge. It didn't take long before a lot of heads were hanging over a hunk of rail, puking seasick guts out. I was among the first. That evening I slept—well, I tried to—in my allotted hammock. I had never been that ill in my life. Measles, chicken pox were vacations compared to this. That did it. From then on I slept up on deck with scores of other sufferers. In a couple of days, the fresh air and calmer seas seemed to right my own body of a ship, and food, at last, could happily be ingested and stay put.

No one knew our destination, but scuttlebutt was rife. Days passed in healthy comradeship, and the nights held star-filled glory. None of the rumors I heard proved correct. We all knew the ship was headed south-west but we wound up docking at a port in Hawaii called Red Hill—just for a few days, while equipment was loaded on the already over-stuffed vessel. But we got our liberty in Honolulu, where I ran into a couple of pals from home, Bernie Galipeau and Dean Houghton. We got crocked one night and decided to get tattoos. The waiting line was so long we soon tired of hanging around, when there were so many other bars we hadn't hit. The following morning I was happier with my hangover than I would have been with a tattoo. I have a snapshot somewhere of the three of us in our whites, arms about each other, tipsy smiles. It looks like an old ad for *On the Town*.

Earlier that evening we had sat on a hill a mile from an outdoor movie screen and watched *Sweet and Low Down*, in which Lynn Bari sings "I'm Making Believe." (Years later I learned it wasn't Lynn doing the singing. Even later, she and I did a play together called *French Postcards*.) I loved the song, and of course sang it to Costello when I was back on board.

The next stop, I think, was Kwajalein Atoll in the Marshall Islands, where we dropped off a lot of guys. (We left some in Hawaii, too.) We arrived in the afternoon. A bunch of older guys were detailed to work; the rest of us were free to roam around, and eventually ended up at another outdoor movie theater, where the film had already started.

Costello and I grabbed a couple of beers and headed up to the top plank. It was a little before dusk, and dark enough to see the film: *Since You Went Away* with Claudette Colbert, Jennifer Jones, and Shirley Temple. We clinked our beer cans and settled back against the fence, ready to make jest at the wartime flick. That didn't last very long. Soon we were both involved with the plot and especially the music. There we sat in the fading light, both of us getting moist around the edges, singing along with the featured song:

> *We strolled the lane together*
> *Laughed at the rain together*
> *Sang love's refrain together*
> *And we'd both pretend it would never end*
> *One day we cried together*
> *Cast love aside together*
> *You're gone from me, but in my memory*
> *We always will be together*

We felt just like we had on the train from boot camp to California—but somehow a bit more personal.

Chapter 5 —————

On to the west went the 38th Battalion. The final destination: Tinian, in the Marianas (which include Guam, Rota and Saipan). When we left the ship, loaded with all sorts of combat gear we knew nothing about, including a Carbine rifle, it was like a Marx Brothers comedy. Clamoring hand-over-hand down the cargo net, I lost footing or grip or just plain slipped. I crashed down into the Landing Ship Tank waiting to ferry us ashore. Everything flew in different directions to applause and laughter. I immediately acquired the nickname, "Arms, Legs and Asshole."

No one, at least the boots, realized what a serious and perilous undertaking this whole thing was. Most of the heavy equipment hit the beach ahead of us. We were the first battalion to land after the island had been made pretty much secure by the wave of Marines that had preceded us by a number of weeks. With all the half-assed rivalries among the different branches of servicemen, the Marines and Seabees were always buddy-buddy. We really respected one another and were honest comrades all during the war and after. Most of the active fighting when we hit Tinian was being waged on Saipan, an island not too far away. We could watch the bombings and anti-aircraft firing after dark like fireworks.

There were still a lot of Japanese on Tinian, mostly hidden in the hills with a minimum of firepower. Still, on the afternoon when we hit the beach, Japanese planes were strafing us as we clamored out of the LST and took shelter under Caterpillars and stuff piled there. In a strange way, there seemed to be little fear involved. Crawling around under a Caterpillar that day, I lost my wallet, and all I could think of was the sixty-five bucks I'd won playing blackjack on the troop ship. I didn't even have the sense to worry about losing my Navy I.D. card—a Captain's Mass Offense.

The strafing subsided as darkness approached, then disappeared completely.

We dug in for the night not far from the beach. There were tents close together and a ring of guards stationed around the temporary area. First duty, however, was to dig a huge hole for our Commander. Remember the character Captain Queeg in that court-martial movie *The Caine Mutiny*, and the steel balls he kept with him all the time? Well, we had our own odd Commander. Rezac, by name. His foible was a xylophone that he kept with him all the time, carted around by a personally selected quartet of unlucky underlings. In the quiet of the night, even that first exhausted evening on Tinian, we'd hear him hammering away on the thing. That evening was a premiere hearing for us boots just joining the 38th. Three diverse groups now made up the battalion: the boots (mostly age eighteen), the "old salts" (who were twenty to twenty-two and had served in the Aleutians on Adak or Kodiak) and the old codgers, age forty or so, who were the real professionals (formally civilian) and knew what they were doing and would teach us. Or try to.

Late that first night, we heard gunfire. The eleven guys on guard had been sniped and shot by stray Japanese. These were, as far as I know, the only losses the 38th incurred during our stretch on the island. A messenger for the Marine Island Command arrived early the following morning with orders from on high to get our collective butts the hell out of there. We had managed to set up camp right smack in an area known to still hide several of the enemy. We got the hell out in a hurry—xylophone first.

When we finally settled down into life in the secure section, it was really very pleasant. Four men to a tent. It was like a small village, with street names and gardens by most tents—probably the most civilian kind of existence you could ask for. We were assigned to jobs according to our individual skills, and began our six-day work weeks. I lasted two days on a jackhammer; the guys got tired of picking me and the hammer out of a hole. We had a (staggered) day off each week, a G.I. day. We could go swimming, explore cautiously or lay about and read. We had a beer tent, post-office tent, pay tent, and a not-too-bad mess hall. Well, the cook was inventive with Spam. I wound up working in the disbursing office, not a job I was looking for. I wanted to do something that would allow me to "strike" (go after a rank or rating) for a Carpenter First Class. I thought that would be fun.

Instead I ended up being a Storekeeper First Striker. I grew to really enjoy the job, since I got to pay the 1,100 guys every month, and the work around the office was negligible. Jake, the chief (three-striper), really ran things; although technically, Ensign Bowker—fresh from Annapolis—was ranking officer. I used to goof off regularly with D.N. I called him by his initials; Seabees didn't do much saluting or Sir-ing. He always called me Stretch. He was maybe four years my senior. He'd requisition a jeep from the car pool, tell Jake we had to attend to something at headquarters, and off we'd go exploring. He'd never fired a carbine either, although we always took one along on those jaunts. Never had to use it. I remember those banana trees with fruit that was smaller than a Chiquita. It was yellowish-green outside and pink inside, and it tasted sweeter, maybe because we felt like we were stealing.

Another job I had was running the beer hall. We were allotted one case of cola and one of beer (usually Lucky Lager, a California brand) per month. There was a hitch, however. You could drink all the soda you wanted, until the twenty-four cans were gone, but the beer was restricted to a maximum of two cans a night. To the dismay of heavy guzzlers, I had to invent a sort of rationing card in the interest of comparative sobriety. The guzzlers didn't hold it against me; they knew the rules, although they constantly tried to outwit the system.

And outwit me. Midnight oil was burning nearly every night in several tents while the forgers went to work. I had to constantly keep changing the cards to stay half a jump ahead. They also made deals with the scarce non-drinkers in the outfit to use their beer rations. I began to know the guys fairly well, since I saw them six nights a week; and I would pretend I didn't know it was their second (sometimes third) trip through the line. I became sort of popular, or at least well-known, more from the nightly booze tent than from the monthly, miniscule pay tent. (Now, thanks to the Internet and a bunch of my films still playing on TV, I hear from a bunch of old 38ers.)

Costello and I fell into a daily routine. We didn't share the same tent, but we did share the same head, and we would have our first cigarette of the day together. The after-teeth-brushing one. Our second would be the breakfast-chow-line one. Whichever of us got on line first would save a space for the other. Then the after-mess cig before we went to work. Cos, on a surveying crew, would hop on the big truck that took him and a large gang of others out to where the work on an airstrip was going on; I hiked to Jake, D.N. and the disbursing office. There was a huge water tower near our office and, even with my acrophobia, I'd climb all those steps every morning to watch the truck wind its way through the jungle. I'd wait until it disappeared from view, then I'd climb down and go in to work. Why, I don't know.

A section of the beach had been heavily bombed before we arrived, and there were craggy shoals and deep caverns in the bluest water I'd ever seen. All sorts of colorful tropical fish swarmed around. (Before anyone had television sets, we had our own Discovery Channel.) We'd swim, lie side-by-side in the coral sand on our bellies and talk about our girlfriends back home. I wrote Joanie almost every week. We received mail very irregularly, so when I heard from her there'd be maybe three letters from her at once. I'd check the dates from the cancellation and read them in order, no more than one a day, like taking a vitamin tablet. I'd tell Cos all about her, and sing "Alone With Joan" for him. He told me about his dates in Springfield, Massachusetts, his home. We'd hunt for and collect some truly beautiful little cone-shaped shells. Some had purple or pink stripes, some a kind of speckled design. When we got really lucky, we'd find the rare cats-eye, a special, priceless discovery.

Even better, of course, were our conversations. We told each other everything. Costello, Irish and Catholic, had a quick wit and a wonderful sly way of telling a story. I'd never felt closer to anyone before, and I basked in our friendship. I always had a great group of buddies, girls and guys, neighbors, classmates, fellow actors, but this was so special it's impossible to describe.

My third job was only on Sundays. I lugged around and played a portable Estes organ at three or four diverse services. The green organ was made in Brattleboro, Vermont, just up Woodford mountain from Bennington, so I felt as if I had a bit of home with me on Sunday. You pumped the peddles with both feet and swelled the tone by pushing little wing-like things in or out with your knees. It was great fun. I made up the music as I went along, sort of somber and churchlike. No one was aware it was pure Carpenter fakery. I had no music to read, but I did minor variations on "The Old Rugged Cross," "Fairest Lord Jesus" and other hymns that I could play by ear, altering the chords and melody just enough to not be an out-and-out steal.

When we eventually built a recreation hall, there was an honest-to-God piano. I wrote Dar and asked her to send me some sheet music of current hits so that I could add to my repertoire of by-ear pop songs. She may have mailed more, but I remember only two, folded into eights to fit an envelope. (I hated that. It was worse than breaking the spine of a book.) I was thrilled to learn "Tico-Tico" and "Don't Fence Me In." I still have the copies, scotch-taped to near extinction.

After a bit, a few other Seabee units joined us on the island, and one of them had an outdoor movie. It was not a long jaunt from our "village," and it was a terrific addition to the shortage of entertainment available at the 38th. Cos and I went often, about every time they changed the movie. We'd walk, arms loosely flung around each other's shoulders, yakking away. Sand bags on a slope were the seats, but comfortable as hell when you were with a good buddy. We all hooted and yelled at the screen, laughing at over-sentimental slush, as we considered it then.

But sometimes things really got quiet, and a muffled sob or two could be heard during a film like *None but the Lonely Heart* with Cary Grant and Ethel Barrymore. I really teared up at that, so I was happy to hear many other guys honking their noses toward the end. I wouldn't have admitted it at the time, but I was a big old sentimental slob down deep. I even got jeered at by admitting once that I cried so easily—even at *Bowling For Dollars* on TV. There was something heartbreaking to me about watching all those hard-working men and women trying so desperately to make a meager killing in their few moments in public, and mostly failing.

Only once, I think, did a USO show come to the Marine base. We all couldn't wait to get to it. It was a disaster. No stars, no one anybody knew, and the show was really shabby. The "comic" was some dirty-mouthed guy with a complexion as bad as his timing. But we applauded anyway, more in thanks for their having come ten thousand miles to entertain us than for the show itself.

I never even thought about the theater all the time I was there. I was so far away from Broadway, and it was important to me to concentrate on the job at hand, whatever it was. On one of my jeep treks with D.N., we went to a big airstrip where most of the work was going on. The first time I saw a B-29, it looked as monstrous as the Empire State Building tipped over on its side. Today it would probably seem like a Piper Cub compared to even one of the commuter-to-hub jobs you can't stand up in.

Cos and I would sometimes have a brief falling-out over some foolish thing, which was healthy. Total bliss gets to be dull. The breaks never lasted for long, and we'd be buddies again in short order. When he wanted a special favor, he had a trump card over me: my lost I.D. card. I never told anyone except him about losing it. It was as if I were Damocles and he held the single hair attached to the sword hanging over my head. He made great comical threats about turning me in "to the xylophone master" if I didn't do whatever. Of course, he never told anyone.

Time waits for no one
It passes you by
It rolls on forever
Like the clouds in the sky
Time waits for no one
Goes on endlessly ...

I'm making believe that you're in
    my arms
Though I know you're so far away
Making believe I'm talking to you
Wish you could hear what I say

Back when World War II was raging, there were countless songs for lovestruck, lonely guys to sing. These were two of my favorites.

One morning a notice was posted in the mess hall: Anyone who took a special written test the following morning would get a half-day off. Nearly nine hundred guys filed in for the exam, me included, looking for that precious half-day. I can't remember much about the test. I hurried through it to get as much time off as possible, then immediately forgot about the whole thing.

Weeks later, an All-Nav order (really big-time) was posted. They were recruiting four men from our outfit to return to the States for V-12 college training to be an officer. I had scored third. I was in sad shock. Had I known what the damned test was for, I would never have taken it. I didn't want to go to college. I didn't want a career in the Navy. I didn't want to leave my outfit. And I certainly didn't want to leave my best friend in the world. Cos made a huge joke of the whole thing; how I was Mister I.Q., and all that.

But this was serious. An All-Nav order was irreversible. I didn't have a clue what to do. How the hell could I get out of this mess? If I went home to the states, I'd want to go back to work on the stage. Cos came up with a plan. Tell them you lost your I.D., he said; then they won't consider sending you away. So off to the Executive Officer I went. I pleaded with the man to take whoever had come in fifth; that I didn't want to be an officer, Sir, and that the vacancy could be filled easily by the next man. No soap, he said, but in stronger words. Impossible! An All-Nav order MUST be obeyed.

Scared to death, I swallowed hard and blurted out my terrible secret. "Well, Sir, I lost my Navy I.D. card." I had reached up and broken the hair holding the sword of doom. He simply turned to the yeoman working at the desk and said, "Type up a new I.D. for this sailor." Turning back to me, he said, "You're on your way stateside, Seaman Carpenter. Congratulations." He disappeared into his inner conclave.

I left the office with a new I.D. and a very heavy heart. This was ten times worse than leaving Mr. Simmons's office without being able to sign that chorus contract. How would I tell Costello? How the hell could I say goodbye?

He solved that problem in an odd way: He kept out of sight. I couldn't find him for the entire two days before I had to leave. No one I asked knew where he was. He didn't show up at the head for the tooth routine, or at chow line. Nowhere. I cleaned out my tent, packing my ditty bag to overflowing. I never saw Cos, right up to the time I was to board a small plane to Saipan. I was sure, somehow, that he'd show up at the plane before it took off. He didn't. This was my first airplane ride. It would be a short one. Barely up, and minutes later I'd be in Saipan. I was too sad to be scared of flying. I sat by one of the two windows on the thing, my eyes searching the strip for anything that looked like a surveying crew, desperately hoping to catch a last look at the friend I'd been forced to leave. As we took off I kept waving my hand at the tiny window in case he happened to be watching the takeoff.

The tears were really flowing, and I kept blowing my nose. The other three guys thought I was just frightened of flying. That was okay by me.

So Costello was no more. Well, not quite. I kept remembering times we'd shared. Getting zonked on something called Torpedo Juice or Coral Cocktail, which was practically pure alcohol distilled from fermented local fruit. Really hard to come by. I did a lot of cajoling in my beer-line capacity to arrange that. One time, after we'd had plenty of beat but were hard-up for a nightcap, we resorted to a drink made with Vitalis hair tonic and grapefruit juice. It's a wonder we survived. Many more adventures played in my head all the way back to the U.S.A., as though watching a movie with the two of us as stars.

In Saipan we switched to a larger plane and proceeded on to Hawaii. We landed there on the same day F.D.R. died. Then we continued by ship to San Francisco. The four of us really got loaded that first night back on American soil. We shared one room and our hangovers the next day. I met several other guys snared from active service. They all seemed overjoyed at being away from the hot war. If I'd come from a destroyer, I probably would have been happy, too. And maybe they hadn't had to leave behind them the most important person ever.

We were assigned to different colleges for pre-V-12 (to help us get used to school again) for a two-week period. Then we'd have a chance to choose the school we wanted to attend. I made up my mind that I wanted to be as close to Broadway as I could get, and had decided on Columbia University. Meanwhile I was assigned to Princeton for the pre-weeks. The second night at Princeton, at around three in the morning, my appendix ruptured. I was rushed to the Brooklyn Naval Hospital for an emergency operation.

I awoke sometime the next day and discovered I was in a huge ward, nearly as jammed as the troop ship, but at least I wasn't in a four-tiered swinging hammock. The bed was narrow, but it was a real hospital one. And there were several rows of these, cheek-by-jowl in the place. A radio was loudly tuned to the Arthur Godfrey show, I remember. I'm sure a lot of the guys there were in worse shape than I, although I was hurting like the dickens. I guess aspirin was the pain reliever of choice. I could have used something a tad stronger.

But I began to get better. Slowly. Operation techniques were hardly as zip-a-dee-do-dah as they are nowadays. I was at the Naval Hospital for nearly two weeks. It wasn't really bad at all, except the necessary episodes with the bedpan. A thoughtful medic would always roll screens around my bed, which was damn near smack in the middle of the ward, for privacy. Then he'd crank up the bed. I'd be in a quasi-sitting stance, head and shoulders above the screens. I'd try to scrunch down out of view and the bedpan would be scooted out from under me.

Of course the rest of the ward, to a man, knew what was going on and razzed the hell out of me. I was so damn tall, it was really impossible to find a hidden position and accomplish the necessary task. After several tries and different angles, I finally had to call it quits. I don't think I had a real B.M. until I was ambulatory. (Which is probably more than you want to know. Sorry about that.)

When I returned to Princeton, the entire pre-V weeks were all but two days over. And I was too late to choose Columbia. I'd been assigned to Trinity College in Hartford, Connecticut. That wasn't too bad; it was fairly close to the city. (I adjust easily. The old Pollyanna complex: The frigging glass is always half-full.)

The second morning at Trinity when we raced outside the dorm to line up for roll-call, I felt sort of peculiar standing there in the second row. Then, dizzy. I began crumbling over, then … blackout. I was taken away by ambulance. I recall coming to my senses in that moving vehicle and thinking what a bunch of miles I was piling up in meat wagons. Off I went to the St. Albans Navy Hospital on Long Island. And the tests began. I was punctured and probed from head to toe; all sorts of blood samplings were taken and analyzed. I was sweating-hot one minute and freezing the next.

I was told that my temperature broke all kinds of records. I ate aspirin tablets like peanuts. The bed was really my friend. This was the first time ever I wasn't bouncing around with the usual high-test energy. I was happy to lay stretched out between the sheets, hardly moving a muscle. Even the hospital food began to taste good after a few days. I knew I must have been mending.

Then the day arrived that changed things around. I was taken into a small room where a teaching doctor had four young medical students observe his technique for doing a spinal tap. He was really excited when I was wheeled in. He told the quartet, in effect: Aha, good skinny specimen. He wielded a syringe that looked big enough to baste a turkey, with a needle long enough for knitting. He jabbed it somewhere into the lower back. That was followed by a vocal "oops!" and the withdrawal of the knitting needle. Then another jab, and a "There we go!" And that song was ended. But the "melody" sure lingered on. Turns out he'd withdrawn too much fluid.

The result of this unintended accident was odd. As long as I stayed lying flat on the bed with no pillow, I was fine. The minute I sat up, my head felt as if were in a giant vise and someone was tightening the screw. Incredible pain. So I stayed prone. For ages, it seemed. Whatever jungle bug had caused the fever had disappeared, but this new thing persisted for weeks. Meanwhile I was eligible for liberty every other night. I didn't want to waste that. I'd grab my pass, race for the subway platform, stretch out on a bench until the train arrived, dash in and lie as flat as I could in the car. Other riders would look at this sailor on his back with a bit of a disapproving sniff on their faces. I'd smile up at them and say, "I'm not drunk. It's a health thing." I wonder what they thought that meant.

One time I visited Liam Dunn on Morton Street in the Village. I arrived while he was out. Someone let me into the building, and I went up to his floor and lay down in the hall in front of his apartment, and fell asleep. I woke when a cold finger touched my neck. It belonged to Liam. Thinking I was dead, he was feeling for a pulse. He had to pick up all the spilled groceries he'd dropped when he came up the stairs and spotted me. That tickled the hell out of me. He looked pale and perturbed. Probably because I hadn't shuffled off my moral coil, he wasn't very amused, but that didn't last long. Liam had a fantastic sense of the ridiculous; he laughed at himself, and could tell jokes better than anyone I ever met. He was able to tell the same story over and over, embroidering every time, so you'd be in hysterics long before he had gotten to the familiar punch line.

The head-crushing syndrome eased up after a bit, and while on liberty I began playing piano, for tips, in bars from the Village to the St. Albans area on Long Island. I think the place there was called the Sunrise. How apt: One evening the customers kept buying me Manhattans. I hit eighteen or nineteen. And boy, did they hit back. I'd never been so sick. The troop-ship seasickness had been a trip through a magic garden in comparison. I haven't had a Manhattan since. I'd order Vitalis and grapefruit juice before drinking another one of those.

Tips were great because of the uniform, and I quickly learned to decline kind offers of drinks. During the day, in St. Albans, I taught a radio class to other inmates, as we called ourselves. That was a kick.

The war in Europe was winding down, and before we knew it we were celebrating V.E. Day. And I was in Manhattan, auditioning for every show I could. Soon I was up for several. One of them, *The Happy Time*, was about a Canadian family. (Years later Kander and Ebb wrote a musical of the same name, not terribly successful, based on the same material.) I also had a shot as a replacement for the part of Chip in *On the Town*. This was a show I was crazy about and had seen twice. The guy playing the role (Cris Alexander) was up for another show and was leaving the cast. I auditioned for the lyricists and bookwriters, Betty Comden and Adolph Green, on the mezzanine floor of the Martin Beck Theater. A piano was there. Maybe it still is. I sang "Come Up to My Place" from a lead sheet, although I already knew most of it from having seen the show twice. (I had the facility then to hear a song in the theater and go home and play it by ear and heart on the ol' 88. That facility, like youth, faded away a long time ago.) Betty and Adolph liked me and the prospects were high. I'm sure that my sailor uniform helped enormously.

Well, *The Happy Time* (to be produced by Leland Hayward) was postponed.

As it turned out, Cris was leaving *On the Town* for a part in that same show. So he withdrew his notice, and I was out of luck for both shows. That's the biz.

On liberty in the city one day, I read for a play called *A Sound of Hunting*. I was offered the supporting role of Daggert. It was to begin rehearsals in October. This was now the end of August. A week later, on September 2, 1945, Japan surrendered. What a weird, indefinable feeling it was to put the pieces together and realize what we'd been doing on Tinian. The 38th had built the airstrip from which Enola Gay (the B-29) took off to end the war. What terrible mixed feelings. Yes, we had helped to end the war in the Pacific, but we'd been responsible for killing all those innocent Japanese people. An awful feeling in the gut. Part of it is still there. It'll always be. At St. Albans I requested a Captain's Mass, and was granted one.

The base commander was very understanding when I explained about the play I'd read for and how it was going into rehearsal the next month, and that this was my life's work. He kept nodding and smiling, and I cut my summation short. The Navy was very interested in getting the men back into civilian life as smoothly as possible. They were discharging guys every day now. I was in line, he told me, for mustering-out as soon as my papers (in Washington because of the V-12 thing) came in. I'd already been surveyed, as they called it.

He gave me the entire month of October as leave, on two conditions. I had to check with the hospital twice each day, and when my papers arrived from D.C. I could come out, get my discharge and my hundred bucks and be on my way. The other condition was, I couldn't get an extension on the generous leave. I even had permission to wear civvies, but had to keep my uniform handy for the mustering-out ceremony. I thanked him profusely and saluted, and was out of there on the first day of October, happily heading back to Broadway.

Chapter 6 —————————

Rehearsals for *A Sound of Hunting* began around October 16. The play was written by Harry Brown; the others in the cast included Frank Lovejoy, Sam Levene and a new guy named Burton Lancaster. It was a heavy drama about G.I.s in Italy during the war. Things were sailing along with the play until suddenly it was October 31—and Washington still hadn't sent my papers to the hospital. The civvies came off, the bell-bottoms went back on, and I had to leave the cast. I was heartbroken. Who knew when another play would come along? The tardy papers arrived on November 9. I became a civilian—nine days too late. But Pollyanna that I was, I felt sure that something would pop up.

A Sound of Hunting opened without me on Broadway on November 20 and closed after twenty-three performances. One week after I was discharged, I auditioned for and got a job in a revue called *Three to Make Ready*. *Three to Make Ready* tried out in Philly and Boston, opened in New York on March 7, ran nearly a year, then toured. I had lucked out.

After two quick-folding plays, it was wonderful to settle in for a healthy run in a hit. *Three to Make Ready* was the third in a series of successful revues by Nancy Hamilton, who wrote the sketches and lyrics; and Morgan "Buddy" Lewis, who wrote the music. What a talented duo!

One for the Money and *Two for the Show* had introduced a bunch of then-unknowns like Eve Arden, Alfred Drake, Gene Kelly, Betty Hutton and Keenan Wynn. One of Nancy and Buddy's delicious tunes, "How High the Moon," became a standard. *Three to Make Ready* was the first revue in the series to have an established star: Ray Bolger, who was fantastic and the big reason for the show's healthy run. He was a real nice person. (I wish I could say as much for his wife, who was a pain in the butt.) He did give me a real scare early in rehearsal, though, when he complained to John Murray Anderson, the director, that he couldn't possibly do a scarecrow number since there was another scarecrow in the show. He pointed dramatically at me. My heart stopped. There goes this show, down the drain for me, I thought. Of course, he was kidding. For several long seconds, however, I was sure I was a goner.

"Entire Production Devised and Staged by John Murray Anderson" was his forever billing. I think it had begun with *Jumbo*, and he always used it for *Ringling Bros. and Barnum & Bailey Circus*. He oversaw everything. In *Three to Make Ready*, Margaret Webster (known for her Shakespeare stagings) was sketch director and Bob Sydney was the choreographer. But Murray was boss. He was maybe the most memorable character I ever met. He had mood swings you wouldn't believe—always comical—and a truly perverse sense of humor. He could dead-pan you into a serene state and then hit you with a zinger. He loved telling stories on himself. I remember one of them. When he and his wife were running a theater school in New York, one of his students was a very plain girl from New England. He thought she was as bad as she was plain. After a few classes, he told her that she should save herself the money and future embarrassment, pack her belongings and head back home. He really believed he was being kind. Her name was Bette Davis. He would chortle after telling this, tears oozing from the corners of his eyes. He always oozed tears when he laughed.

He had special names for everyone. Hugh Martin (the songwriting partner of Ralph Blane) was Birdseed, Ralph was Blockbuster. Who knew why? That pair, by the way, wrote hit after hit, including "The Boy Next Door," "Have Yourself a Merry Little Christmas" and "The Trolley Song," all standards today and forever.

Murray called Bob Sydney "Evil." I was "Mascarp." He picked on me all through rehearsals. I was sure he hated me. During one number, four dancing couples sat at tables in a nightclub set, all of them smoking. For some reason I was stationed as far upstage center as I could get. While we were rehearsing, my hind end was practically up against the heating pipes on the empty stage. John, with his ever-present bullhorn, stood somewhere out front counting loudly: "One, two, three, four, inhale, two, three, four, exhale, two, three, four …" over and over. The kids would sometimes choke, and he'd scream, "AGAIN!" He stopped for the tiniest reasons, and they'd have to start over from the top. At one point he screamed: "STOP!" Everybody froze. "Mascarp," he shrieked, "you moved! Stand perfectly still." I thought I was at strict attention back there. How could he even see if I'd moved slightly? The eight exhausted and by-now bored dancers shot me deadly looks. I stared straight ahead. And they took the thing from the top yet another time.

I'm sure we spent two hours on this smoking routine.

Shortly before lunch break, Murray stopped for the umpteenth time. "Mascarp," he boomed, "turn and face upstage." Like a big stupe I screwed up the courage and asked why.

"Because at this point in the show you'll be wearing a very expensive costume, and I want the audience to see the back of it." I faced the pipes.

Now my New York professional life had really begun, and I settled into it with happy confidence. As soon as I'd found out that I'd been surveyed and was on my way out of the service, I had bravely rented a brownstone apartment at 134 East 47th Street between Lexington and Third Avenues. It was one very big room, built in back on the main building on the ground floor. There was a narrow passageway (maybe twelve feet long and windowed on one side) leading from the building. A small fridge and stove were in the passageway; a basin and running water were in the room itself. The john was in the hallway, and the bathtub and shower were up on the second floor. The super, Hugh (Elihu) Harrison, and his wife Vivian occupied the ground-floor apartment.

My room had an immense fireplace (I'm six-foot-three and could almost stand inside it) and a pair of twin beds against the back wall—as Murray would say, "one very slightly used." He called my place "Tart's Tomb." The furnishings consisted of a sofa, a chest of drawers, a table with four chairs, and a pair of comfortable old armchairs. Liberty after liberty from St. Albans, I gathered pans, silverware, dishes, etc.; there were meager cooking utensils in the meager kitchen.

I loved the place. When I had begun my October leave to appear in *A Sound of Hunting*, the first thing I did was rent a piano. I've never lived anywhere without one since.

Now, while waiting to begin rehearsals for *Three to Make Ready*, I did more radio, which I always thought was like stealing. You went into a studio, read a script, got a check and went on to another radio show. I got a kick out of the elevators in the old CBS building at Madison and 53rd. On Monday mornings, the guys would "converse" with one another between floors, everyone cupping one hand to an ear to listen to his own voice. "Have a good weekend? Fine. How's the wife? That's good. The kids okay?" Everybody talking. Nobody listening. It always broke me up.

I also signed with Society of Models and did photo shoots for tabloid magazines like *True Confessions*, *True Romances* and *True Crime*. Sometimes I was a pitiful victim, sometimes a baby-faced killer or a raving maniac. Great fun.

On Sundays I missed the routine of going to church, so I shopped around my neighborhood for a place. I tried a small Catholic church east of Third Avenue, but I didn't understand much about it. And there was no Joan beside me. I tried a big place on Park Avenue. I think it was Episcopalian. I didn't know any of the hymns and the "sermon" was really nothing but the fiscal possibilities of merging with the Methodists or somebody. Nothing churchlike at all. I gave up religion in New York for a while.

The main reason I loved that east-side neighborhood is that I was just two blocks away from my love, Jeanne Shelby. She lived with her roommate Minette on 49th between Lexington and Third. We spent as much time as possible together, often eating at a tiny, six-steps-down restaurant called the Blue Bowl on 48th. Comfort food, home-cooked, very inexpensive. It was difficult to inflate the bill to a dollar. The portions were tiny, however. There were eleven, sometimes twelve peas in a portion. I used to count. Still, the tapioca pudding was terrific.

I had lost track of my best Seabee buddy Costello. He had sent me one of his rare, short, almost impersonal letters while I was still in St. Albans. It ended with a postscript that the 38th was splitting up, and part of it was moving from Tinian to Guam. Cos was among those reassigned. No new Battalion number. I had no way to contact him now. That was before V-J Day. I'd gotten no word from him since. That was too long a time and it worried me.

I had talked to Liam Dunn a little about Cos before. Now I told him everything, tiny details about our time together, how miserable I felt about having to leave him and return stateside; I blurted out every twinge of feeling I still had about my best friend in the world and how I didn't know whether he was even alive or not. I wasn't even conscious of the tears streaking down my cheeks. It felt as if I were confessing to a priest (confessing what?) or an analyst. Liam seemed to be both at the moment. He consoled, sympathized, said all the right things to calm me down. Finally, several minutes later, when I was comparatively sane again, he quietly told me it was obvious that I loved Cos. I told Liam, of course I do, just like I love you. He smiled at me a long time, I remember, and said, without a trace of his usually constant humor: "I think this is different." That statement, not fully understood, hung with me for a long, quasi-haunted time.

Before I left that night to return to St. Alban's Hospital, he invited me to a small party he was throwing in two days. He ordered me to be there. I said I would show up (it would be another liberty night) at the Beverly Hotel, where he'd acquired the use of Anne Nichols's penthouse apartment for the evening. She was the author of *Abie's Irish Rose*. Liam had been doing a production of it in Philly recently, and had, in his leprechaunish way, become great friends with the famous author.

What a revealing party that turned out to be—great fun, very memorable and very drunken. Liam's cousin, Jeannie Hathersol (or something close) was a semi-classy hoot. There were three or four other guests, including one huge surprise: Charles Bowlby, from the cast of *Bright Boy*. He had changed his name to Colby. He said he had gotten tired of the nickname "Toilet." He seemed different, somehow. I suppose I did to him, too. To him. At any rate, at one drunken point that late evening with a twelve-inch 78 of "Laura" blasting through the penthouse, the two of us found ourselves out on the small balcony overlooking Lexington Avenue and 51st, hanging halfway over the concrete railing and then on the outdoor glider there.

Suddenly, Charlie threw his arms around me and kissed me full on the lips for what seemed an eternity. When we broke apart I gasped for air, feeling really dizzy—partly due to the booze, but mostly to the kiss. I had never been kissed by a man before. It was thrilling. Electric. Like a shock. Well, it *was* a shock. I leapt about like an idiot, climbing up on the railing and holding the post with one hand and waving my glass with the other as I swung out over Lex, which was way too many floors below. Charlie rescued me, but he was unable to calm me down or shut me up. I jolted through the apartment happily proclaiming to the world: "I kissed a man. I kissed another man." I have no notion what anybody thought. Didn't give a rat's ass. "I kissed Ole Toilet Bowlby. And it was GREAT!"

At the hospital the following morning I was hung over, and nothing seemed very great. Shame and guilt fought each other inside me for attention. I gave them equal time, and gave myself a severe talking-to. What the hell did I think I was doing? Was I nuts? I had no idea. Then, to make things even worse that day, I received a very strange letter from our xylophone commander's yeoman. It was funny hearing from him; I hardly knew him. His gossipy letter was written as though we had been great buddies on the island. I didn't know most of the guys he was writing about. I couldn't even remember what he looked like. His letter gushed on and on about life in the 38th as if he were doing a puff piece for some newspaper.

Toward the end of all this crap, which didn't interest me in the least, was a question about Costello. He wanted to know if I ever heard from him, or were we "just like two ships that only passed in the night." It sounded kind of snide to me, as if he were in on some joke I didn't get.

But it got me thinking about the previous night's shenanigans. And Cos. My god, what would he have thought of that whole penthouse scene? I suddenly felt that I'd betrayed him and he would never forgive me for being so foolish. Probably never speak to me again. Or just beat the hell out of me. Heavy, heavy remorse descended. I hadn't even given him a thought the night before; I was just getting loaded and making an asshole of myself.

After a day or two, things began sorting themselves out. I was con-centrating on the radio classes, looking for future work on liberty days, and playing piano at night. The place I played most often was a below-street-level bar on MacDougal Street in the Village. It had an old upright against a side wall. There was a railing around it—a good safety mea-sure. The crowd was mixed, but mostly male. One evening a pair of ladies leaned over my rail and requested "I Love You Truly." I segued into it and they sashayed, hand in hand into the bathroom.

It didn't take very long to figure out what kind of bar this was. Not only did I not mind it, I found myself liking all the attention. I was just a young sailor with a mop of blond hair. The bar dug me. I didn't like myself much those days, but it didn't stop me from stuffing myself at the atten-tion table. I flirted with everyone for tips. They fell for the act. At the end of my shift I'd stuff all the cash into the pocket of my pea coat and head, sometimes hornily, back to St. Albans.

There was one night, just before I found and rented my place on 47th, when I came very close to … if not real love, at least to a mutually fulfilled passion and lifelong loving friendship. A young Harvard student, in town visiting his mom and brother, met me in a bar on the east side and we fell into conversation. I mean real conversation, about life, politics, books; not bar-talk, pickup bull. His name was Lewis Freedman, and we took to each other in an instant. He'd buy a round: beer for him, highball for me. Then I'd buy a round: scotch for him, highball for me. It tickled me, because he was paying less for his rounds. This turned into a routine that went on for years. I always ended up spending more. But he'd grin and remind me I was getting what I wanted when he bought.

We ended up that first night together at the Shelton Hotel on Lex-ington and 48th, the same hotel where I had stayed when I came to town to see *Lady in the Dark*. The single bed we shared was large enough. We were all over it and each other like a pin-less wresting match. We explored everything, laughed ourselves silly, and had an unforgettable adventure together.

Later, when I was in Boston with *Three to Make Ready*, I visited him on campus. He was anxious to hear my new tunes, and we went into Adams House and found a piano. While I was playing something like "I'm a Little Afraid," for Lewis, General George Marshall was outside delivering a commencement address. That turned out to be the Marshall Plan, which helped put Europe back together after World War II.

Lewis, who years later became head of PBS in New York, always avowed that between the Marshall Plan or Carp's new songs (with Caroline, who he met, of course, when I was ensconced in the Tomb) he'd pick the songs anytime. Now that's true friendship.

One night during *Three to Make Ready* he came to my dressing room accompanied by someone he introduced as Fleming. "Extend for the Mascarp, Fleming," he ordered, and the man lifted his leg straight up over his head, as if doing a perpendicular split. I asked the guy his real name. He told me it was Robert Alton and that he was from Bennington, too. He said he'd changed his name from Hart because of the Vermont hard 'a's. He said people couldn't do anything with Alton. Then he rolled it off his tongue, like *Awl*ton.

An old chum from junior high, Caroline Phillips, was now living in New York, and we reconnected. As kids in Bennington, we had written songs together all the time. Once we wrote a musical version of *The Story of Fairyfoot*, from the old *Book House* children's anthology. It was about a place where everyone had feet as big as canal boats; a child with normal-size feet is found and becomes the laughing stock of the kingdom. Caroline wrote wonderful lyrics. I learned a lot from her. Her Dad, Judson Philips, was a best-selling mystery novelist who wrote under the name Hugh Pentecost. Caroline's mother, Georgiana Philips, was a writer as well, but as far as I remember she published only one novel, *Summer of Good Hope*. Georgiana, Caroline and her maternal grandparents lived in Old Bennington, which meant money. It was up on the hill by the Old First Church, looking down on the peons in the village below. The centerpiece was the Bennington Battle Monument, the tallest of its kind in the world and the biggest phallic symbol you ever saw. From wherever you enter the town you can't help seeing it, proudly erected and braving the fiercest New England storms.

Caroline's folks were divorced—a sin in those days—and I never met her father until years later. I was always a little scared when I dined at the beautiful old home of Caroline's grandparents, the Cushmans. Would I use the proper fork? What was that little bowl of water with a hunk of lemon for after dessert?

Caroline had written a play for me in eighth grade. It was a hoot. The opening was:

KING: Come, come, Griselda, the soup is getting cold.

PRINCESS: But, Father, I've told you I shan't sit down until I find someone to risk his neck for me.

How's that for a grabber?

Anyway, together again in New York, we wrote like crazy. Song after song, mostly about the futility of love. Some titles: "It's Time To Fall in Love Again," "No Enchantment," "I'm A Little Afraid." You get the idea. Teen cynicism was the soup du jour for us. Of course we sold none of our songs, although I'd haunt the halls of the Brill Building on Broadway every chance I could grab. I went from door to door, floor to floor. It was hard to break in. I didn't know anybody in the music biz; even people who did had almost as tough a time getting someone to listen to their songs as I.

We saw *Carousel* and scoffed at the sentimentality; we had both seen *Oklahoma* and thought it simpleminded. Now, as we worked on a revue to be called *Couch in the Corner*, we decided to do a sendup of the two Rodgers & Hammerstein shows. It would have parodies of both scores mixed up. We couldn't choose between calling it *Oklasel* or *Caryhoma*.

When I arrived for the first day of rehearsal for *Three to Make Ready*, the twenty-one cast members were listening to the songs, sung by lyricist Nancy Hamilton. I heard a long musical piece called "Wisconsin, or Kenosha Canoe"—a version of *An American Tragedy* as if it had been written by Rodgers and Hammerstein. I couldn't believe it. I phoned Caroline as soon as I got home and we carried on about how they'd stolen our idea. We were outraged, but at the same time sort of flattered that we'd come up with an idea really Broadway-worthy. (A couple of years later, when I was writing a lot of special material for cabaret, five writers, including me, wrote a number called "Love Is a Four-Letter Name"—all in about a week. Maybe nothing is really original.)

Now, in late November 1945, I had to put all the radio, modeling, and collaborating with Caroline on hold during rehearsals for *Three to Make Ready*.

What a wonderful cast! Ray Bolger starred, and the supporting players included Brenda Forbes, Rose Ingraham, Gordon MacRae, Bibi Osterwald, Harold Lang, Jane Deering, Meg Mundy, Garry Davis, me, ten dancers, *and* Arthur Godfrey.

I was hired primarily for the sketches, but everyone sang and danced as well. I was in hog heaven. When we finally moved on to Boston that blistery cold December, just before Christmas, it was truly exciting. One of the biggest goose-pimply experiences of a lifetime was sitting in a ballroom at the Bradford Hotel, hearing the full orchestra, for the first time, play the songs we'd rehearsed with just piano and drums. Wow! Believe me, there's nothing like it. The entire company was crying and clapping and clutching one another, eagerly awaiting the chance to get onstage with the sets.

We were opening at the Shubert, where *Dream with Music* had been my nightly destination after *Career Angel*. I hadn't been in Boston since, and was thrilled to be playing the big house across the street now. Plus, I was in a musical. We'd lost the talented Hugh Martin, who'd moved on for more work with "Blockbuster" (Ralph Blane). Now the pit pianist was a wiry, balding gentleman named Joe Moon. He had a spectacular sense of humor and a modest wooden leg. He could make the piano sing and dance. Shortly before opening night, after leaving through the stage door, he hit a long strip of black ice on the sidewalk of Tremont Street. Down he crashed, his leg detaching itself and slipping out of his pants leg and sliding down the slope of Tremont, shoe and sock attached. Passersby screamed in horror; two cars collided mid-street; chaos reigned. Joe sat there bundled against the harsh wind, watching his gallivanting leg careen away and laughing like crazy. "It's all right, it's all right," he kept calling out to the stunned group that had gathered. With a smile as big as his name, he tried to calm everybody down. "It's really okay," he said, laughing. "I have a spare leg at the hotel." That dispersed the crowd. Most of them probably thought he was out of his head.

Two of us helped Joe back to the Touraine, where he was staying. He was overjoyed to have shocked so many. He did, indeed, have an extra at the hotel. But we retrieved the runaway on our way there. Wes Craven would have loved the scene.

I had stayed at the Touraine during *Career Angel*—four to the room. This time I had my own room at a hotel called the Avery, a couple of blocks farther from the theater. They had a very reasonable rate for actors. From that time on I claimed it as my home whenever I played Boston. I used to claim that it was the only hotel I knew that one could, if one cared to, get the clap in before the ink was dry on the registration card. It did have, well, relaxed rules, as well as tiny rooms and a busy after-show bar called the Oval. Forevermore I called the hotel the Ovary.

After the out-of-town tryouts, *Three to Make Ready* opened on March 7, 1946 at the Adelphi Theatre on 54th Street between Sixth and Seventh Avenues. It's now gone. The reviews were good to excellent and we settled in for a nine-month run, moving along the way to the Broadhurst on 44th—right next door to the Shubert, where I'd done my first scale-singing audition for Mr. Simmons.

On opening night, Ray Bolger presented the entire cast with gifts. This was a surprise—but the gifts themselves inspired muffled merriment among everyone, especially the ladies, who all received compacts (picked out by his wife, Gwen) with their names gracefully and daintily inscribed on one side. On the other, the entire allotted space was covered with the words FROM RAY BOLGER. The men fared a tad better. They got cuff links. Each one was printed with its recipient's initials. Turn it over, and it said, in the largest letters possible: FROM RAY BOLGER. A heartfelt gesture by Ray had turned into a joke by his spouse. He kept apologizing for weeks about the "engraving" mistake.

Onstage, however, he stopped the show at every performance, especially with a wonderful number called "The Old Soft Shoe." Godfrey, strumming his uke, did okay with "A Lovely, Lazy Kind of Day." (Gordon MacRae did a better job of it when Arthur left the show.) "Kenosha Canoe," the twenty-minute mini-musical that closed the first act—like idiots, Caroline and I were sure they'd swiped the whole idea from us—was a hoot. Its songs included "Off Ter the Nuttin' Party," "I Cain't Say Snow," and a finale a la *Oklahoma!*

> *We're gonna miss Wisconsin when we're bouncin' through*
> *the good ol' USA*
> *Miss that eight-month freeze, that smell of cheese*
> *When the breeze comes wheezing down the bay*
> *Where the mail comes once in months and months*
> *But the Lunts keep comin' every May*

Another high point for me was when Bolger, in black boat-neck sweater, black pants and a red kerchief around his neck, swaggered out, stuck one foot on a rock and sang: "I gotter do a soliloquy." I suppose that's all tame by today's standards. But I loved it.

Murray had an artist's knack for opening the curtains on a beautiful picture. Some were backlit, as in the number "Barnaby Beach," where everyone stood on stage in various poses, stock-still and seemingly in black silhouette; then the lights would reveal everyone in yellow and green as they came to life. The curtain would always close on another lovely picture. In another favorite of mine, Brenda Forbes, wearing a tatty tutu, sang a sad song called "Born for Better Things" while sitting dejectedly on an old chair. At the end of the number, a voice from offstage called, "Ready?" She sighed and answered, "Yes, Mister Degas," then assumed the exact pose of one of his best-known works. As she held the pose, two V-cut portals irised in, framing her. Fade out. Heartbreaking.

There was a very funny sketch that opened with Bolger standing on the closed lid of the john in his pajamas and a bathrobe that he couldn't get to stay closed, because he was busy holding up the pull-chained overhead water tank that had broken loose from the wall. He yells for his wife (played by Rose Ingraham) to come help. She rushes in, not knowing what to do. He tells her to grab the phone and call for a plumber. She runs offstage, races back on with a stool and a phone on a very long chord. She sits, calls and converses with the plumber for a long time, while behind her things are going from really bad to extremely worse.

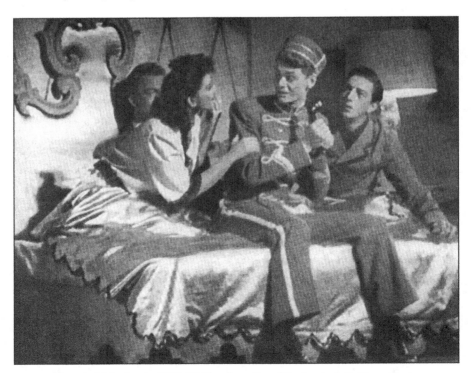

Three to Make Ready, 1946: "Bellboy," a satire of the Lunts. L-R: Garry Davis, Rose Ingraham, me, Ray Bolger.

Somehow, as she watched every show from out front, Gwen decided that Ingraham was upstaging her husband. How on earth could she have figured that? He was right up against the flat with water splashing all over him, losing his robe and about to lose his pajama bottoms. At one matinee, Gwen hatched a plan. She snuck backstage during the show against strict orders by the stage manager, and tied off the phone chord by two thirds so it would only reach a few feet from the wings.

Of course Rosie was unaware of this, so when she rushed off, grabbed the stool and phone and raced back on, she tripped, props flying out of her hands. Knowing immediately who was responsible, Rose scrambled up—to hell with the scene—and tore offstage in time to see Gwen escaping out the stage door and onto 53rd. Rose chased Gwen, who was in costume (robe and hair in curlers), all the way to Sixth Avenue, yelling, "I'M GONNA BREAK EVERY BONE IN YOUR IDIOT HEAD!" Rose didn't catch her, but from that day on Mrs. B. kept her distance. She never came backstage again, even after a show.

Murray dined off the story for ages. He congratulated Rosie, even though—or maybe because—she'd broken the golden rule of "the show must go on." Murray was perverse. He would have loved it if all the guys in the show had suddenly turned up for a performance with completely shaved heads.

Now with my days free—except for Wednesday and Saturday matinees—I plunged into a work routine that's impossible for me to believe now. Back I went to modeling, radio, and a new thing, television, which fascinated the hell out of me. We worked in an old radio studio at NBC that had been converted for this weird medium. The lights were water-cooled, there were cables everywhere and huge stationary cameras, and we actors had to wear a sort of greenish make-up. (This, of course, was black-and-white TV.) The show was called *Campus Hoopla*. It was twenty minutes long and starred Vivian Allen, Larry Douglas and me. Lou Little, a coach at Columbia, did a sports spot on every show.

The set was a soda shop with a booth or two, a short fountain bar, and a small place where we could dance and sing a bit. The big thing was that this was NBC's very first show with a sponsor: U.S. Rubber, which made Keds. That didn't affect our salaries, however, which were slave-labor low because we had no union coverage. The T in AFTRA hadn't been added yet. I think we all got twenty or twenty-five dollars a show. The show wouldn't pay musicians' union minimums, so we had to use recorded music for accompaniment. But *Campus Hoopla* gave jobs to two pretty gals who played cheerleaders and did the commercials as cheers:

> *Keds are keen*
> *Keds are neat*
> *Keds are best for the family feet*
> *Wear 'em!*

They'd jump up on the "wear 'em!" Peggy Lobbin and Eva Marie Saint. Later on, Eva landed the only female role in Josh Logan's *Mister Roberts*, and we all celebrated at the Blue Ribbon German restaurant on 43rd. But a few weeks later, after rehearsals for the show had begun, Logan told her she was being replaced by Jocelyn Brando (yeah, his sister), but asked Eva if she'd remain on as understudy. She agreed, happily. It was her first show, and she'd do anything. What a wonderful lady, and a trouper. Most young actresses would have skulked away in high dudgeon at being replaced. We celebrated the understudy job as well. How I loved her.

When NBC got a mobile trailer, I did the first remote for them, emceeing a show televised at the Village Barn on Eighth Street. They kept me busy. When the Sunday night alternating shows—*Goodyear Theater* and *Philco Playhouse*—began, I worked every week on those shows as well. Paychecks depended on the size of the role. Some weeks I was in the bellhop category, some weeks I had a leading role, so I made from fifteen to fifty bucks. But I worked steadily. Between 1946 and '49, when I went to MGM, I did more TV work than any other actor in New York. I know that's saying a lot. But it's true. God knows it's not a brag. It's almost a laugh at those fees. I certainly worked with a bunch of very talented writers and actors. I kept learning. That was part of the fun.

During its run, *Three to Make Ready* moved to the Broadhurst on 44th Street, and on summer nights a loading door would be left open at the back of the theater. Between acts I used to hang out there by the alley for a breath of fresh air. Often I stood there with a gal from the musical *Lute Song*, which was playing at the Plymouth on 45th. She was in the chorus, and had a bit part as a lady-in-waiting. Her name was Nancy Davis, and she was a lot of fun. This was her Broadway debut. She told me she'd toured with ZaSu Pitts in a show called *Ramshackle Inn*. We became cigarette buddies. We talked about our families, our hopes. Her adoptive father was a big-time doctor in Chicago, I think. Later we met again at MGM and even later at the White House.

One Wednesday between the matinee and evening shows, I walked across town to the Tomb. It was summer, and I felt weakish; maybe I was coming down with a cold or something. Once home, I warmed up a can of soup and tried to take a nap. I couldn't, so I decided to go back to the theater early. As I passed the lobby going to the stage door, there was Costello at the THIS PERFORMANCE ONLY window. My knees buckled. I ducked inside the stage door, grabbed the phone, and called Caroline. All I got out was, "Costello's back."

"I'll meet you backstage after," she said quickly.

There was a skit in the revue called "The Sad Sack." All the men were in it. Bolger, who ate in the theater between shows, saw me passing his dressing room; he kept the door open for extra air. He said I looked like I'd just seen a ghost, was I all right? I said I was fine, and that an old navy buddy was seeing the show tonight. I was just a little nervous, that's all. He wanted to know his name. Like a stupe, I told him.

Mr. B. had told the other actors in "The Sad Sack" that an old buddy named Costello was out front. So they called me by his name (instead of "Beanpole") for the entire sketch. They tossed it in ever time they could, even ad-libbing "Ain't that right, Costello?" several times between regular lines. I must have looked to the audience as if I'd added extra rouge makeup.

I was (still am) one of the first to get out of the theater after a performance; I moved so fast that people waiting for the star's autograph probably thought I was one of the stagehands. That evening, shaky with fever, I was like a greyhound getting out of the gate. I scrubbed off the Max Factor and raced to the stage door. Caroline, as promised, was there waiting. So were Costello and his cousin. I carried a snapshot of Cos in my wallet, so my personal Florence Nightingale recognized him, and had already introduced herself before I came out. Thank heaven for her. She was magnificent, and, boy, did I need all the help I could get.

Cos and I shook hands almost formally and exchanged hi's. Caroline herded us around the corner and up Broadway to Howard Johnson's at 46th. The girls preceded us, chatting up a storm about the show. Cos and I tagged along wordlessly behind them. My mind kept channeling back to Tinian, like a newsreel. I had quick mental flashbacks to scene after scene of us together during our months on the island. Now we were walking up Broadway like strangers, no longer with our arms around each other's shoulders. I couldn't open my mouth. I had no clue how to break this unexpected ice.

When we were seated in the restaurant, Cos across the table from me, we stared at each other. The girls seemed to disappear; the place seemed completely empty. We were all alone, just like at the beach cove on a G.I. day. Cos finally spoke, while looking at me apologetically, wistfully. I'll never forget those very first words.

"I guess we hadn't been getting along so hot the last few days before you left. I wanted to come see you off, but I couldn't. I waved a shovel at the plane when you took off but I guess you didn't see it."

When I found my voice I told him I'd been waving from the plane window but guessed he wouldn't have seen that either. I didn't tell him about the tears. Now, sitting in the middle of a crowded restaurant, I was trying desperately to keep the water pipes from bursting again. He told me he was staying somewhere out on Long Island with his aunt and the cousin he'd brought along to the show. He wrote down the address and what subway and train to take so I could visit the following day. We had to have a good ol' buddy-buddy talk and catch up, he said.

We parted with what would have been a hug if I hadn't turned it into a handshake and a slap on the back instead. What the hell was wrong with me? I couldn't for the life of me figure me out.

Somehow, the next morning, I managed to pull myself partially together—enough to make the pilgrimage out to Costello's aunt's home. His cousin, whose name I've forgotten at the moment, was off somewhere. We went out and walked around the small village, warming up to each other once more. Reminiscing, laughing and pretty much picking up where we'd left off, which seemed like ages ago. We were smoking and schmoozing about nothing and yet everything. I was still ill, yet I don't believe I've ever been so completely happy and at ease in my entire life.

Then he said something that threw me for a complete loss. "You know, I've been back in the States for nearly three months now and I haven't dated a single girl. I think maybe I'm getting a little queer or something." He chuckled and kicked a small stone off the sidewalk. I was stunned. I turned mute, but managed a chuckle back. Why didn't I say something? Was he telling me he felt as deeply about me as I did about him? Here was a door edged open, begging for further discussion.

I didn't, to my everlasting regret, take even a baby step toward that door. I changed the subject. And we were back to more Tinian trivia. After lunch—I managed a cup of tea and that was about it—I promised to keep in touch. I came back into the city and totally fell apart. I was a nervous wreck, and my feverish mind was racing to all kinds of places I didn't want to go. Everything seemed out of kilter. I was afraid Cos would pick up vibrations about me, that he'd somehow know the things I'd done just before leaving the Navy. Now he was suggesting (confessing?) that he …

I couldn't believe this. Did he say that because he thought I might be, too? Why in hell hadn't I opened my dumb mouth and said something? Anything? Wouldn't he have understood? No. Maybe. I didn't know. *Why hadn't I said something?*

I missed doing the show that night and on Friday as well. Caroline had called a doctor, who arrived with her at the Tomb the afternoon I returned from the Cos visit. I was having what was then called a nervous breakdown. Whatever it may be called these days, it ain't a bucket of Midwestern guffaws. I don't know what drugs the doc gave me, but they helped. I slept a lot, losing my fever and dulling a bit of whatever psychosis was screwing up my cemented head. By the time I felt strong enough, physically and mentally, to call Costello at his aunt's, he'd already returned to his home in Springfield, Massachusetts.

I returned, still a little shaky, to the show for the Saturday matinee. Those two shows were the only ones I'd ever missed. Everyone knows working is the best therapy, and losing oneself completely in a show is absolutely the best. You can't worry about yourself when you're someone else. I took a ton of kidding from the dancing guys. They were merciless. Were Costello and I off on a second honeymoon? Had we tied the knot? "You look like you lost weight. I can guess what from." All that camp crap. They used to kid me about being a bottle blond. My hair did look lighter under the stage lights. I was dumb enough to counter their accusation by pointing to the hair on my arm. "See, look, it's the same color." One guy said, "You probably soak in a bathtub of peroxide." I learned to just take the flak and smile.

Chapter 7 ———————

I rebounded to health much quicker than the doc had guessed. The American Theater Wing had programs for returning vets in almost every phase of the business, and by day I was playing piano for the dancer and choreographer Peter Birch's tap classes, among my other pursuits. The pupils included Tony Charmoli, who went on to become one of the biggest choreographers in the business. Aside from learning tap, I got to study ballet. I knew I'd never make a ballet dancer, and I looked ridiculous in tights; during class at a Carnegie Hall studio I always tried to hide in the back row, but that was impossible because of the mirrors on every wall. The classes were good exercise, though, and I got to use some of the steps in a comedic fashion later on. The only thing I regretted about that class was losing my wallet, which contained the only picture of Costello I had. But I found a good friend, Duane Thorpe. He was a very good dancer from Athol, Massachusetts. More on him later.

I also reconnected with Charlie Colby, with whom I'd shared that passionate kiss at the Beverly Hotel. When we were in *Bright Boy*, we had tossed around an idea for a musical; he'd do the book and I'd do the score. Now we started it in earnest. I'm sure Charlie had forgotten the drunken penthouse smack, but I'd remember it forever. I never spoke of it, though, and we became good friends and collaborators on that musical, which we called *Cleopatra Had Morals*. I happily recall the last line of act one. One of Cleo's handmaidens came into her chamber to announce that Caesar wouldn't be available to join her for lunch; he'd gone off to invade France. Said Cleo in a voice that we hoped would sound like Mae West: "Of all the gall!" Curtain.

Just before Christmas of 1946, *Three to Make Ready* closed after 327 performances. Then we took to the road. Playing in Chicago at the Blackstone Theatre, I was now earning 150 bucks a week. A fortune. My weekly letters from home still closed with the "get-a-real-job" bit, although I'd

Ex-soldiers take to tap dancing with real zest in the course taught by Peter Birch who is a featured dancer in *Carousel*. No cash outlay is required of any student in the Theatre Wing's school. They are all veterans studying under the GI Bill of Rights. Prominent people in the arts are their teachers. Agnes De Mille is chairman of the dance division.
Photos by Irving Haberman, PM

Playing piano for a veterans' tap class sponsored by the G.I. Bill, 1946.

never been out of work. I got a brainstorm. I phoned Greenburg's Furniture in Bennington and asked if they had one of those new automatic washing machines. The sales guy said, "Yes, indeed." I told them to take one over to the Lyons District and install it in my folks' house, and I'd send a money order. The weekly letter still arrived, but the tag line disappeared. I guess Dar and Cart, seeing proof-positive sitting there in their kitchen every morning, figured the kid was doing okay.

But my stomach wasn't doing so hot. After having kept up a breakneck work pace for so long, I had developed ulcers, and was on something called Sippy powders, little glassine envelopes of chalk. Booze was forbidden, and I was on a bland diet. It didn't bother me. That was my taste anyway. I left my tonsils in Old Chicago, so I missed some more performances. The ulcers hung in there, but the throat healed quickly, and I was back on stage in jig time, lifting a heftier partner in "Off Ter the Nuttin' Party." The thin-as-tissue-paper Meg Mundy didn't tour; she remained in New York, and soon was starring in the Jean-Paul Sartre play *The Respectful Prostitute.*

The wonderful Julie Wilson—later everyone's favorite cabaret diva—was now my partner. Kaye Ballard, the incredible comedienne, joined us on the road as well. We became (and stayed) close buddies. Bill Tabbert, who would make his mark as Lt. Cable in *South Pacific*, replaced Gordon MacRae. We were a big hit in Chicago. We got better notices there than we had in New York. Claudia Cassidy, the dreaded critic for the *Trib*, even had some very fine words for me: "You can't miss Carleton Carpenter, who looks so tautly young … and who has so much fun he may pay the management at the end of the week." I was surprised and thrilled.

I stayed in a place on the near North Side nicknamed Estuary House. The manager, Bob Thiebolt, ran the establishment replete with hot and cold running guests, mostly theater folk. What a wild and nutty place. One party would end just as another was gaining depth. Not really good for my ulcers, but a hell of a time for my libido.

We had a long and prosperous run in Chicago, and it was a sad time when we had to say goodbye to our mess of new friends. I can't remember all the cities we played—I think not too many—but we did play Philly again. While we were at the Shubert house, the *On the Town* road company was at the Forrest. We all mixed and mingled and spent too many late nights at the Variety Club. I met a gal name Helen Forrest (not the singer, though I did meet her later), and another dancer by the name of Glen Tetley. I really hit it off with both of them and they, in different ways, would become parts of my life. Helen and her lover Bob Cobert would stay in the Tomb whenever I was out of town; eventually they took the place over when I moved out.

One other note about the Chicago run of *Three to Make Ready*: I'd had new pictures taken, and did quite a hunk of modeling during our stay, mostly for the Sears catalog. After one fairly long session at the studio on the North Side, it was getting late in the afternoon, and I decided I had to take a taxi in order to get back to the theater on time. Trouble loomed. It was snowing and blowing like crazy; the wind whipped around blindingly. I wandered over to some main drag to hail a cab. There was no one to be found. You honestly couldn't see six feet in front of you. The city was really earning its famous adjective, *windy*. I kept plowing (almost literally) ahead, not quite knowing where the devil I was, the gale-like blizzard pushing me along from behind. Few cars passed me. No taxis. I kept on. Suddenly I realized I was up on the Outer Drive with no way to turn back. I figured I had at least two miles to go—and that because of the fierce wind, my only option was at my back.

Somehow, frozen and shaking, I made it off that hated ramp and down the street to the Blackstone and into the warmth of the theater. When my fingers became un-numbed enough to take my mail out of the wall box by the doorman's cubicle, there was a letter, with enclosed brochure, inviting me to join the Naval Reserve. That brochure, with its colored pictures of a South Sea Island somewhere, really looked inviting at that moment. Believe me, I was more than sorely tempted to sign up.

It was great getting home to the Tomb. I had treated Elihu Harrison, the superintendant, and his wife to good seats for the Broadway opening of *Three to Make Ready*, and had instantly become his favorite tenant. Now they welcomed me home like a long-lost son. They'd taken care of the apartment (something I wasn't wont to do), and it was sparkling clean and waiting with freshly laundered sheets on both the twin I used and the one I rarely slept in.

What a pair, the Harrisons. Hugh would always volunteer to be a quasi-maître'd at my parties. He really hosted most of them, like my big Christmas one in 1946. He loved to mix with the often celebrated guests and to amusingly introduce people—who already knew each other well— to one another.

Hugh was entertaining in other ways as well. The loo (let's be English) in the hallway abutted the super's apt. There was unfailingly a newspaper on the floor. And it was always the wrong way around, if one wanted to read while sitting and taking care of business (a family euphemism). That was impossible, but one could listen, often much too early, to the couple on the other side of the wall. They argued a lot. And loudly. One favorite overheard exchange:

ELIHU [who was given on regular occasions to booze]: Get back in that bed, you brown bitch!

WIFE: You know my name's not bitch. It's Vivian.

Then back to work I went, making the rounds. I landed a new play within ten days. It all seemed to easy in those days. The rounds were actually great fun, and a way of seeing and swapping stories with many old acquaintances on the prowl for jobs. These trips from one casting office to another, from one agent to another were daily. Few actors had exclusive contracts with one representative.

Maynard Morris, who had an office on Madison Avenue, was very influential then. His secretary, a Miss Kaye, was inclined to feel even more powerful than her boss. Once when I went to visit, his waiting room, which was really just a bit of an indent in the hall opposite the bank of elevators, was overflowing. There was one dilapidated couch whose springs were nonexistent; you were so low to the floor on the thin cushions that it was of no comfort whatever. On this day the sagging couch overloaded, but we all dutifully gave our names to the receptionist behind the sliding glass panel and found a spot of wall to lean against.

Suddenly, after what seemed ages, the door to the inner sanctum swung open. A very tiny, very ancient character actress tried desperately to rise from her sunken seat on the couch. Helping hands finally got her on her feet. She padded across to the door, grandly held open by the imperious Miss Kaye. "I'm here to see Mr. Morris," the old actress stated in a lovely voice polished by years of footlight experience. There was a pause, theatrical by intent, as Miss Kaye framed herself in the doorway.

"I'm sorry," she said. "Mr. Morris is seeing no one today. He's casting." And she drew the door tightly shut—oxymoronically speaking.

Other puzzling things happened to me in agent's offices. One day I sat in yet another jammed outer office, waiting to see another important person, a lady with a hard-hearted reputation. She was very hard to make an appointment with, so you took your chances with the daily throng. As she scanned the congregation, we waited hopefully for a nod and a pointing finger and the single word, "You." Only one time did I get the finger, so to speak. I was allowed inside her office to leave a picture and resume and to be quizzed by the great lady about my experience. She gave me perhaps three minutes. After being dismissed, I turned to leave, but she had one additional piece of advice to give me.

"Carpenter," she warned, "watch that height." I bobbed my head up and down, assuring her I would.

Next up on my Broadway resume was a truly forgotten and forgettable comedy, *The Magic Touch*, written by two Charlies, Raddock and Sherman. I knew this show would be a natural for ol' Professor Upham, the magician. The producer, John Morris Chanin, had an office high up in the Chanin Building on 42nd and Lex. I read for the part of a character named Larry Masters. I didn't get to read the entire play before auditioning, but I was hired for the role. I never really got to read the total masterpiece, since it was forever being rewritten.

After a confusing rehearsal period, we hit the road for a pre-Broadway tour. We hit unusual places like Buffalo and Newark. I shared a dressing room with an extremely bizarre gentleman named Le Roi Operti—whose grandfather or great grandfather, I forget which, had written *The*

The Magic Touch, 1947. Sid Melton is second from left, Sara Anderson seated.
Photo by Lucas Pritchard.

Black Crook, assumed to be the first Broadway musical—and two midgets. (They disappeared somewhere around the ninth rewrite.)

After a suddenly postponed New York opening night—the reason was never fully explained to the cast—we opened officially rose at the International Theatre in Columbus Square (long gone) on September 3, 1947. It was the first play of the new theatrical season. You never read such notices. I saved them all. A couple of headlines: "THE SEASON IS NOT YET OPEN!" "THE CURTAIN GOES UP, THE THUMBS GO DOWN."

The critics really had a chance to strut their stuff. The reviews were comic masterpieces, each one topping the last with glorious putdowns. And with very good cause. We staggered through twelve performances and folded. How we held on that long will forever remain a mystery. I couldn't have been happier, since I was already rehearsing in a new play during the day. I had given my two-week notice before the opening, hoping they'd replace me before the fateful night. But they didn't. I double-shifted for those two weeks instead.

I thought back to our run at Shea's Theatre in Buffalo. A squadron of pidgeons hovered just above the stage door and would bomb away at the cast when we tried to dash from Shea's to eatery. I had never before realized how astute and critically correct those birds could be. I'm sure they had caught an early performance.

Our leading lady Frances Comstock, smart lady she, took to carrying an umbrella. I became great friends with Frances and her husband, who designed and built all those amazingly beautiful signs for the main terminal of Grand Central. I also became close pals with two of the costars, Hope Emerson and Burke McHugh. Burke claimed that his father had the loneliest job in the world: He was head of the Democratic Party in Vermont. Burke, who took over my role after my two-week sentence, sometime later opened a bar on 9th Street in the Village; there the still-unknown baby Barbra displayed and wowed the world with that heavenly voice. (Burke did say she dressed like a homeless soul, in rags.)

Another cast-member, Howard Smith, was directed to indulge in huge, cheek-slapping, coffee-spurting takes. He was a very accomplished actor, as he displayed two seasons later in *Death of a Salesman*. As a company we hung closely together—joined by our terrific state manager, Perry Bruskin—until our official hanging by the critics.

Meantime, over at the other ranch, I was playing a sailor in a play I honestly liked called *The Big People*. It was directed by Martin Ritt (who taught me how to do a legitimate double-take) and featured a talented cast headed by Ernest Truex. This play, disguised as a comedy, dealt with an important theme, bigotry, in its slyest and ultimately most obscene and overt form.

The entire play took place in a bar setting created by the famed Boris Aronson; it was dominated by a huge moose head with a neck about six feet long, that made it extend above and beyond the bar stools. To put it mildly, the moose head snatched the audience's attention.

Mini-synopsis: A group of short people (led by Truex) are trying to recruit and organize a defense against the tall ones, who, they are convinced, are trying to take over the world. Things become complicated, sometimes comically, and lots of trouble ensues. Finally, just as things come to some sort of mutual understanding, another group arrives, wildly declaring its own war: the blue-eyed people against the brown-eyed.

Try as he might, Stanley Young, the playwright, couldn't pull the third act together. After a tryout in Philly we folded the play, never coming into New York. But for years to come, that play haunted me, and eventually I decided it would be a wonderful basis for a musical—a serious one. By the time I located Mr. Young, he had passed away. His widow was very helpful; she put me in touch with some professor at the University of Texas, to which Young had willed all his papers. They found a copy of the script and sent it on to me. I had permission from his wife to do whatever I wanted with it. But after reading it again after all those years, I couldn't come up with a proper hook to musicalize the piece. I still think there's a viable germ in it somewhere. Maybe it'll hit me yet.

While we were playing in Philly, Jeanne Shelby was there as well, in the tryout of a musical called *Music in My Heart*, based on the melodies of Tchaikovsky. But with our constant rehearsing, we could only get together for one Sunday dinner. Her show did come into town, but lasted only briefly.

Now, en-Tombed once more on 47th Street, I plunged into a really heavy schedule of live TV shows. At NBC, I did the *Philco Television Playhouse*, which presented old standbys like *The Torchbearers* by George Kelly (Grace's uncle), and *Three-Cornered Moon* and F. Hugh Herbert's *For Love or Money*. Herbert was the Neil Simon of the 1940s. I also acted in many, many originals by the string of talented writers then working for television.

During a break in rehearsals for some show, Nina Foch and I were gabbing about canasta while an older character actress named Leona Powers knitted away. Ms. Powers, a Broadway and touring veteran, tended to talk constantly about her career. It was always "my" show or "my" company. Her boasting was comical, never really high-handed. But on this day she was uncharacteristically quiet. Thinking that perhaps something was troubling her, I turned and asked her if she'd ever played canasta, which was new then. "Oh, I'm sure I have," she said. "I've played every little city and hamlet in the country."

One day, out of the wide blue, my life was invaded by a guy I'd met in Chicago during the tour of *Three to Make Ready*. Kaye Ballard, who was a friend of his, had introduced us; she thought we'd hit it off, since he had done a lot of magic shows. We did. He was a nice kid, and we saw each other a few times in the Windy. Now he was at my door in New York, saying he needed a place to stay. (I learned later he had an aunt living in the city.) He took over the lesser-used twin. He made a great dessert, called trifle, which was Jello and fruit and sponge cake.

Anyway, Little Kimmer, as John Murray Anderson called him, was ensconced. The day I turned twenty-one, Little Kimmer jokingly threatened me by saying he was going to the police and turn me in for harboring a minor. He was nineteen. I laughed, but suddenly I realized that our friendship wasn't tight enough for roommate-ville. Was I going to allow this to happen? Basically, although I love people and am gregarious, deep inside I am a loner, not a commitment-maker. I even hated signing contracts. I'm not a joiner, except for unions.

All of a sudden one early evening, Costello was at the door. We went down Third Avenue to the German American Beer Hall, then up to a bar on Second Avenue called the Old Nickelodeon. Jack Lemmon was playing piano, and there was a contest to see who could sing "By the Beautiful Sea" the fastest. I won, and we had more free beer than a party of six could have handled. When I asked Cos how he had found me, he said in his off-handed manner: "I keep track of you." That was all. We parted, late and loaded, without any meaningful conversation. But the night was magically dreamlike for me.

My dancer friend Glen Tetley was back in the city after having toured with *On the Town*, and he and I reunited. He was passionately devoted to modern dance. He had studied with one of the great pioneers of that art, Hanya Holm, and had spent much time in Colorado working with her. He became a real role model to me. This was a serious and tremendously talented man, very strict with himself, gentle and sweet to others. I respected him so much. Having fallen luckily into constant work, I had spent most of my time treating everything more or less as a lark. I began to realize that work meant more than that, and how terrifically fortunate I was. Funny how much more satisfying work becomes the more you really involve yourself in it. I'm ashamed to admit that I sometimes strayed from the complete dedication a project should have elicited from me, but thanks to Glen's example I slowly became better. And so did my work.

Tetley went on to become a famous choreographer and head of dance groups in several countries. He is gone now. He never knew the lasting effect his dedication to art had on my life.

Before long, L.K. had talked me into moving from the Tomb. I don't know why I went along with the idea, but I turned the place over to my friends Helen and Bob Cobert. I moved into an old brownstone on 29th Street. I heard that the place had been a morgue, whether that was true or not, that's what the house was called: the Morgue. From the Tomb to the Morgue. Was I on some kind of weird trip? In a way, I was.

The scene there felt like a commune. Presiding over the occupants was a talented music writer named Al Moritz, who with his grand piano and a roommate named Syd occupied the entire parlor floor. The floors above were all single bedrooms, and the kitchen in the basement had a tiled floor that slanted in from all sides toward a drain in the center—for blood from the corpses, one assumes.

Our fellow boarders (cultists?) were a wonderful bunch of people. Joan, Scully, and Meredith were among the women; Neal was an elegant gentleman from Baltimore whose room was in the basement, just off the kitchen. There were two refrigerators; we all had our own special sections, but we shared. A huge table covered the drain in the floor. Sometimes we divided the cooking, depending on schedules, but usually everyone did his or her own.

Not bad at all—except for one major flaw. The room that Little Kimmer and I shared had but one bed. That might have been okay if it hadn't been for the ancient mattress, whose springs were overstretched and sagged toward the center. I had to hang on to my side of the bed to avoid being constantly in contact with L.K. I don't like sharing a bed. (Still don't, except sometimes.) It didn't bother L.K., but it riled the hell out of me. I was working every day and wanted my roomie to do the same. Once in a while he'd take a temporary job somewhere, but these gigs never lasted for long, and I found myself nagging him like an old fishwife. I hated doing it, and I'm sure it didn't tickle him much either.

Every morning I'd leave for one TV rehearsal or another, happy to be off by myself for the day. I was beginning to feel trapped; more and more I longed for the freedom to be alone. One sunny Sunday, while taking a solitary stroll over to Fifth and heading uptown, I passed a church with a sign out front. It proclaimed: "Where old-fashioned friendliness still survives." The following Sunday, I decided to give religion another go-round.

My co-cultist Joan and I checked it out together. She was very tall, had a booming laugh, and was great all-around company. We sat in the balcony—well, upstairs. The hymns were familiar, the church very pretty, and the minister, who wore glasses, had a great smile. Sunlight streamed in on him from the high windows, lighting him in a very theatrical fashion. He himself seemed very much at home on his stage, the pulpit. The sermon was a humdinger, and dead on target to something close to my heart. In essence, it said: "Move to the back of the bus, you s.o.b., so others can get on and share a ride." I was hooked. So was Joan. Our Sunday mornings were now booked.

Sunday afternoons often involved Moritz soirees on the parlor floor. Guests arrived to be entertained by him at the grand piano and to share tea and talk. Very proper. Inmates from the upstairs could always attend—well, almost always. Some Sundays would be closed to us because Al might be auditioning material for a new show. Those were strictly business afternoons.

On one non-biz Sunday, the new faces included a fascinating lady who carried herself like a star. Short haircut, high cheekbones, and eyes that could thrill you if you were lucky enough to have them focus on you. She was the most stylish lady I'd ever met. A rag thrown around her shoulders would seem like the chicest thing one could imagine. She could radiate and warm any room she happened to be in. Okay, I'll back off. I was in awe. We'll leave it at that.

She had lived in Hollywood and met many movie people. When questioned about someone, she obligingly gave her personal insight with honesty and grace, perhaps adding a personal anecdote. Ladylike charm poured forth, until Esther Williams's name was mentioned.

She paused. Thoughtfully she took off her horn-rimmed glasses, then replaced and removed them once again. After a Pinteresque pause, the glasses were replaced, sides tapped, and a hand was placed on her crossed knee. "Esther Williams," she repeated softly, leaning forward a smidge and placing the other hand on her hip. "I really don't know what to say about Esther except, if you want a big fuck, she's it." It was not at all unkind, simply a statement of physical fact. I fell to the floor laughing and hugging her knees.

I was at her knees from then on, at times literally, for years and years. Her name was Jay Presson—later, Jay Presson Allen. She became the wildly and determinedly talented writer and director of three Broadway hits: *The Prime of Miss Jean Brodie*, *Forty Carats*, and *Tru*. But she was always a little odd with me.

Some time later she spoke to me about Neal, the gent in the always neat basement apartment, which included a spinet piano I often used. On most Sundays, Neal prepared and served the delicacies we fingered down. Jay said that when she was rich and famous she wanted to hire him as majordomo of her estate. The man from Baltimore had innate elegance, flawless manners and a quietly sly sense of humor. Even his laughter was gentle. And it was all for real; there wasn't a phony molecule in his body.

One Sunday evening, Joan and I decided to give the old-fashion hymn-sing in the basement of the church a try. There was a fair-size group of warblers and a rather large lady at the old upright piano. I shared a hymnal with a lady on my left. Joan shared with a man on her right. On our way to this event we pledged to behave ourselves, although we were both giggling at the thought of attending the thing. We would be strong and proper. That never happened. The very first hymn announced was new to us both, but we turned to the page as the choristers collectively cleared their throats. Then the lady of the keyboard gave us the intro. It was strictly a Shubert pick-up. Da da, da dum dum dum. I felt a slight nudge from Joan's elbow. I bit my lip and plunged into "In my heart there rings a melody," reading the music line. It was precisely the harmony of "Ev'rything's Up to Date in Kansas City" from *Oklahoma*. After the second line, "Rings a melody of heaven's harmony," my shoulders began to jiggle.

I could feel Joan beginning to crack, too. We kept singing and tried to hold on. Tears started oozing from my eyes, and as the second stanza began we were goners. We handed our hymnals to our stern sharers and fled, never looking back. We couldn't stop roaring with laughter. Why is it that when you want to keep yourself from breaking up it's impossible? And at ridiculous things one can't explain, like someone dropping a fork, and because of the timing it's the funniest thing in the word. There's a "go figure" for you. It was obvious the gal at the piano had played for many theater auditions.

We never tried the hymn-sing again, although we did continue on most Sundays to go to the church. But before long, the place became so popular that there were long lines waiting to get in. I had discovered the church shortly before the world did. It was the Marble Collegiate, and the actor-pastor was Norman Vincent Peale.

Things at the Morgue were getting touchy. I was trying to get L.K. a job. Using Neal's piano, I prepared him for an audition for a new musical, *Birdseed*, that Hugh Martin was doing. I taught him "I'll Build A Stairway to Paradise" and went along and played for him. My predicament with Little Kimmer was about to end. He didn't get the show, but he caught the eye of the composer, who would shortly whisk him off to Europe, and out of that hated bed in the Morgue.

Just prior to the whisking, Cos showed up one night. How he ferreted me out there I'll never know, but another magical drunken evening ensued. Serious talk was avoided, as always. I'd so often wondered what would happen if we spent more than twenty minutes together sober. We never gave it a chance. We just loved being in each other's company. I wanted more than just the occasional one night of carousing. But it was better than nothing. Or was it? Thereafter, I never really managed to have a committed emotional life. Cos was constantly there in the back of my mind. Just when I thought maybe I'd shaken this idyllic, platonic notion, he'd make an unexpected appearance to bring the whole thing roaring back to me. It certainly wasn't a very adult situation.

Professionally, at least, things were booming. I had a contract with CBS television for a show called *Places, Please*, which aired on Mondays, Wednesdays, and Fridays from 7:15 to 7:30 p.m. We did the show at the old Maxine Elliott Theatre on 38th Street. I played Stretch, the stage manager. William Lee was Pop, the doorman, and Barry Wood was the host. The stage was bare except for a few props—maybe a ladder or table or a couple of chairs and a grand piano. *Places, Please* showcased the talents of Broadway understudies and other pros with much talent but little exposure. On one show, a very young Eddie Fisher came up from Philly to sing "It's Magic." There were maybe three turns a night, four if one was a duet.

The trouble with all these TV shows I was doing is that hardly anyone had a television set, so the audiences were miniscule. It was a big deal when Boston got the coaxial cable, and an even bigger one when Chicago joined the network. However, the work was a great joy for me. The pay was as small as the audience: seventy-five bucks a week for three shows. And I couldn't leave town with a play or a musical, so Broadway was on hold for the nonce.

I had moved from 134 to 156 East 47th Street. Bob and Helen were still at the Tomb. I was so happy to be on my own again, with a bed to myself, and back in the old familiar part of the city. Every evening after *Places, Please* I was playing piano at a place called Rainbow Bar and Grill on 3rd Avenue between 43rd and 44th, almost under the El. A tiny four-octave piano stood by the entrance, next to the window. Murray Anderson told me I should tap on the window like a Swedish whore to get people in. The regulars in the place were mostly folks who lived nearby in Tudor City. The food was plain Italian; the boss was kindly, and paid me in cash each night. There was no TV, of course, or even radio or jukebox—just me and the midget 48.

During the day, I was rehearsing with eleven others at the Charles Weidman Studio for Leonard Sillman, the *New Faces* gent. This was to be an intimate revue for a nightclub. We rehearsed gratis for weeks on end—eight of us plus a singing quartet called, I think, the Skylarks. (One of the young singers was Jack Rollins, Rollins, later the producer of many Woody Allen films.) Jay Presson was in it with me, an added bliss. I didn't have to show up for *Places, Please* until six p.m. It was a short hour-and-a-half, thrice-weekly gig; a brief rundown of that night's program and we hit the air.

One early evening, helping to move a piano around onstage, I felt a pain in my groin. Oops, I've ruptured myself, thought I, figuring I knew my body like a pro. (This notion was probably instilled in me while I played Dr. Health in grade school.) A couple of days later it was really hurting, so I went to see Dr. Bill Eisenbrandt, who I'd met during the Morgue safari. "You've a rupture on the right side," he confirmed. I bought a truss with a little felt-covered, water-filled ball on one end, which held in the hunk of loose gut. It was painless, although funny-looking. I happily displayed it to anyone who was interested.

Shortly after Chicago got the coaxial, another show joined us at the Maxine Elliott on Sunday night: *Toast of the Town*. It was emceed by a newspaper columnist with a bland visage and an amazing lack of personality, but it had a great singer, Monica Lewis. The show eventually became very popular; it ran a helluva lot longer than *Places*. Retitled *The Ed Sullivan Show*, it moved several blocks uptown to what became the Ed Sullivan Theater.

Leonard Sillman, for whom I was still rehearsing, was part con man and part creator, with charm he could turn on with winning assurance at the drop of an eyelid. I later sat in on a backer's audition where he had the money-heavy crowd in the palm of his hand. I was mesmerized. As he gave brief outlines of unwritten sketches and asked the sweet, talented composer, Arthur Siegel, to play a few bars of tunes not yet set to paper, the greenbackers were already reaching for their wallets or checkbooks. They didn't even know what the proposed endeavor was actually about. It was rumored that one wealthy widow had invested and lost over one million dollars, yet she kept coming back to the siren song that Sillman voiced so adeptly.

Even though I was working day and night, I still grabbed a few minutes to audition for upcoming Broadway shows. At one point I was seriously under consideration for two musicals when Leonard called me into his office on East 42nd Street. He wanted me to sign an agreement that I would be available if and when he finalized a deal with a lady named Muriel Abbott to book our *New Faces* club revue into the Palmer House in Chicago and the Persian Room at the Plaza in New York. I told him I was up for a couple of Broadway shows. He answered that this agreement was just to show Miss Abbott she would get the revue she'd watched at the Weidman studio. Of course, he assured me, a Broadway show was more important, and if I got one it would be terrific. This paper was just a formality. I would be replaced. I signed. He wished me all the luck in the world, patting me on the back as I left his office.

Two weeks later, after a callback audition, I got *Along Fifth Avenue*, a revue starring Nancy Walker. We would start rehearsals the following Thursday. I raced over to Sillman's office to give him the great news, beaming like an idiot. What great timing: *Places, Please* had finished its last show the previous week. Leonard hit the ceiling, rising from his chair in a wild rage, his face purpling. *"No way in hell are you leaving my show!"* he screamed. My jaw dropped several inches. He fumbled around in a desk drawer and came out with a piece of paper and leaned forward, waving it in my face.

"But you said—" I started.

"No buts. I have a signed contract with you."

"But I signed a contract for the show."

"Well, get out of it!" he commanded, voice amps increasing.

"I can't. We start rehearsals next Thursday."

"Tell 'em you're sick. Tell 'em something. Anything. We're set for the Plaza and I want you. And I've got you. Legally." He kept waving that damned "formality" agreement at me.

"I can't just lie to Arthur Lesser." He was the producer.

"That sonofabitch!" Sillman began to pace back and forth behind his desk.

Finally he cried out in triumph: "I've got it. Go to the hospital. Get your goddamn hernia sewn up. I'll pay for it."

I called Mr. Lesser's office. Not bothering to hide my extreme disappointment, I told him I had to have an operation. Then I called Dr. Bill, who booked a room at the Lexington Hospital (now gone) for the following morning. He told me to shave myself "down there" the best I could, and that the hospital would complete the job when I checked into my room. I called Sillman and told him I'd be at the hospital in the morning. He said he'd send someone over with a check. He did. As I lay in bed, getting drowsy from the pre-op shot, a nurse came in with a check. One hundred dollars, made out to me. She held a chart board and gave me a pen to endorse it. I could hardly turn the check over, I was losing ground so quickly; but I gripped the pen as tightly as I could to sign my name on the back. Typed in capital letters across the top of the check were the words:

THIS IS A LOAN

A husky actor who'd been in the play *The Big People*—he'd also played a sailor—helped me home and carried me up the four flights to my place at 156 East 47th. My mother had come down and was there waiting for me. She slept on the couch in the one room apartment. There was a stall shower in the place next to the sink and stove, but the john was out in the hall. It was so small you couldn't turn around in it. Dar said she had to look both ways, open the door, get skirts up and pants down, and then back into it in order to pee. It was handier to be a man on that floor.

Quick note: When I'd moved into this new home, the first thing I did was rent a piano. The company had to rig up a hoist from the roof and haul it up from the street, remove the window, and get it in through there—a production enjoyed by everybody in the old skinny brownstone.

A week later, Sillman had me jumping off tables downstairs in the Plaza Hotel's Rendez-vous room, where we were still rehearsing for the grand opening upstairs in the Persian Room. (The Rendez-vous later became a cabaret, Plaza 9-, then a movie theater.) A first novel by a Southern kid had just come out; it dealt explicitly with homosexuality, and sported a provocative photo of the author on the back of the jacket: a pouty, poetic face gazing straight into the lens as he sprawled on a divan. That picture (and a mass of pre-publishing flack) helped drive up the sales. During rehearsal one morning, Leonard came rushing back from the men's room. He stopped us mid-skit and announced: "You'll never guess who was standing beside me at the next urinal. That short Southern belle, who wrote the book everyone's going nuts over. If I'd listed a little to the left, I could have caught him right in the lisp." Truman Capote. The book was his first novel, *Other Voices, Other Rooms*. Not exactly your typical Norman Rockwell moment.

One evening after my nightly gig at the Rainbow, I went with Murray to the all-night dress runthrough of Ringling Bros. and Barnum & Bailey Circus at the Garden in Madison Square between 49th and 50th off Eighth Avenue. The season for the circus had officially begun here in New York. After the indoor run here, it would go back under canvas and tour. His credit was prominent: "Devised and Directed by JOHN MURRAY ANDERSON" (in a box). This was really his element and he gloried in it.

Spectacles with hundreds of people and animals were his best-loved productions. He was king of a whole nation of performers. A man he called N.P. (for Name Pending), Dick Barstow, was the choreographer; Miles White (Murray called him "Eccentric") was the costumer. Jerry Banks was in charge of the clowns—a division called Clown Alley.

All the animals were loved, taught and cared for by a host of trainers. But Murray was *the boss*. Bullhorn in hand. He knew how much I loved the circus and how I'd been taken every year down to Menands (a spit away from downtown Albany, just across the Hudson from Troy) to catch an afternoon show, even if it meant losing a day of school. I was a circus nut. I thought it was the best possible life that anyone could be lucky enough to have. Menands was the closest the "big show" ever got to Bennington. Some smaller ones came in awhile, and of course I caught those. But, c'mon, Ringling Brothers and Barnum & Bailey was the heavy cream.

Now here I sat next to John Murray Anderson, the man who ran the entire operation from high up in the bleachers at the Garden so Murray could keep his keen eyes on everything. It was incredibly exciting for me, but it must have been elongated torture for the cast, the roustabouts, riggers, orchestra and especially the animals. Otto Schmidt, the elephant trainer, was putting his charges through their paces in spite of a constant bellowing from Murray's bullhorn: "Ruth," he screamed, knowing all their names, "get back there. Don't crowd. Modock, stop swaying around. Pay attention. Bertha, what the devil are you doing? Can't you hear the music? Emily, for gawdsake, keep up with the others, you're ruining the whole symmetry of the number." On and on he ranted away. It was now about four a.m.

Suddenly, one of the largest of the verbally attacked group lifted its trunk and trumpeted triumphantly. The Garden grew very still, and everything seemed to freeze. Then the elephants joined trunks to tails in a long line and walked majestically out of the arena. Murray was stunned. Trainer Schmidt stood alone down there on the track. "You see, Murray," Otto called, "You can yell at people like that. But elephants won't take it." And he strode away from rehearsal. The perverse Murray put the bullhorn down and laughed like I'd never seen before, eyes streaming tears. He slapped his legs, he slapped me on the arm, he couldn't stop laughing. He really adored being put down by a group of proud elephants.

In 1944, after the terrible Ringling Bros. fire that killed 186 people in Hartford, Connecticut, the circus abandoned the canvas and played only indoor arenas. For me, part of the wonderful aura vanished. But the troop was happy to be beyond the two-buckets-of-water allowance per day. There were also better living quarters on the train. Still later, another edition of the show was added. Now there were two touring units; Red and Blue.

New Faces at the Persian Room was a huge success and an innovation, a miniature revue in a nightclub. It was the forerunner of the inventive Julius Monk revues, most of which had healthy runs and introduced many well-known and talented performers. Our show was sleek, chic, funny and elegant. The ladies wore specially designed dresses, all beautifully tailored to fit their individual personalities. All were black and white. The gentlemen wore tuxedos or full-dress tailcoat evening clothes, also, of course, black and white.

Our notices were raves, or close to, and we enjoyed a happy twelve-week run. We'd been booked for only six. And, of course, Sillman deducted twenty-five bucks from my first four weeks of paychecks.

Chapter 8 ⸻

J ust before I'd wound up the cabaret gig, my agent called with an audition appointment. She explained nothing about it except where to
go and what time. She ended the short telephone call with: "And for
God's sake, look young."

I shaved as close as I could without actually drawing blood, and
wore a button-down white shirt with my old black navy sweater over it.
I checked the mirror. The twenty-one-year-old face stared back at me.
Was that young enough? Who knew? Off I went. The office was full of
guys about my age, maybe a bit younger, and all a helluva lot shorter. I
hunkered down on my heels in a corner, trying my best, as warned, to
"watch that height." Reading over the two pages a lady had handed me,
I realized this was no play. This was a movie. I still didn't care anything
about Hollywood. During *Three to Make Ready*, two other contracts had
been proffered. Columbia and MGM. I politely resisted.

Now, I thought, I'm here. I'll read anyway. And I did. I thanked the
men I read for and went home. An hour later came another call from the
agent. They would like to do a screen test with me for the role, she said. I
told her okay. I wasn't all that thrilled, but at least it wasn't for a long-term
contract or anything. I tested with a really nice girl named Susan, who
had already secured a part. We sat at a table for the scene, which never
ended up in the film). I was playing her small-town boyfriend. We did
just one take. Then we went to another room where they filmed us just
standing side by side. She was so short (or I was so tall) that they had her
standing on something called an apple box. It looked like a Sand Springs
Ginger Ale case, only higher. Then Susan left and they sat me on a stool,
filming me from all sides in tight closeup.

As I faced front again, the man I thought was the director—he turned
out to be the producer—began asking me about my background. My face
must have been jumping all over the place, because he told me, with a

laugh, to be a bit more relaxed and less facially expressive. It was my first (and probably best) piece of movie-acting direction. One did not act for the camera. One thought. The camera would do the rest.

The film was Louis de Rochement's *Lost Boundaries*, directed by Alfred L. Werker and shot in and around Portsmouth, New Hampshire. It was based on the true story of a Negro doctor and his family who had lived in Keene (also New Hampshire) and had passed for white for twenty years. In his first starring role, Mel Ferrer was playing the doctor, Beatrice Pearson his wife. Susan Douglas, the gal I tested with, played the teenage daughter, Richard Hylton the son. A wonderful supporting cast included the great Canada Lee, William Greaves, and Parker Fennelly. I played Andy, the daughter's boyfriend.

There was a scene where the son brings his college roommate home on vacation so they can continue working on a musical they're writing together. As I read the script (credited to a Virginia Shaler), I thought it needed something ahead of a part where the son and his friend arrive and are asked to perform.

I had an idea. I wrote out a new scene to precede my character's entrance, including a song I'd recently written before getting the film, called

Susan Douglas and I in *Lost Boundaries*.

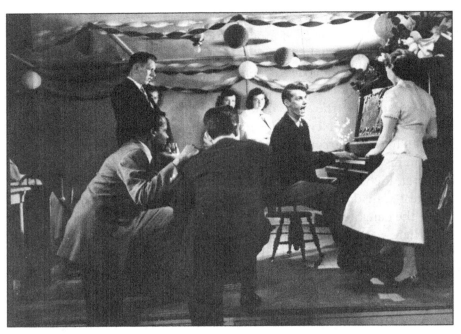

Performing my song "I Wouldn't Mind" in *Lost Boundaries*, 1949.

"I Wouldn't Mind." I phoned Mr. de Rochemont from the old Rockingham Hotel in Portsmouth, where the cast was staying. He lived fairly close by in a town called Newington. I asked if I could come out and discuss an idea with him. He heartily agreed, even sending a car to pick me up. The house was enormous, the living room with a grand piano spectacular. He introduced me to his wife, joined her on the sofa, and asked what my idea was.

Too dumb to be cowed by the house or the producer, I pulled out my pages and dove right in. I ended by sitting at the piano and singing the tune. When I finished, they were both beaming. Mr. de Rochemont said he liked the new scene and the song. We'll see, he said, rising to see me out. When I thanked them and told Mrs. de Rochemont how nice it was to meet her, she smiled and said: "I think you've improved my scene no end."

On the way back to the hotel I kept thinking about the "my scene" thing. Then it dawned on me that Mrs. de Rochemont was Virginia Shaler. I'd had the gall to sit there in front of the screenwriter and read my changes right in her own home. I felt awful. I was so ashamed, I hid in my room the rest of the day and didn't go down for dinner; I just went to bed, expecting some terrible fate from my colossal faux pas.

The next morning, under my door (and the doors of all the other actors) were new pages, exactly as I'd written them. That's the way that section of film was shot. The song with me playing and singing was done live on the set, not pre-recorded.

I finished my four-week stint at four hundred dollars per and returned to New York and forgot about it. The gang at the Rainbow welcomed me back after the long hiatus, and the next day it seemed as if I'd never been away. I had a batch of new Tune-Dex cards (three-by-five cards with the melody, chords and lyrics of songs). New ones came out every month—Hit Paraders, current show tunes and a few real oldies; a fun mix. With them, I could fill most requests.

I had run into Duane Thorpe again, and he was having a rough time finding work as a dancer. He was also looking for cheaper digs. When a small room became vacant at 156, I rented it for him. It was down at the end of the hall from me. He spent a bunch of time at the Rainbow, and every so often would fill in for me when I took the rare bathroom break. Thorpe didn't read music, but he had learned "Star Dust" by ear. That was his entire repertoire—that one Parish-Carmichael song. He would play it straight, as a waltz, a tango, a cha-cha, rumba, whatever. It was a hoot. We'd split the tips.

That bar, strangely enough, began to become very popular with the after-show crowd from Broadway, and on many occasions it was jammed not only with chorus kids but with the stars, like Henry Fonda. He was starring in *Mr. Roberts*, a huge hit at the time. There were also performers from posh boîtes like the new Le Directoire, where Kay Thompson was holding forth with the Williams Brothers. Baby Andy became a semi-regular at the Rainbow, and sometimes sang with me at the forty-eight.

The place became a very eclectic, fun group hangout. Most important, we never lost any of the original neighborhood customers. They enjoyed the mix even when it threatened to get a smidge out of control. One star, who shall remain nameless, did a split on the bar late on a Saturday night. Many years later, in Paris, at a tiny, really dark downstairs after-hours dive, a complete stranger (American) came over to my table—how he could see in the near-blackout, I'll never know—and told me how much he had enjoyed the Rainbow Bar on Third Avenue, and thanked me. This was even after the El had been torn down.

The circus was back again at the Garden, and I told Murray I'd join up if there was a spot. He reintroduced me to Jerry Banks, the head of Clown Alley, who set up an audition. Yes, to be a clown. I walked funny anyway, so that was a plus. I pranced around the track, stopping now and then to walk with palms flat on the ground, knees locked, head up with back parallel to the sawdust. Since I was sort of double-jointed, could do splits, and had long, skinny arms that dangled chimp-like down my sides, and because Jerry liked the sketch I'd done for my planned clown make-up, I passed with flying colors. I was on cloud ten.

It was a young kid's dream come true: to run away with the circus. I was much too old for this. Would I ever grow up? I told Thorpe, and he turned green before my eyes. He wanted to be a clown, too. I talked to Banks for him. No soap. Clown Alley was full-up. But maybe he could get a job with the head of wardrobe, and perhaps move into clowning later on. That idea suited Thorpe just fine, so I invited the wardrobe man out for drinks after the show that night. We went to an old hangout of mine called the Metropole on the corner of 48th and 7th. Helen McArdle, a favorite there and a pal of mine, sang a la Beatrice Kay (the singing star known as the "Gay '90s Girl") up in the middle of the big oval bar. Thorpe and I kept the drinks flowing into our prey, and by the time the three of us staggered from the bar, we were best buddies. And Thorpe had a job.

He started work immediately. I was to start with the circus the next week. But a new play came up at the Theatre Guild and I signed for it instead of hitting the road. Murray congratulated me and told me to stick with the theatre. I knew he was relieved I hadn't signed on to be a clown. Thorpe started out by hauling wardrobe trunks around Clown Alley and moved up through the ranks. He spent the rest of his life (nearly fifty years) with Ringling Bros. I'd see him every year in New York or wherever I was. And we wrote—well, he did—often. I'm not much of a letter writer but I was better with my dear old friend than anyone else.

The Theatre Guild job was a new play *Out of Dust*, by Lynn Riggs, the man who had written *Green Grow the Lilacs*, which was later adapted into *Oklahoma*.

Out of Dust, a western drama, would be directed by Mary Hunter. (Later on she directed the Jerome Robbins production of *Peter Pan*.) Just before rehearsals began, I got an invitation from the New York office of Louis de Rochemont to attend a screening of *Lost Boundaries* at the tiny Preview Theatre atop a building on Broadway around 48th Street. The following evening I took the elevator to the top floor and sat in the last row, sort of hiding. I was fascinated, but scared. It thrilled me to see one of the credits:

Song – "I Wouldn't Mind" by Carleton Carpenter

Then the film began. Everything was fine until I showed up, rushing in tardily from work, at the dance. Oh, God, I looked terrible. Clumsy, jitterbugging all over the place. Sitting at the piano, singing in unforgiving close-up, I looked like Donald Duck. I couldn't stand looking at myself. It was torture. I hated everything about the whole performance. I stuck it out until just before the cast credits rolled. I raced out the door before the lights came up. Two elevators were standing open, waiting for the screening crowd to emerge. I told the guy to take me down. He said they'd all be out in a minute or two. I said, "I HAVE TO GO DOWN NOW!" He gave me a strange look, but closed the door and down we went. He knew a maniac was about to burst. I ran all the way across town to 156, up the flights and into the empty safety of my room. I drank a lot of vodka and spent the rest of the night on my knees praying to God to make me a good actor, while knowing I was probably begging for the impossible.

Thank goodness I had a stage play to start working on. I did not, by any stretch of anyone's fertile imagination, have a face for the screen. We rehearsed at the Guild on 53rd near the Museum of Modern Art. Ms. Hunter was a marvelous director and I felt like an actor again. The cast included William Redfield, Berry Kroeger and the dynamic Helen Craig, wife of the film actor John Beal. There were rewrites, but the melodrama began to slowly come together. We were going to move on to Westport, Connecticut, to rehearse further and try out at the Playhouse Theatre there.

Then I received a phone call from Costello's cousin. She was in near-hysterics. She told me Cos was very, very ill, not making much sense and walking around the house all the time in a bathrobe, clutching a souvenir program of *Three to Make Ready*. Maybe if could go to Springfield there might be some way I could help.

I never hesitated. I told her I'd go at once. After I hung up I knew what I had to do. I went to Mary Hunter and told her I had a friend who needed my help and I had to go to him. If I could, I'd return to the cast; if not, I wouldn't be able to help it. This was something I simply had to do. She was wonderful. She said she completely understood and hoped my friend would get better.

I took the first plane I could get from LaGuardia to Springfield. A small rickety thing, but I was too anxious about Cos to be scared. After taking a cab to his home, I saw a woman I assumed to be his mother rocking on the front porch. I introduced myself and asked to see Cos. She kept rocking. After what seemed an eternity, she told me he wasn't there. They had taken him away, she said quietly. When I asked where he was she told me it was some veteran hospital. I told her I'd go there, but she said they wouldn't let anybody see him. I left this poor empty shell of a lady and went to find a taxi. I didn't know where to look, but I eventually located one with the help of somebody and went to the vet hospital. I would get in. I made up my mind. Nothing was going to stop me.

God knows how, I talked myself in to meet with his doctor. It was getting very late in the day. Almost dark. He was getting ready to leave but stayed with me. We talked. I told him how close Cos and I had been on Tinian and what great friends we were. He said he knew all that, but I wouldn't really want to see him. I said I most certainly would. The doc explained that Cos had been given a series of shock treatments. It seemed he'd been at the place for a couple of weeks. Apparently his cousin hadn't been told.

I begged the doc to let me see him for a minute or two. He finally agreed, but warned that I wouldn't like it.

I was taken to a small room and told to wait. I smoked nervously and paced around, then sat on one of the hard chairs in the cell-like space. Two male attendants brought him in and sat him down, then left us alone. We stared at each other for a long time. He looked awful—thin, with several days' growth of beard. He was just sort of lumped there in pj's and a frail hospital robe. Suddenly he gave me a lop-sided grin and said: "I look pretty terrific, right?"

He began to talk a bit. He rambled some about the fun times we'd had and how he was now locked up in this joint. I didn't say much. I nodded and smiled a lot, agreeing with whatever he was saying as his mood swung wildly from one thing to another. He'd go from smiling and talking almost amorously to exposing himself to me and spitting.

It was a nightmare. I wouldn't let myself break down and give in to tears, and after the worst nine or ten minutes in my life, the attendants came in and took him away.

I couldn't figure anything out. I was a nervous and physical wreck. What could I do? Where could I go? Could I even go on? I fled from the hospital into the evening, gulping at the air. I honestly felt my life was over. I felt everything was my fault and I was helpless to do anything about it. I wandered out to some highway and hitched a ride in some big truck, just wanting—and needing—to get the hell away. The friendly driver wanted to make conversation but I wasn't much use to him. My head was so full of … I don't know what.

The driver kept up his gab and I tried to focus in on it to drive all the stuff out of my brain. In a way, it helped. I concentrated so hard on everything he was rattling on about, it began to settle me down a bit. When I suddenly asked him which way we were headed, he roared with laughter. It turned out to be north. Then it suddenly hit me. This was the night I was supposed to be in Keene, New Hampshire for the premiere of *Lost Boundaries*. By some stroke of fate, he was headed in that general direction. When I told him my destination, he said he was sorry; he'd be turning off about an hour's drive before there. Fine, I said. I'd use the old thumb again. I was trying to jolly myself up, but it was really impossible.

He dropped me off and said, "Thanks for the company" before I could say "Thanks for the ride." Two more hitches and I arrived in Keene. A policeman escorted me to the home of the Johnsons, the real-life doctor and his family who were portrayed in the film. It was nearly midnight when we arrived, but the after-premiere party was still going on in the huge tent beside their house. The whole cast was there, along with most of the crew and about half of Keene. Everybody was having a high old time. Boy, did people drink a lot in those days. I was hugged and kissed by the film gang and locals alike. I grabbed myself a stiff vodka and let the music and general bonhomie lull me part of the way out of the terrible funk I was in. Apparently the film had been a success. I couldn't catch up with the pervading mood, but I did my damnedest, finally getting a ride back to the city with one of the cast in the oncoming dawn.

I rejoined *Out of Dust*, which moved on to Westport. In my off time I hung out there with a great gal, Nancy Ryan, and a bunch of her local pals. Among them was a baby Stephen Sondheim, three years my junior. We played our songs for each other whenever there was a piano around and enjoyed each other's work. He was still in the common thirty-two-bar stage, like me. Unfortunately, I never moved much beyond that standard style. You know what happened to him and his.

Out of Dust remained in the expensive dust of Connecticut, never moving on to Broadway. Meanwhile, *Lost Boundaries* opened to raves at the Astor Theatre on Broadway, where it remained for a little over eleven months. The reviews for the film were something sensational. Amazingly, most of them singled out my performance for special mention. I thought the movie critics must have been a bunch of real stupes.

This picture was a real breakthrough for civil liberty for black Americans. Not only did it win the Cannes award but, in typical Hollywood me-too filmmaking, caused Fox to rush out a film called *Pinky* and another studio to change the central character, a Jewish soldier, in the filming of Arthur Laurents's thoughtful play about anti-Semitism, *Home of the Brave*, to a young black soldier, beautifully played by James Edwards. To everyone's credit, all three were successful and flourished.

Along with the continuing TV work, I landed semi-regular roles on the hit radio show, *The Aldrich Family*. I played Toby and Charlie. We performed the broadcasts in front of live audiences. After we'd done one episode, the cast would return to do a repeat performance for the West Coast. Before each show, we'd assemble behind curtains and the announcer would introduce the leading actors. "Ladies and gentlemen, Mr. Aldrich, played by House Jameson." The house would applaud and House would step through and take a bow. Then would come Mrs. Aldrich, Katharine Raht. Applause, step through, bow. Homer, Jackie Kelk. Loud applause, step through, bow. And finally Henry Aldrich, himself, played by Ezra Stone. Thunderous applause, step through, sudden momentary cessation of applause. Then it picked up and carried through the bow. Cause of cessation: the shock of recognition. Stone was not only fast approaching middle age, but was also quite rotund and more than quite bald. The rest of us supporting players always listened for that brief moment and it never failed to crack us up.

Ezra, an old pro, warmed up every audience until they were ready to laugh their collective heads off during the broadcast. When the ONE MINUTE TO AIR warning was hard, he always wound up by fumbling his script until it flew from his hands and scattered all over the stage. The audience would let out a huge gasp of horror. Then he'd produce another script from his back pocket and away we'd go.

The show was directed by a gentle, talented veteran, Ed Durer. Because we were all playing teenagers, the scripts were actually marked where and on what lines our voices should crack. It was choreographed hormonal vocal breakage. Ah, how I miss the fun and thievery of radio.

Murray was staging new shows at Billy Rose's Diamond Horseshoe, in the basement of what had once been the Paramount Hotel on 46th Street, just a few doors west of the Hotel Edison. I often sat in on rehearsals and then later would see them in all their glittery glory when the shows opened. There was always a small array of leggy, gorgeous showgirls—bruisers, in Murray-speak. He called the chorus girls Ponies. Always on the lookout, he had personally discovered many of them, often in Europe. One of them—from Sweden? Norway? Finland?—was named Siri. She was truly a traffic-stopping beauty who stood six-foot-one and had a cautionary wit, which of course Murray adored. She often came out with some remarkable (and true) pronouncement at the exact wrong time to exactly the wrong person. I loved her, and we used to hang out together.

Murray had worked often with Billy Rose, beginning with the musical *Jumbo* in 1935. They'd collaborated on a gigantic exposition that Rose produced for some Texas event. It was a huge outdoor event with an immense stage in the middle of nowhere. In the grand finale, a herd of buffalo raced from beyond a hill, headed down a fenced-in track, then charged onto and across the stage and off. At the final tech runthrough and light check, Murray stood onstage as he conferred with his lighting man, Carlton Winckler, who was out in the audience. Finally Murray decided it was time for the buffalo run. He went way over and upstage right to blow the whistle cue. This was followed by a shotgun blast, the signal to release the animals. Out they came. When they were halfway down the track, Murray bullhorned: "All right. Hold them right there." He turned back to Winckler to instruct: "Now, change those gels to my special lavender." Rose grabbed Murray and barely got him out of the path of the thundering stampede.

When Rose's partner at the Horseshow, Nicky Blair, decided to go it alone, he opened the Carnival, a place on 50th Street across from the Garden. Murray went with him and staged the shows for the big room. I think Martha Raye was the first headliner. I remember seeing Ed Wynn and his bicycle. Richard Barstow was the choreographer—Murray called him N.P., for "Name Pending"—and Carlton Winckler did the lighting. They were the usual suspects who worked faithfully with Murray. I hung out mostly at the big oval bar where Nicky someone played piano. Dorothy Kilgallen always seemed to be there, sometimes with Johnnie Ray, with whom she was allegedly in love.

Speaking of Johnny: One night when Dar was visiting, we went out somewhere to play bridge. After taking her home to 156, I was set to meet Johnnie at the Blue Angel. When I turned from Lex onto 55th, I saw two fire trucks in front of the place. Herbert Jacoby (who co-owned the Angel with Max Gordon) stood stoically on the sidewalk near the entrance. He said to me in those soft French tones: "Your friend has set fire to a banquette in the bar. Please remove him." I bowed, then went in and got Johnny, several sheets aflap, out and into a cab. Damage to the boite was minimal. (We probably went across town to the Carnival.)

My other favorite haunts throughout that era were Le Ruban Bleu, which was run by Julius Monk; the tiny bar at Sardi's; and anywhere Helen McArdle was singing. Each time she opened in a new place, I tried to appear at her opening night and present her with yellow roses, her favorite. Then there were a bunch of gay bars, mostly on the East Side, that were known as the Bird Circuit.

Julius was a character. He emceed the always chic, funny, or breathtakingly wonderful acts with his standard intro. It was forever delivered in his very, very soft—it would quiet even the noisiest audience—Southern twang, overlayed with an acquired British accent: "Ladies and gentlemen, may I direct your attention and applause to … " whomever. He said it with the solemnity of a gentle undertaker.

Some of my favorite of his acts were Jane Dulo, (James) Kirkwood and (Lee) Goodman (for whom I wrote material), James Shelton, Sylvia Syms … I'll stop there. There were too many.

I hung out at Number One Fifth Avenue, too. All kinds of terrific performers got their start there, with Hal Fonville and Bob Downey at the duo pianos. I studied with Hal from time to time. He was a good voice coach who lived at the Osborne on 57th off Seventh Avenue. Most of the time I coached with Bob Fram, who lived farther west on 57th. Bob was a very jolly gent, slightly overweight, whose studio—actually his living room—was jammed with hundreds of stuffed elephants. He was great at finding old show tunes I didn't know, and he would accompany me at auditions. He was a good cook, and became a dear friend. Dar was so impressed by his elephant display that she started a collection of her own. I added to it with any foreign trip I took. It grew fairly large, but nowhere near the size of Fram's. Bob had quite a big-name clientele. I'll mention only a couple of pals: Bibi Osterwald (who later married Justin Arndt, the bassist from the trio at Le Ruban Bleu) and Elaine Stritch.

Then there was the doorway (a gate, really) through which I passed often, on 48th just east of Third. When buzzed open, it led into a small courtyard, like an English mews. One of the three or four apartments belonged to Len Hanna, the heir to the family that owned practically everything in Cleveland, Ohio. In partnership with Cole Porter and other rich pals, Len opened a ritzy restaurant called 1-2-3, at 123 East 54th Street. Roger Stearns, the pianist there—some claimed he was Porter's lover—introduced us. Roger played ripply, ornate show tunes at odd tempi. He was impossible to sing along with. The offbeat attraction of the place was a lady palm reader. She read me many times and made me an almost complete believer.

Anyway, probably just because I lived around the corner, Hanna invited me several times to his home for dinner—usually whenever Cole was dining there. What a wondrous treat for me! The conversation at the elegantly set and served table was priceless, even better than the food, which was five-star. Hanna had a chef as well as butler. (I can remember how lucky I'd felt as a kid growing up with those proper meals with the Cushmans of Old Bennington.) There were never more than four or five of us at Len's. Ethel Merman's pianist was sometimes there. He lived in the neighborhood, too. I had sense enough to keep my mouth shut and ears open. Some of the gossip I didn't understand, but the fun language and delivery were delightful. Cole was always very sweet to me. Well, I was young and sort of cute. Maybe I was part dinner decoration. I didn't care.

When given the chance, I would add a bit of wit to the mix. I always felt relaxed and enjoyed those evenings, never feeling out of place. I loved the risqué talk. That was the operative word, risqué, as in the material done by the naughty singer-pianists of the day, like Dwight Fiske and Spivy, the proprietor of Spivy's Roof.

Work never stopped: TV, radio, the occasional modeling job and the steadiness of the Rainbow. One day, an agent named Arnold Hosquith called me from the New York office of Warner Bros., wanting me to come in to read for a film that was to star Bette Davis and an unknown young actor. Me? Hadn't they seen *Lost Boundaries*? Didn't they know I wasn't right for the silver screen? I began to think perhaps I should try again. Even though I hated myself "up there," I'd fooled the critics. Maybe I could do something I wouldn't be ashamed of.

I went way west on 56th, almost to the Hudson River. The script was based on a novel called *The Two Worlds of Johnny Truro*, written by George Sklar, who was later blacklisted by the loathsome House Un-American Activities Committee (HUAC). The script was, I thought, sensationally good. It was about a love affair between an older woman and a lanky teenager—well, eighteen or nineteen; grown-up, really. I thought I was a natural for it. So did the East Coast division of Warner Bros.

Everything looked set to go. Then Miss Davis pulled out of the project. That was the end of *Two Worlds*, for the time being. A few months later, shortly after I had arrived at MGM, the film came back on the Warner Bros. schedule and they wanted to get me on loan, to star opposite Ruth Roman. Warner's shelved it again. The film was never made—here. A few years later in France, however, they made *Devil in the Flesh* with Gérard Philipe. It became an international smash.

The deal in New York had hardly fallen through when MGM again offered me a seven-year contract. This time I was eager to make another flick, and I signed, but only after screwing my less-than-Leo-the-lion-sized courage to the sticking post. I inked the thing—and remember how I feel about contracts; this was a mother-grabber—at the Loew's office in the State Theatre building on Broadway, below Duffy Square. When they gave me an envelope with an air ticket to California, I asked if I could have the fare in cash instead. I know they thought I was nuts, but they forked it over. I had a reason, which I'll explain shortly.

I was to report to Billy Grady, the head of casting, at the Culver City lot on September 14th. That was a month away. When I left the office with the dreaded contract folded in my pocket, I started back across town to 156. I got as far as Sixth Avenue. *In the Good Old Summertime* was playing at Radio City. I bought a ticket, headed for the balcony (you could smoke, sneakily), and lost myself in that musical, which was based on *The Shop Around the Corner*. Judy Garland was sensational. "Play That Barbershop Chord": wow! I began to feel better about heading for MGM. Maybe I'd get to see or even work with that lady. Oh, sure. Lotsa luck.

That weekend, the actor Ed Durer, who was a friend of Jimmy Kirkwood's, invited me up to his home in Pound Ridge, Westchester. Ed, Jimmy, and I were all going to a swimming party somewhere closeby. Jim and Ed had been there before, so when we arrived I knocked on the front door. They disappeared around a corner of the house. The door opened. There stood our hostess, Tallulah Bankhead, in all her naked glory. "Come in, darling," she drawled. "I watch you all the time on that big test-tube television. What's your name again?" I told her, trying to concentrate only on her face. "We're out back at the pool. I'm sure I have something to fit your skinny flat ass, if you want covering up. Come along."

I followed her into what she had named "Windows." With her lack of modesty, she might as well have lived in a house of glass. She waved her arms about, everything on her bouncing, while she gave me what she described as the "nickel" tour. She tossed some shorts at me and said, "Put 'em on. If you must. We'll be out back." And she was gone. I put the bathing suit on and joined the party, in full fluid swing, at the pool.

I won't clatter a bunch of names at you; instead I'll concentrate on our naked hostess—glass in hand, half in the water, boobies afloat, and holding forth about her latest project. She was Hollywood-bound, she stated, to star in the movie version of *The Glass Menagerie*. (Years earlier it had played at the same theater, the Playhouse, where I'd debuted in *Bright Boy*. Laurette Taylor was the star.) "Of course the billing was a bit of a problem," explained Tallulah. "Those two so-called movie names, Kirk Douglas and Jane what's-her-name, Wyman, will be foolishly billed above me. BUT"—she took a big swig of whatever she was drinking—"beneath in the SAME SIZE print it'll say 'TALLULAH BANKHEAD AS AMELIA.'"

Applause and huzzahs from the guests. Actually, she'd only tested for the role. She didn't get it. Gertrude Lawrence, my first star crush, played the Taylor role in the film. (Two degrees of separation?)

Back home, it was time to get ready for my move to "the coast." I packed everything at 156. Books, 78s, even jars of pennies. First I headed for Vermont. In Troy, New York, I made arrangements to rent a trailer, and went on up to Bennington. I convinced my folks of an adventurous trip across the 48. It was a hard sell, but I closed the deal. Dar and Cart became almost as giddy as me as they anticipated the trek. Cart drove down and hooked the thing up to the family car while I helped Dar pack stuff.

The next morning we were up before the sun, but it already looked like a great day for the journey's first leg. After our last Vermont meal, oatmeal, the house was locked (Cart checked twice) and we were finally off. I was so happy I'd carefully planned to travel cross-country instead of flying. The folks had never been farther west than Lake Erie. They'd really never had much time alone together in a car, or a vacation together. It was mid-afternoon when we trailered onto 47th Street East.

The entire block was jammed with people. It looked like a party, with streamers and balloons and folks hanging halfway out of windows. Well, it *was* a party, and it was for me. I'd lived most of my life on this block, between Lexington Avenue and 147 and 159 Third Avenue with the elevated tracks over Third. I was up, down, and across, hugging and kissing everybody goodbye. What a wonderful surprise! What great folks! And what timing! Once again, Steinway had the hooks on the roof, and my old, rented piano was on its dangling way down to the sidewalk from the windowless fourth-floor apartment. It was just like a scene from the movie about Gershwin, *Rhapsody in Blue.*

Now poor Cart had to maneuver the car and trailer around so we could get going. We made it out of the city and only as far as Easton, Pennsylvania on that first day. Then we made camp in a pasture and cooked our first meal en route. That cross-country trip was thrilling for Dar and Cart, and fun. But it was slow going, dragging that load. By the time we got to the home of my Aunt Bobbie (Dar's youngest sister) and Uncle Tom in Broken Arrow, Oklahoma, I knew I'd have to fly ahead in order to make my first studio appointment on time. Tom worked for American Airlines and arranged a flight out of Tulsa for me. The folks would come out, stay with me for a day or two, and then head north to visit Cart's sister, Aunt Elizabeth and her husband in Washington. Then they'd head back East.

That was an experience the two of them would feast off of for the rest of their lives. I love the story about Cart stopping fairly early one afternoon for gas. He suggested Dar and he should eat out that night (which meant not cooking along the road). They entered a diner and slid into a booth. Cart ordered a beer. "I'm exhausted," he said. "Why?" asked Dar. "Well, I've been driving for hours." "Nonsense," she scoffed. "I've driven every inch of the way. All you've done is hold the wheel."

If you saw *A Star Is Born*, you'll know what my first day at MGM was like. After I'd met with Mr. Grady, someone took me from one office to another, starting with publicity. Everyone was busy, and smiled at me without making eye contact. In each department, to a man or woman, they said, "Nice to have you with us," and went on with their work. Welcome to the golden age of motion pictures at Metro-Goldwyn-Mayer.

Chapter 9

Now here I was in LaLa Land: alone, except for one friend I had met at St. Albans Hospital, an ex-marine named Paul Savage. He'd been in one of my radio classes in New York. Paul was a sweet giant of a man—six-foot-seven, I think—who wanted to be an actor when he got out of the service. I took him to an agent I knew, Al Ochs, another giant about as tall as Paul. Al tried unsuccessfully to land him work. Savage headed west. He was the only contact I had in Hollywood. He was living at a place on Franklin Avenue called Villa Carlotta. When I looked him up, he was so pleased to see me that he moved to a larger apartment and I shared it with him. He saved money, and it was inexpensive for me.

But it wasn't very convenient to the studio. I took, I believe, three buses every day to get to work. Public transport in L.A. was sort of impossible. It was at least an hour-long jaunt each way. (It hasn't improved much since.) I had no agent to hold my hand. Before I had left New York, I'd signed with a wonderful gal (rare in agentry) named Maggie Lindley. She was working for the Paul Small Agency at the time, although I'd met her originally when she worked at A&S Lyons along with Milton Goldman. The Small Agency was to open an office in Hollywood, and Maggie headed west to run it. That's why I signed with them.

Months later, the Small office opened for business in a tiny place on Sunset Boulevard. Paul was a large, vulgar, cigar-smoking, feet-on-the-desk archetype. There's a famous story about the time he was introduced at some big industry affair in San Francisco. Jay C. Flippen, a warm and lovable character actor, did the intro: "You've all heard of the actor's actor, the singer's singer, the writer's writer. I'd like you to meet the one and only shit heel's shit heel, Paul Small." A joke, but not far from the marrow.

Maggie, who had been in the business all her adult life, finally became so sickened with him and the whole semi-sleazy industry that she quit. She moved to Mexico and opened a restaurant. Great lady, too honest for Hollywood. Soon after, I left Small for another agency, MCA, where a young Jay Kanter (the agent, at various times, for Marilyn Monroe, Grace Kelly, and Marlon Brando) was assigned to me.

In my first days at MGM, I was put to work on an almost purely technical task at Metro: I dubbed the voice of a young actor in a film called *The Outriders*. This was done in a radio-like studio on the lot, the "loop" stage. Small stretches of film kept repeating on a screen as I listened through earphones and read the dialogue to the actor's lip movement. It turned out I was pretty good at it. Later I'd have to loop my own voice for outdoor shots that had too much traffic or wind noise. Once I did it for nearly an entire feature in which I starred with a lion.

That lot was incredible. It was a complete village in itself. Restaurant, barber shop, dentist, hospital, police and fire departments, lumber yards, paint shops, you name it. And all those fantastic soundstages. The first time I walked into one, the thing that impressed me the most was the work of the art department on the background scenery. You could stand with your nose practically up against a flat and, because of the exquisite perspective, swear you were looking a mile or more beyond. There was nothing that perfect on Broadway. What artists, and craftsmen. It's no wonder that studios back then rarely went on location. They stuck with the soundstages.

Shortly after reporting for duty, I ran into the dancer-choreographer Robert Alton (né Hart), the high-kicker Murray had called Fleming. Maybe because of our mutual Bennington roots, he treated me like an old friend. At any rate, the instant friendship was welcome indeed. He even invited me for dinner at his place in Pacific Palisades. There I met Lotte, his housekeeper, and was allowed to watch him rehearse a new act for Kay Thompson and two dancers (Buzz Miller and George Martin, I think). Sitting in a chair, he actually directed with his legs.

I also met a producer named Jack Cummings, and learned I'd been put under contract primarily for an upcoming film called *The Tender Hours*, which he was producing. But before that started I was rushed into a film to be directed by Vincent Minnelli: *Father of the Bride*, with Elizabeth Taylor and Spencer Tracy. I played one of her ex-boyfriends who became chief usher at the wedding, escorting Joan Bennett to her seat. I waved my raincoat around way too much during the rainy wedding rehearsals. I also had one tiny little gem of a scene with Mr. Tracy at the reception. It involved a couple of cokes. I received no mention in the credits. I guess it was part of Metro's long-range build-up plan for me.

Father of the Bride, 1950.

I have to confess, the most beautiful thing I ever saw during my time at MGM was the young Ms. Taylor early in the AM, before makeup or hair. Those lavender eyes and that flawless skin could make one ache. She was also a great gal, in love, at that moment, with a young football star, Glenn Davis. She loved dancing, and we spent the time between setups jitterbugging around some corner of the stage.

We worked six days a week and sometimes even on Sundays. When not in front of the camera or rehearsing, we were taken over by the publicity department for interviews with the dozens of fan magazines and columnists, or to do photo shoots for stories or studio portraits. The execs in the Thalberg Building kept everyone hopping. They got their money's worth, but I was thrilled to earn the four-hundred-dollar check I picked up weekly from the cashier's window around the corner from the commissary.

With Debbie Reynolds in *Three Little Words*, 1950.

While still shooting *Father of the Bride*, I was ordered to another stage to do a number in a musical about the lives of the famous songwriting team of the 1920s and '30s, Bert Kalmar and Harry Ruby. It was called *Three Little Words*. My song was "I Wanna Be Loved by You," a vaudeville turn that Helen Kane and her husband Dan Healy had performed years earlier. The gal playing Helen mugged to Miss Kane's own voice. I just mugged. Neither of us had a line.

The young girl was Debbie Reynolds. Prior to this she had been signed to a Warner Bros. contract after mugging to a Betty Hutton record in a Burbank contest and winning the "Miss Personality" title. After giving her a part in *The Daughter of Rosie O'Grady*, the studio had dropped her, but Solly Biano, a casting guy at Warner's, suggested her to Metro for the job of dubbing Kane. Debbie was certainly Miss Personality in person. She was cute as a bunny. Jack Cummings, the producer of *Three Little Words*, liked the way we looked together when he saw the rushes of that number. He signed her to play opposite me in *The Tender Hours*. Originally her character, Melba, was supposed to have been a short, chubby kid with a crush on my character, Billy. Deb was anything but chubby, and we did look good together. I was tickled that we'd get to team up again. We really hit it off, onscreen and off.

Bob Alton was working on MGM's film version of *Annie Get Your Gun*. It had been delayed because of its star Judy Garland's breakdown and lengthy stay in a Boston hospital. Although Alton had been hired to direct and choreograph the Garland version, George Sydney took over when Garland was replaced by Betty Hutton. (I always wished it could have been Betty Garrett.) The wait between the two versions was so long that the voice of Howard Keel—a super guy, straight from a budding Broadway career—had dropped a bit and needed new orchestrations.

I went to a screening room one day with Bob and he ran the Garland footage for me: a couple of complete (edited) numbers and several partial takes from others. These tapes, showing a tired, overworked Judy, would eventually be pirated and sold all over the place as camp. What an awful thing. Some so-called film buffs are shameless.

Once she was back, the studio rushed Garland into a new musical, *Summer Stock*, opposite Gene Kelly. She was healthy, sassy and a tad tubby, which was somewhat disguised by clever wardrobe wizardry. I was cast as Artie, the piano player and mechanic of the acting group that descends on Garland's farm to put on a show in the barn. Its star would be Judy's sister, played by Gloria DeHaven. Marjorie Main played the cook on the farm.

Now I was not only working with Miss Garland, but also with someone who shared my mother's maiden name—although Marjorie Main was a pseudonym; she was born Mary Tomlinson.

I got two big shocks. Kelly, like Fred Astaire, always rehearsed wearing a cap. Gene wore a baseball cap. Both were bald. I couldn't believe it. But on the set, ready to shoot, they both had toupees that were undetectable, even in extreme closeup. Metro magic. The second and even greater shock came from Marjorie Main. Off camera, as soon as "cut" was called, she'd pull a tight mesh over her face and hold it tightly to her neck. She was afraid of germs. Ma Kettle, afraid of germs? Well, she was. She wore gloves all the time. Marjorie carried a change purse, and when she had to pay for anything she made them reach in and take the coins. She never touched money. The hair person on the set had to unseal a new comb to adjust her do, which for this role was usually unkempt. She also kept canned goods in her Cadillac, and never allowed anyone in her portable dressing room for fear of contamination. Publicity took a shot of the two of us in front of the thing with her name on the door between us. Both of us thumbed toward it and beamed—after she had removed her gloves, of course. It really broke me up, but naturally I couldn't laugh.

When the picture was released, the *Bennington Banner* ran the shot on the front page. It was headlined, "Carp with Marjorie Main, not his Mom." After a new setup for a scene, the assistant director would call, "Ready, Miss Main," and off would come the veil, the mask, the gloves. She'd wade through muck to replace her stand-in. Marjorie was a conundrum.

Judy was wonderful and treated me like an old pal, sitting with me between takes on my piano bench with her arm, Costello-like, around my shoulder. Charles Walters, the director, was terrific to me too. But Mr. Kelly was another puzzle to me. He did odd things, always with a smile. He might come onto the set when Walters had configured the gang of us. Finding he was to be next to me, he'd say: "Is that where the director put you, Carp? (I was always Carp.) I'd say, "Yes, sir." Then he'd move somewhere else and say to Mr. Walters, "Chuck, I think I ought to be over here." I couldn't figure out why he didn't like me. Was I too tall? Maybe, although I did manage to sit, squat, or lean on something most of the time for the whole film, except in one song, "Dig, Dig, Dig." At one point I'm standing against a wall. He dances by and does a huge take at my height. Off camera, he told me he'd seen me at the Persian Room in *New Faces*. With a big smile he said, "Carp, you'll be a big star on gaucherie alone." I had to look the word up when I got home.

Summer Stock, 1950: Gene Kelly, Phil Silvers, and me.

So there were rewards, but I always felt there was a knife at my back.

There were times when I left the studio nearly in tears. He was so strangely mean, but always with a smile. That smile never extended as far up as his eyes, however. I know Judy and Chuck Walters noticed his behavior with me.

Judy reminded me of "Kimmer"—my old friend, Kaye Ballard. They were both built sort of the same way: bosoms to butts, with not much in between. They also shared identical laughs and offbeat, off-the-wall humor. Both were loving, loyal, heartwarming company. Watching *Summer Stock* now, you can spot Judy's fluctuating weight. The first song she shot, "If You Feel Like Singing, Sing," was shot as she took a shower. Then she got into overalls, designed, like the rest of her clothes, by Helen Rose. They couldn't quite disguise her excess poundage, which she began losing in the course of shooting.

One number, "Happy Harvest," is sort of a hoot to watch. As in all pictures, parts were shot out of sequence, and Judy had three distinct weights in that one song, which she sang while driving a new tracker home. Pieces were shot on the set, on a back lot and on the process stage, where the actor is stationary and the filmed background rolls behind you. Weeks passed between the shooting of each part, so you can watch the happy farm girl change from robust to medium to thin.

By the time she did "Get Happy," she was back to her slimmed-down best. When the film was released, lots of fans thought the number was cut from some previous movie and added to *Summer Stock*. I was nearly finished with *The Tender Hours*, and I sneaked in to watch several days of shooting. It turned out to be the very last thing Garland shot at MGM.

When she was unable to do the next film slated for her, *Royal Wedding*, she was replaced by the talented lady I had chased after in *The Tender Hours*, Jane Powell. After all those years and all the millions she'd earned for Metro, Judy was released from her contract. Sad news. But some wonderful things were still in store for that special lady.

After "Get Happy" was in the can, Mr. Kelly wanted another number to balance the two stars on screen presence. I was called off the set of *The Tender Hours* to do a short intro with Gene before he filmed "You, Wonderful You," in which he tap-danced on a sheet of newspaper placed on a creaking board in the barn. The chorus gang, which included the brilliant Carol Haney, had been signed for a certain length of time, I think ten or twelve weeks. We'd all become very close-knit, like family; and when they were finishing up I tossed a cocktail party for them in the rehearsal hall. Judy got wind of the farewell bash and cornered me, saying: "Aren't I one of the kids?" Who would turn the lady down?

She showed up with Roger Edens in tow. I "just happened" to have brought a lead sheet for a song I'd written especially for her weeks ago, but which I thought I'd never have the chance to do for her. That day, at my party, I didn't have to. Edens sat down at the piano with my lead sheet. Judy scrunched beside him on the bench. Sight-reading, she sang "Let Go of Your Heart" twice through, the second time ad-libbing a new harmonizing line above the melody. (As soon as I got home I wrote it down, adding it to the song.) Tears were pouring down my face at the joy of hearing it the way I had heard it in my head while composing the thing. She hugged and kissed me. So did Roger. I'd never been this happy before.

Wow, do I wish that tape recorders had been invented back then. I haven't let anyone sing that song since—and it's a pretty good number. I heard it performed once, at its best.

By this time, several changes in my life had occurred. Dar and Cart arrived at Villa Carlotta, dropped off my junk and headed north. Bob

Alton offered me his old house on Centinella, which he still owned because of the apartment behind it where his housekeeper Lotte lived. Savage moved to smaller digs in Hollywood, where he found work in a Shakespeare revival. I saw it, and he was quite good. His young fellow actor Dewey Martin, who later married Peggy Lee, was even better. The Centinella place was practically a stone's throw from Culver City and the studio. It was furnished ornately in semi-baroque fashion (including a high-camp canopy bed) and a big fireplace in the living room. I had to keep the place in neat shape and did, with Lotte's help. What a money-saving gift. And I bought my first car, a (very) used Plymouth coupe. One of the *Summer Stock* gang gave me a doorknob kind of doohicky that you put on the steering wheel for one-hand turnage. A forerunner of power steering? Now I could park in the special lot close to the main gate, set aside for contract players. If I wasn't a big shot, at least I was a BB.

In *The Tender Hours* I now had a real role, that of Billy Finley. Roy Roland directed and Busby Berkeley did the dance sequences, almost forever on the boom, a crane that could carry him way up above the set. We used to sing, "Somewhere there's Busby, how high the boom," a parody of the Nancy Hamilton-Morgan Lewis hit. The cast included Jane Powell (whom I still see and adore), Ricardo Montalban, Deb, the beautiful Ann Harding and Louis Calhern, who I first met on a set when we were ready to shoot. On the first walkthrough for marks, he suddenly looked up at me and boomed: "My gawd, boy, you look like a praying mantis." Well, he hit that smack on the nose. Our friendship was sealed.

I told him I'd seen him in several Broadway shows, including a quick folderoo called *The Wooden Dish*. That seemed to impress the hell out of him. What a joy he was. Also in the cast were Lillian Bronson, Dorothy Neuman, Billy Gray and baby Tommy Reddig. My father in the flick, Clint Sundburg, was a hoot. He had my favorite line. Looking out on the ruins of the elaborate fireworks display accidently touched off on that holiday eve, he deadpanned: "Well, it's been a grand and a glorious third."

While rehearsing a number with Jane, "The Oceanna Roll," I looked through the stack of old-fashioned, oversized sheet music on the piano. I spied a copy of an old novelty tune, written by Arthur Fields and Walter Donovan and published in 1914. When the vocal arranger, Saul Chaplin, took a break, I sat down on the bench and ran over it. I called Deb over and we sang it quietly together. We both got a kick out of it. In the script, we were to be in Janie's "The Oceanna Roll" and in another song, "That's How I Need You," at a player piano. That was it.

"Aba Daba Honeymoon" from *Two Weeks with Love*.

A couple of days later, on a break, I spotted Jack Cummings, the producer, as he headed for the hall. I grabbed Debbie and dashed for Saul at the keyboard. "Play it as fast as you can," I said, and the two of us were "just happening" to be singing it when Mr. Cummings came in. When we finished rattling through it, he came over to the piano and said: "That sounds like a great number for the two of you."

That's how "Aba Daba Honeymoon" happened. After the rushes on that filmed song and dance were shown, another number was stuck in for us, "Row, Row, Row." For that song I wrote the ad-libs in the verse. Both records sold over a million copies, earning us gold records and MGM recording contracts. By the time *The Tender Hours* was released it carried a new title—its third, in fact. It was briefly called *Kissimmee in the Catskills*; finally they named it *Two Weeks with Love*. When it was re-released later on, some theatres billed it as *Aba Daba Honeymoon*, with smaller letters below saying *Two Weeks with Love*.

Most of the credit for that song should go to Busby and his assistant, Jack Baker, for their staging. Same with "Row, Row, Row," which I loved for all the old vaudeville hoofing. The film was a Technicolor jellybean, as my friend Ruth Waterbury, who worked for Louella Parsons, called it. It's a kind of movie long-gone from the screen. I say sadly; some say happily. But "I Wanna Be Loved by You" and the fast chorus part of "Aba Daba Honeymoon" were brought back years later in *That's Entertainment*.

Singing "Row, Row, Row" with Debbie in *Two Weeks with Love*, 1950.

That's one nice thing about films: They hang around, showing up on the tube now and then. With plays, the curtain falls and that's it. But I can't help it; I'm still stagestruck. An old lady friend, now gone, once told me I'd never retire. "You'll die off stage right," she predicted. (At this juncture, I wonder if I should always exit left.)

Around that time, I had my first studio-arranged date, with a young gal from publicity. They fitted me out in a tux and we took in the premiere of *The Heiress*. Lights and cameras were flashing and heavy-duty stars abounded. My eyes were all over the place, like a knee-buckled fan. In the lobby, an old gal came over to me when I wasn't looking and tapped me on the arm. I turned, looked down and saw the wonderful lady who had played James Stewart's ma in the now-classic *It's a Wonderful Life*. Miss Beulah Bondi was smiling up at me. Before I could find my voice she said, "I thought you were so honest and dear in *Lost Boundaries*. My first compliment from a real-life movie star! I hugged her and kissed her full on the lips. She patted me on the cheek and thanked me. I said, "No, no, thank you," but she waved it away and filed into the theater, adjusting the fur stole she sported. Now that I was her number-one fan, Miss Bondi helped me reconsider the role of Andy in my film debut. When it was later shown on TV, I watched it as if Andy were someone else, and found myself thinking, that kid wasn't all that bad—even though he still looked a bit like Donald Duck at the piano.

My first "steady" was an actress in her teens, Joan Evans, who at fifteen had played the title character in *Roseanna McCoy*. Her parents were Dale Eunson and Katherine Albert, two screenwriters whose credits would later include *How to Marry a Millionaire*. Our dates were set up by her folks, who invited me to dinner (sort of like an audition), thinking I was the hot new kid at Metro and that we could get lots of ink in the press as the latest teen twosome. They were very up front about the whole arrangement. I was eight years older than Joan but still playing kids. (My character in *Two Weeks* was sixteen.) Joan played older (but not much) than her age. We all took to one another immediately, and I apparently passed whatever inspection there was. The three of them, even young Joan, were bright, funny Hollywood pros.

They were right on the nose with their plan for us. For the next three years, Joan and I were the most photographed couple in or on the town. Even at the Oscars, and this was when all the really big stars still attended, we usually wound up on the front page of the papers the following morning. The fanzines went mad for us, and fan mail at Samuel Goldwyn

On the town with Joan Evans.

(Joan's studio) and MGM zoomed out of sight. The power of press puffery. Joan and I always had a ball together. Lots of times I'd take her home and then play bridge with her folks for hours. Sometimes Joanie and I would show up someplace, let the press flash away, then sneak off early so I could get to the bridge table and she'd get her beauty sleep. The Eunsons were great friends and gave me a lot. As for sex, however, I was taking care of that on my own with a lovely redhead. I'll get to her later.

During the last weeks of shooting *Two Weeks*, a script arrived at Centinella from Louis de Rochemont. I tore into it at once. It was called *The Whistle at Eaton Falls*, and it was about labor and management relations. His films were always about something important. Halfway through the screenplay I came across a blank page—well, almost blank. In the middle of the page was one line: PLACE FOR CARP'S SONG. Studios made money from picture grosses and from the loaning-out of contract players to other studios. A loan-out was brokered for my services in *The Whistle at Eaton Falls*. I would make four hundred a week. De Rochement paid Metro ten thousand per. So everyone was happy. MGM was making a tidy profit, and I was getting the chance to go back to New Hampshire and work for the great man. And location shooting was really much more fun than studio stage work.

He had assembled an incredible cast: Lloyd Bridges, Dorothy Gish (yes, the sister of Lillian), Anne Francis, Diana Douglas, James Westerfield, Murray Hamilton, Lenore Lonergan, Parker Fennelly, Anne Seymour, and two men making their debuts on film, Ernest Borgnine and

Anne Francis and I in *The Whistle at Eaton Falls*, 1951.

Arthur O'Connell. (O'Connell had had bits in a couple of other pies, but this was his first real role.) Robert Siodmak directed.

They welcomed me back to the Rockingham Hotel like a beloved relative and the joy of the work began. The company stayed together, ate together, acted together *and* (almost every evening) drank together. What a wild and lovable gang of talent. We nearly rocked the ol' Rockingham off its historic haunches.

I've saved one cast member for special attention. Talking about degrees of separation, the actress who played, to absolute scary perfection, the threatening bitch of the film was Helen Shields—the sweet lady who had read with me when I auditioned for my first Broadway play, *Bright Boy*. It turned out she was the wife of the Navy playwright Lt. John Boruff. How about them Granny Smiths! Anne Francis was my love in the flick and my love to this day; we shared drinks and dancing often at the rockin' Rock, but it was Diana Douglas, separated from husband Kirk, with whom I shared the sheets, briefly. (Later in New York I babysat her sons Joel and Michael.) Westerfield, a fabulous raconteur and brilliant actor—he won New York Drama Critics' Circle Awards for his roles on Broadway in *Detective Story* and *The Madwoman of Chaillot*. He was a large man whose chin tended to edge toward his shoulder. He claimed that if he ever ran for public office, his campaign slogan would be: "Pitiful Jim for Alderman." He also professed, over drinks, that if his young bride, then performing in a ballet company in Canada, didn't put in an appearance that coming Sunday, he'd have to take matters into his own hands: "I may have to indulge in a little … what some people call … self-abuse."

Midway through the filming, I got a phone message at the hotel to call Northfield, Vermont. Norwich University. It was Costello, again from out of nowhere. I managed a two-day weekend away from the set and bussed over to the Military School he was now attending. When I returned the call, he'd been very cheery, like his old self, and advised me on which room and dorm I should head for. I couldn't wait to see him again. The bus ride seemed to take forever, but it was a short trip. Northfield is south of Montpelier.

When I located the room, I found a note telling me to meet him some other place. I went there only to find another note; he'd be at a bar in town. That's where I found him, sitting alone in a booth, nursing a heavy drink. I slid in opposite him, waving for a drink. His first words were again startling: "Guess I was in pretty bad shape last time you saw me. Didn't think you'd ever want to see me again. Sorry. Had to start without you." He slugged back his drink. "You look terrific."

"So do you. Really terrific." I meant that with all my heart.

"You're a big movie star now," he said.

"Bullshit," I told him. He said he didn't remember too much about our brief last meeting. Lying, I said I didn't, either. (How could I ever forget an episode like that?) Cos said he was a couple of drinks up on me. I doubled the next two, trying to catch up. But we actually talked for a change. He enjoyed the all-male military college, but wasn't intending to rejoin the service. He was studying engineering. I told him I sometimes missed not having gone to college—well, the experience and social side of it, not the career studies. I would only have been learning to do what I was already doing.

It was a beautiful late afternoon and I was getting happily pissed with my dear old friend. We really tied a healthy one on. We chowed on spaghetti and I spent the night in an empty bunk across from him. We sang to each other, like we had on the troop train; mostly oldies from the war years. We had a great time together. It was a welcome eraser for the blackboard of the Vets Hospital.

I headed back to Portsmouth late Sunday morning after a down-off-campus town breakfast. We shook hand at the bus station. Again, I wanted to hug him goodbye. Would we ever meet up again? I never could figure what was going on in that red head of his, so of course the handshake was it, and the wave through the window when the bus pulled out, like the shovel-wave on Tinian.

It turned out I wrote a couple of songs for *The Whistle at Eaton Falls*. One of them, "Ev'ry Other Day," was sung by Anne Francis and me at a benefit dance sequence. It was Anne's first singing attempt—prerecorded, of course. She was a smidge off-pitch, but that worked out fine for the scene since we were supposed to be very nervous singing in public on a stage in front of a big local orchestra. It was sort of sweet. The other was a number called "Saturday Square Dance" that I did solo. Jack Shaindlin, the music scorer, used "Ev'ry Other Day" as a theme all through the pic, and later I recorded it for MGM Records backed with an old, old favorite of mine, "It's a Million to One You're in Love." It hit the charts for a few weeks, but it wasn't a big deal. George Simon Music published it with a movie cover on the sheet music: Lloyd and Diana, Anne and me. "I Wouldn't Mind," published earlier by Chappell, had had a movie cover as well, with Mel Ferrer and Beatrice Pearson. Both songs were ASCAP, as all my music would be.

A character actress named Doro Merande—maybe you remember her hung up on a coat hanger in *The Russians Are Coming, The Russians Are Coming*—was a long-faced lady, very much the funny, cranky curmudgeon. (Is that being pleonastically reduntant?) She was ensconced in the Rockingham with the rest of us. Doro complained to the desk often about a family with very young kids in the room next to hers. They were keeping her awake. When no noticeable change in her neighbors' loud habits came about, she took matters into her own hands. She set her alarm for four-thirty a.m. or so, then when it rang, she proceeded to pelt the wall with books until she could hear crying and muffled adult complaints. Then she smiled and caught another good hour of sleep. Tit for tat, she said when she told me the story of her revenge on the set later. Goofy gal.

Some of the scenes were directed by Louis de Rochemont himself in order to stick to budget. I remember one in particular, a love scene between Anne and me in a parked car. He used mostly closeups, even a couple of ECUs (extreme closeups), and only a few takes so the editor would have to cut it the way he filmed it. I guess he wanted to get his money's worth out of me, after all the loot Metro had charged. Well, I also knew he liked my work. He told once he wished I'd never signed with MGM and that he had been able to put me under personal contract. It was far and away the best compliment I'd ever received.

Chapter 10 ———————

As soon as I finished my shooting, I flew back to Metro to begin work on a big western, based on a Luke Short story, called *Vengeance Valley*. A word about the state of MGM in those days. Things were happening that I didn't realize when I'd first come on the lot. There was a big division taking place. Dore Schary, the former head of RKO, had been hired by the studio as chief of production, but he hadn't actually appeared on the scene until around the time I returned from loan-out.

Now there were two rival camps, Louis B. Mayer's glittering entertainment films and Mr. Schary's serious "message" pictures. The clash of these two factions eventually led to the ouster of longtime boss Mayer from the throne in the Thalberg Building, where the crown had seemingly been his to flaunt forever. Schary himself was bounced from his post in 1956. He went on to write and produce the Broadway play *Sunrise at Campobello* and took home five Tony Awards.

The other war, between North and South Korea, was now in full, frightening swing. Young kids, undertrained and underequipped to deal with the brutally cold temperature, were being shipped back to the States (many to Ft. Ord, near Monterey) by the score. Every Sunday, a bunch of us entertainers would bus north to the Fort Hospital: Keenan Wynn and his wife Betsy; Jim Backus (Mr. Magoo) and his wife; Bill Warfield, the glorious singer who had sung "Ol' Man River" in MGM's version of *Show Boat*; Howard Keel; Bobby Tucker (vocal arranger, coach, and pianist extraordinaire); Deb; and me. I called us the Keenan Wynn Players. We were the core regulars, but others would travel with us once in a while: Ann Miller, Walter Pidgeon, Audrey Totter.

We'd do the wards during the afternoon, then a big show in the theater there on Sunday night. The wards were tough. There were so many youngsters, and too many amputees who'd suffered frostbite. We'd conjure up a brave front, talking and joking with them. Keenan would do anything for a laugh. Every fifteen minutes of so I'd have to go outside to the hall, cry, take some deep breaths, splash cold water on the face and go back in to clown around again. We would travel over the Christmas holidays every year to South Korea; we also went to Iceland, Greenland, Morocco, Libya, Italy (Napoli and Livorno).

Now, back from New Hampshire to prepare for *Vengeance Valley*, I picked up my love life again in Culver City. I'd been going with a contract gal on the sly, because I knew she was some exec's sometime companion. She had beautiful red hair and lived close to the studio with her Mom, Pinky, who was a hoot. We had originally met in the commissary. She was among the regulars at the long table I always sat at. (People at MGM tended to forever use the same table; we only sat at others if we were doing an interview.) We were a mixture at that table: actors, writers, assistant directors, crew. The redhead, Amanda Blake, and I took to each other instantly. Humor was the big thing she shared. She was sort of a standby for Greer Garson, who was waiting for a big picture of her own, *Running of the Tide*, which never got made. Most of the actors were signed as standbys for somebody else. Maybe I was supposed to be a standby for Marshall Thompson, but I doubt it.

Anyway, Amanda and I became fast friends. Without anyone's knowledge we'd meet at the Rococo Ranch (my nickname for the Alton house on Centinella) and romp around like raunchy rogues in that luxe canopied bed. It was great lusty fun, made even more pleasurably passionate because of the secretive nature of it.

Then one morning at our usual long table, Mandy leaned across and whispered, "Good morning, Daddy." That's the closest I ever edged toward a heart attack. I suddenly knew my days at Metro were numbered. Whoever that unknown exec was (I had a hunch but it was later proved wrong), he'd be after my tail if he found out I was the culprit two-timing "his" gal while he was two-timing his wife. Two terrifying weeks dragged by like an eon. Then Mandy, with her deep-throated laugh, told me she'd "fallen off the roof" that morning (another family euphemism). She'd been late. I was elated. I took my first big breath in a long time. I never asked Amanda who her "mentor" was. I figured no gentleman would. The scare ended our lust-making but deepened our forever friendship. Later, of course, she became well-known as Kitty on *Gunsmoke*. We continued to see each other on one coast or the other right up until her death.

A bit of personal medical fact: I'd had ulcers in New York, but they had cleared up and vanished when I moved to Hollywood. Usually it's the other way around. By the time of *Vengeance Valley* Bob Alton was selling the Rococo Ranch, and I rented a small house on Manning Avenue in Westwood. It was a tiny one-bedroom place on a corner, but I loved it. It was mine and I could throw parties there, which I did on an irregular basis, and not worry about fancy decorative furniture being mistreated when free-flowing booze was spilled. It was a neat kind of freedom. I rented a piano and got a new cat, whom I named Bugbee.

The prep work before shooting included a lot of horseback riding on MGM's Western Street backlot, where some of the film would be shot. The rest of it was filmed on a soundstage and, for several weeks, on location in Canon City, Colorado. I had ridden very little as a kid, and even then it was on an old workhorse on someone's farm in Vermont. But now, I took to it quickly—or so I thought. Those studio horses were hams. They'd perk up when they heard the word "action" and relax after "cut." Burt Lancaster, Robert Walker and I would ride around together in the mornings before we left for Colorado. I felt very at home on my screen nag.

With Burt Lancaster and Robert Walker in *Vengeance Valley*, 1951.

But when we headed for location, they brought along Burt's and Bob's horses. Mine was left on the back lot. That didn't worry me; I figured I was practically the Lone Ranger on horseback by then. When I was assigned a spirited little local pinto job, I climbed up onto the western saddle with all the confidence of the truly dumb. Then the wrangler handed me the reins and slapped that eager s.o.b. on the rump. He took off like it was the final stretch at Churchill Downs. I held on for dear life, literally, pulling the reins back with one hand and clutching his mane with the other. I don't know how many miles we flew down some beautiful mountain range, but too many. Fortunately, Silver, or whatever the hell his name was, eventually tired a bit just before my rapidly oncoming demise, and I found enough breath to begin talking to him. It didn't help all that much—I think he only understood Indian—but my soothing tones of endearment must have helped us bond enough to reverse course and find the way back toward the cast and crew. When he spotted them miles later, he raced even faster to join his four-legged brothers. I was limp but alive, and had to bravely endure the roars of derisive laughter from everyone. But after all the hoots, there were huzzahs; I'd passed my first riding test.

That pony and I never really got along, but we arrived at kind of a working truce. The acting company, though, was another close-knit family affair. Location shooting has a tendency to bring that out. It's sort of like being on the road with a touring company. Lancaster was surprised when I reminded him of *A Sound of Hunting*, his Broadway debut. Bobby Walker, playing a villain, was an angel; there were also Joanne Dru and John Ireland (who married later), Hugh O'Brian, Ray Collins (I'd been in *Summer Stock* with him), and Sally Forrest, whom Hughie, my character, ended up with. She got knocked up and had a baby by the bad brother in the story; at the end of the movie they hooked up, but it wasn't in the finished film. A great gang. We'd bowl together evenings—Canon City was no city—and go to Colorado City on Sundays and swim at the Broadmoor.

The director was Richard Thorpe, who'd done *Three Little Words*. It was rumored that he received a healthy bonus for every day he could bring in the film under schedule. He shot straight from the hip, and excellently. Thorpe was a really good craftsman. He knew what he wanted, and was gentle and thoughtful in the ways in which he got that from his actors.

Hughie was a good role. (I also narrated the movie.) Toward the end of the film, Hughie shoots the real villain, John Ireland, who's ready to ambush Lancaster from behind a rock. I ride up, spot him, grab my rifle from the long holster, pull up and shoot him just as he's ready to gun down Burt. I'm leading a posse of five. I had to round a huge rock and pull up the horse on an exact mark, grab and fire and the rest of the posse would file past. Well, my four-legged Indian friend would want to follow the passing horses. Through two rehearsals, the pony wouldn't hold the spot. Third time, camera rolling, I pull up. The pony stays in place. I'm tickled. I reach and grab the rifle and aim. The horse rears up—and the rifle butt smashes into my mouth. Blood spurted all over. Thorpe, scanning the sky, says: "We're losing the sun. Put in a double."

So while I'm in a truck having my lip stitched up, brave Hughie-to-the-rescue—his double, actually—rides by with the posse while someone else shoots Ireland. That's the movies. I got a nice scar, and Dick Thorpe got a nice bonus.

Most important, the film turned out real well—it still plays on TV— and Lancaster and I became great friends, often playing bridge at his house. Burt was a good player. *Vengeance Valley* turned out to be Bobby Walker's last completed film. His next, *My Son John*, wasn't more than half-finished before his sudden death, which I always considered murder, since his doctor, who should have known better, gave him a big shot of some sedative when he was quite drunk. He died within an hour. I had been with him two nights before at the Mocambo, having drinks and watching somebody perform. He was in fine fettle, a tad tipsy (me too) but as far as I could tell in the best of health. Such a dear, gentle guy. *My Son John* was finished by a double, with the addition of some closeups from other films, I was told. It was released a year after *Vengeance Valley*.

I was so busy in my MGM days that there wasn't much time for socializing. One of the very few places I hung out was at the home of the jazz pianist Bobby Tucker, who worked in the music department; and his other half, Johnny Catlett Payne. The two guys were both Southerners, and they were heavenly hosts. Catlett could cook up a storm. I won't tell you his secret recipe for Old Fashioneds.

It was always great musical fun, because they both played piano and had super guests, like the great film arranger and composer Conrad Salinger; Loulie Jean Norman, who had sung on Bing Crosby's radio show and who did much dubbing work in films; and Eileen Farrell, one of many bridge players. Eileen was the opera singer who adored singing old standards and the blues. She and her policeman husband lived in Staten Island but would visit Bobby and Johnny whenever they were in California.

I also spent some of my off-time visiting John Hodiak and Anne Baxter. Both of them were from New York, and their house was modest, lived-in, and usually filled with a gang of game players who were fellow ex-New Yorkers. We had wicked bouts of charades, a game I still love. Few people these days seem to have time for games.

If I had a couple of days in a row without an assignment, I'd hop a plane to New York. I figured I must have bought a fleet or two of American Airlines DC6Bs. We always had to stop at Midway Airport in Chicago. (This was before O'Haire.) I had never lost touch with my pals in Manhattan, or with what was happening on Broadway. The irregular commutes were pretty much the same. I'd stay at the Wellington Hotel at 55th and Seventh, call a bunch of friends, see a show, and usually meet Lewis Freedman for a meal at his Mom's apartment uptown. Florence was a fabulous cook; her brisket was to die for. Her other son, Allen, sometimes joined us. After a show, Lewis and I would head for a local and do the I-buy-you-buy thing. I'd head back to L.A. the next morning.

There was much more of an East Coast-West Coast "conflict" back then. (Everyone is bicoastal now.) Agents, even those with offices in both places, like my agency, MCA, would greet you when you stopped by to say hi with: "So what have you been up to? Haven't seen you in ages." East never knew what West was doing, it seemed, even though I might be playing in a film around the corner. I began to think that New York never went to the movies and L.A. never went to the theater. It tickled the hell out of me. But in a way it was worrisome, since my heart was firmly planted in (or on) the stage.

Only once at Metro did I get to do a play. I'd seen *Remains to Be Seen* on Broadway with Jackie Cooper and Janis Paige; MGM bought the film rights, and they planned a production of it at the Laguna Playhouse. I begged the powers in the Thalberg Building to let me do it, and they agreed. The Laguna was founded and run by Dorothy McGuire, Gregory Peck and Mel Ferrer. A great Equity theater, it was almost always sold out; the subscription list was enormous.

It felt wonderful to be back on the boards again. I did the Cooper part and had visions of doing the film eventually, although Van Johnson got the assignment. Monica Lewis made her stage debut opposite me and we had a ball. There was a terrific supporting cast, including Jesse White, Louis Jean Heydt, and Dick Elliot. Oh, Barry Kelly played the police chief. He was the only one who appeared in the screen version, I believe. But I had the chance to do it onstage, which to me was much better.

Around the time I moved to Westwood, I had met and flipped over a new contract player, Barbara Ruick. Her dad, Mel Ruick, was a studio pianist, and her mom was the actress and later drama teacher Lureen Tuttle. This time it was the real thing. I fell absolutely ass over teakettle in love. So, happily, did Barb. This time, I didn't have to sneak around and hide anything. We moved in together, more or less. Well, we were either at my house or her apartment, a few short blocks away. We spent all our time away from home ("home" being the Metro lot) together. One magical weekend, we even got away to Palm Springs, where we registered at the hotel (or motel) as Mr. and Mrs. We used her manager's last name, so we were Ebbins for two nights and three days. We talked often of marriage, but it was difficult setting an exact time. When I was hot for the altar, it wasn't right for her; when she was ready, I wasn't.

So the affair continued. I was now filming *Fearless Fagan*, based on a true story that had made the cover of *Life*. It was about a young man, Floyd C. Humeston, who gets drafted and takes his pet lion along. Floyd (renamed Hilston in the film) was supposed to do the scenes that featured his now-older, three-hundred-pound pet. I felt sorry for him. After Bill Tuttle, the head of MGM's makeup department, did a death mask of me—which by the way was scary, because you sit there for hours while the Plaster of Paris (or whatever) dries with everything completely covered except for two little straws in the nostrils—he waxed out Floyd's hairline to match mine, dyed his hair (or rather, bleached it) and altered the poor guy's features so he'd look as much like me as possible. At least we were about the same height and weight.

I worked with Floyd on the back lot where Fagan was kept; that required getting used to being around the wild animal and conquering natural fears. I'd drive around an old van with him in the back, with wire netting between us, so he'd get used to me and my particular smells. I learned to try to keep my head lower than his, which was really difficult at times. Gradually I grew bolder—in large part because this would be my first starring role—and would walk with him on a chain leash.

We were getting use to each other and our individual odors, if not exactly becoming bosom buddies. One day, returning to the house on Manning after a workout with Fagan, I drove up, parked my car (I'd traded up to a new yellow Ford convertible) and called for Bugbee. He came running from behind the house, bounding up to me in greeting. About six feet from me he stopped, yowled, flipped over backward from the sudden stop and raced away, fur and tail straight up. I forgot I had stepped in

Feeding my costar in *Fearless Fagan*, 1952.

a puddle of Fagan urine. Bugbee never came back. I threw those old work boots in the garbage out of respect for poor Bug. I loved that cat.

After two days of actual shooting on the film and an accident with one of the extras who got scratched by Fagan's swinging paw, Floyd quit. He went to the front office and told them the lion was too old now and that he couldn't work him anymore.

Next day on the set, a young but still big and heavy lion was brought in from Mel's Animal Farm in the Valley. Because the mane wasn't as big as the real Fagan's, a wig was fashioned in a hurry by some deptartment (Lion Toupees?) on the lot. They could do anything at MGM.

Mel brought the new co-star over to me and shouted, "Up!" Two heavy paws hit my shoulders. It was like having a new pet. I wasn't afraid at all, after the training with the old (now cranky) big cat. So I ended up doing all the animal stuff while waxed and bleached Humeston watched from off the set. We did all sorts of risky things: We got into bed together, I fed him with a bottle, stuff that with today's technology would be a cinch, with no threat of danger. I shot everything with guys with guns just off camera, ready to save my life. I wore a strap under my sleeve of the army shirt so the lion and

I could roll around and wrestle while his teeth were clenched around my arm. Only thing is, when I'd walk in front with him following he usually would sink his teeth into my buttock. If I pulled away they'd sink deeper, so I learned to just let him nip me on the butt and pay no attention. (Footnote: I had scars on my ass for a year and a half after the filming.)

The new kid had strict work habits, or else a built-in cat clock. At five every afternoon, he'd quit taking the commands that were shouted at the dear thing all day long and just stand there. Time to call it a day. I wasn't so lucky. We'd shot without Fagan for at least another hour, sometimes a lot longer. (Because of all that order-shouting, I had to loop almost the entire flick; at least all of the lion stuff.)

The film's director, Stanley Donen, whom I adored, asked Mel how they got the lion to work so well. He was told it was sort of a sex thing: Mel would rub his stomach and groin before coming on the set. I heard about this. The following morning, when Stanley said they were ready for me for the first shot of the day, I just sat there in my chair, my head sort of lolling and my knees slightly apart. Finally he got the message. He came over and grabbed my crotch, and I jumped up and cried: "Ready now." The crew cracked up.

Janet Leigh co-starred. She was scared of the lion, naturally, and hated doing the picture. I don't really blame her. She didn't have much of a part. Several gals had tested for it, including Deb. The one test I wish I had a copy of was Jean Hagen's. The studio thought she looked too old for me, but I was nuts for her and loved working with the lady. I did manage to get Barb assigned to the film for a brief scene as a nurse. I also got the lot to hire Paul Savage to play one of the soldiers. The part wasn't much, but it was a couple of days work.

My old buddy Keenan Wynn gave a flustered and funny performance as the frustrated sergeant, and the darling Ellen Corby was a comic gem. The small black and white film did well at the box office and made a good profit for the studio. But then, most MGM films did; they played in the Loew's Theatres until 1959, when Loew's and MGM split. I did a tour for the picture's openings, mostly in the Midwest. I really enjoyed it. It added to my visibility and Metro's purse. More of the same promotional tours would soon follow. I liked the fans and, luckily, the feeling seemed to be mutual.

Next up on the assignment list was a flick called *My Pal Geechy*, in which I would co-star with Mickey Rooney. MCA wouldn't let me do it, and I had to go on suspension for the five-week shoot. The agency's reason: In *Geechy* I was to play a married man with a child, but the film after that would have me playing a young cowhand just turning twenty-one. MCA wanted my aging to be more gradual. I had looked forward to playing someone closer to my own age, and I put up a brief argument; but I followed my agent's advice. I was replaced by Eddie Bracken and the title, on release, was changed to *A Slight Case of Larceny*.

For years after, whenever we were hoisting a brew or two, Mickey jokingly accused me of not wanting to work with him. But of course, he knew why I couldn't.

During those five unpaid weeks (they'd be tacked on at the end of my seven-year contract) I went east: first to Bennington, where I gathered up my folks and my Aunt Bobby; then to Portsmouth for the opening of *The Whistle at Eaton Falls*. All expenses were paid by de Rochement. The premiere was pretty gala for New England, and great down-home fun. Louis and his wife Virginia loved Dar and Cart on sight, and insisted they take a puppy from their new litter, a fancy breed that slips my mind.

Anyway, the pup was adorable and was immediately christened Whistle. He joined our quartet as we visited Cape Cod and saw Provincetown for the first time. We sneaked the new member of the family into

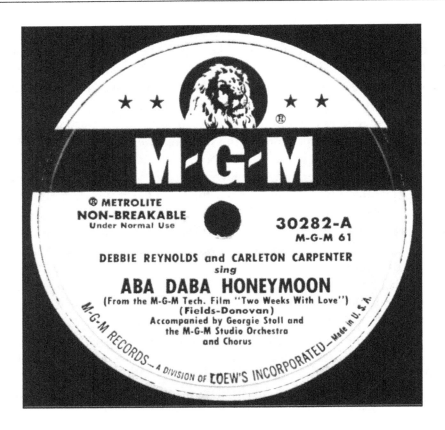

the hotel; no pets were allowed, although some of the human guests were much odder and less housebroken. Our vacation was cut short when we got the news that Grandma Main was ill. She was staying at our house in the Lyons District, and Cart made record time in getting us home to her. She recovered for a spell, but not too many months later I got word at the studio that she'd passed on. I'm peculiar about death. I'm no mourner. I'm a celebrant. The people I was close to are still with me, and I tend to remember all the tender and fun stuff and forget the rest. And I don't like funerals. Or weddings. The occasional memorial service can be life-enhancing and uplifting, sometimes even great fun, with the honoree somehow still there enjoying it too.

Before returning to work after the suspension, I did a short personal-appearance tour for the openings of *Whistle*. Everywhere I went I was fanfared with "Aba Daba." I'd had no idea how big an impact that kooky number had had on people. Even now, people ask me if I'm sick of hearing about it. Well, I'm not. It's nice to be remembered in any context. (The royalties weren't bad either.) It was on the TV version of *Your Hit Parade* for so long, the producers had a terrible time thinking up new ways to stage it. The song was covered by about ten other record labels, but none of them could knock us off the top of the charts, where we remained for months. Even Merv Griffin and Kitty Kallen & Richard Hayes did versions.

Barb and I fell into each other's arms. Alternating beds once more, we resumed our (mostly) monogamous affair. We were asked by Frank Loesser to do the demos for a new score for a movie. It was *Hans Christian Andersen*. We rehearsed at his and his wife Lynn's home before heading for a recording studio on Vine just below Hollywood Boulevard. What a joy dueting on those glorious songs: "Inchworm," "Wonderful Copenhagen," "Thumbelina," "No Two People." Frank did "The King's New Clothes," the title song and others. Barb and I cut "No Two People" for MGM records. It sold well, but not as well as the version by the film's star, Danny Kaye. A friend of ours, Bob Wells, who had co-written "The Christmas Song" with Mel Tormé, wrote a tune for us called "Walkin' in the Rain" for the B-side. Loesser sent us cases of champagne and Scotch for having done the demo session. I didn't drink, but our guests certainly enjoyed them. (Why not? It was Black Label and Dom Perignon.)

We hung out at a couple of special places in West Hollywood: the Ready Room on La Cienega, where Bobby Troup (who wrote "Route 66") held happy sway; and at Café Gala on Sunset. The Gala was run by a singer named Johnny Walsh, and it was a hangout for a quase-in studio crowd. It had great music and a terrific bar that overlooked a vast panorama of L.A. at eventide. The future cabaret king, Bobby Short, made his West Coast debut at that place. A wag at the bar said that Walsh had spotted him in some bar in New York and immediately moved the Bobby westward: "Lock, stock and cock." Just a rumor. But he did live upstairs over the bar.

One night Barb introduced me to a guy she'd sung with in a group called the Whipporwills. His name was Larry Kert. He was the singer Anita Ellis's younger brother. Anita had dubbed for many film stars who weren't the best of singers. But I never understood why they let her dub for Vera-Ellen, whom I'd seen in *A Connecticut Yankee* on Broadway. I loved her soubrette voice. Larry and I hooked up later that night after I'd taken Barb home fairly early. She had a five-a.m. call. That was a brief blip on the non-monogamy screen.

Barb and I also went wherever the Page Cavanaugh Trio was playing, and we'd scat along. On our rare days or half-days off, we spent happy and raucous hours at Arthur Loew, Jr.'s house on Miller Drive. For an out-of-the-way place up off Sunset Boulevard with a tiny three- or four-stool bar under the staircase, that place did one helluva business. There was a constant parade of fun people. And Artie was the funniest, most inventive guy ever. He was an heir to three studio greats: His maternal grandfather was Adolph Zukor, the founder of Paramount; his paternal grandfather, Marcus Loew, had started MGM and Loew's Theatres; and his father was Arthur Loew, Sr., one of MGM's presidents. Artie had also been one of the gang in *Summer Stock*, where we became pals. His cousin Stewart Stern, the screenwriter of several really fantastic films (including *Teresa*, *Rebel Without a Cause*, and *Rachel, Rachel*), shared the house with him. It was a great period in my life. I had a half-assed crush on Artie, and Stewart had a two-thirds-assed crush on me. We sort of chased each other around like a road-company Ritz Brothers, completely zany and, of course, unproductive. There were so many movie names in and out of that mad house that I won't clatter them at you. But a couple of regulars like Mel Tormé and Gore Vidal were lively condiments in the comic stew at that zoo.

Artie, another walking hormone (although by studio necessity I was fairly well reined-in now) would have a lady friend nearly every night as a sleepover guest. Everyone consumed an inordinate amount of alcohol; there were never just one or two nightcaps. The malingerers, and I was always one, would be sipping Martell when Art disappeared upstairs with his current gal. Moments later, back down he'd come to kiss me goodnight and hurry back to his upstairs undertakings.

Finally the studio allowed him to produce a few pictures. The first was an adaptation of Max Shulman's *The Affairs of Dobie Gillis*. Shulman himself was doing the screenplay, and I was to play the lead. Debbie would be my gal; Barb, the other gal. Charlie Trask would be played by Bobby Van. The film was eventually done without me because they switched me to another, bigger budget job that I hated. More about that later. But they gave Dobie to Van and put Bob Fosse in as Dobie's roommate, Charlie. Fosse should have done Gillis, in my opinion.

For now, I plunged into what turned out to be my favorite flick, *Sky Full of Moon*. It was written and directed by Norman Foster, whom I was nuts about. He'd been married at one time to Claudette Colbert and acted with Will Rogers in the original film version of *State Fair*. Now he was married to Sally Blane, sister of Loretta Young. Jan Sterling, maybe my favorite actress of all time, played the girl. How I loved her. The movie was a very simple one. A young, itinerant cowhand, working from ranch to ranch, turns twenty-one; goes to Las Vegas to enter all the events in the

My favorite of my films.

rodeo; meets a girl; loses the girl; enters only one event; loses it; and ends up back on the manure pile at another rancho. That's it. But it was a sweet, touching picture, kind of like a small foreign film. Dear Keenan Wynn was in this one, too.

Foster did the shoot mostly in and around Las Vegas, a great joy for me. We watched rushes together—I'd never done that with a director before—and rehearsed scenes as if it were a play. It's no accident that the love

With Jan Sterling in *Sky Full of Moon*, 1953.

put into the project showed up on the screen. These working conditions were rare, almost nonexistent, in films. I had a very special chance to thank him a few years later. Janie (Jan) always referred to the picture as *Sky Full of Process*, since a long hunk of it, a sequence of a careening car out of control with no brakes, was shot, both closeups and dialogue, on the process stage.

Somewhere along here—you'll have to excuse possible chronological inconsistencies; a storm of stuff was happening over a short period of time—Debbie and I were called into a big exec's office in the Thalberg Building. The papers, both local and national (because of syndication), were running items almost daily, most of them headlined, about planned pics for MGM's new young duo. Louella in the Hearst papers, Hedda in the others; columnists like Mike Connolly in the *Hollywood Reporter* and Army Archerd in *Daily Variety*; the fanzines—the whole fermenting "winegar woiks." The exec asked, "How would you kids like to make some personal appearances around the country?" Then, without pause: "You open in December at the Capitol Theatre in Washington, D.C." A done deal. Well, not quite. I told them it was a fine idea, *if* we could do a real vaudeville act. Not one of those, "I just flew in from Hollywood and my arms are still tired," picture-plugging things. I was given a baffled look, but I raced on. I said I'd put an act together and would let them see it, and if they approved, off we'd go. The Great Powers agreed.

I called Nick Castle, with whom I'd worked on *Summer Stock*. Together we whipped up an act, rehearsed it to within a gasp of its life (Deb was and still is a hard worker) and showcased it to the Great Powers. They gave it a (conferenced) okay.

So the show went on the road, with dear Max (Deb's mom, Maxene) in tow, since her talented offspring was still underage. The three of us got along terrifically. She called me Junior for the rest of her life.

This was the day of movie palaces with rising stages and a big, usually well-known band in the moveable pit to back up several acts between showings of the picture. In the first few theaters we played, we weren't the headliners; we were an Extra Added Attraction, In Person. This meant we did at least four or five shows a day, rarely leaving the movie house. Deb had never been on a stage before, aside from her Miss Burbank school contest; but she learned quickly and took to it like an old pro. She was never nervous before going on. I always had those theater butterflies, and envied her complete lack of them.

Our act opened with the two of us running on from opposite sides of the stage and racing right into the fast chorus of "Aba Daba." Had we

New York's Capitol Theatre, 1951.

known it was going to be such a smash, we would have saved it for last. We segued into "Row, Row, Row," then went back to "Honeymoon" for the extended finish. There was a bit of patter about why I wouldn't date her, which led into "I Wanna Be Loved by You," with Deb sounding remarkably like Helen Kane. During the second chorus she discovered a thread of white knitting wool and began slowly pulling it out, longer and longer, unraveling my undershorts; I reacted with writhing terror. The gag always worked like a charm. She'd run off, I'd sing "Where Did You Get That Girl," then I'd run off as she raced back to sing "I Love the Guy." I'd rejoin her for "You Wonderful You."

The act ran twelve to thirteen minutes. We never mentioned MGM, Hollywood, or any pictures; we just ran on singing and dancing and raced off singing and dancing and sweating. On the bows, I'd come in from the wings and kick high, and Deb would run in under my leg. Sometimes we'd have to do it four or five times. To be immodest, we were a smash. The kids loved us, and would fill the street by the stage door after each show. The reviewers loved us as well. When we played the now-gone Capitol Theatre in New York at 51st and Broadway, *Variety* said it was the best vaudeville act to have ever come out of a studio promo tour, and that we were the greatest young team since the Garland-Rooney duo. What higher praise was there?

A fiscal note: When we played the Loew's houses, we were paid fifteen hundred each per week; when my agent negotiated for a run at the independent Oriental Theatre in Chicago, we each got five thousand per. The first two weekends in Chicago we squeezed in seven, count 'em, seven shows a day on Saturday and Sunday. Incidentally, I was in the film playing there, *Vengeance Valley*, and during our three weeks there Deb was on the cover of *Life*. As I mentioned earlier, the magazine photoshoot had featured the two of us, but a shot of Deb alone was picked for the cover. We were "covered" together on many fanzines and also on *Cash Box*, which gave us an award for our long chart stay for "Aba Daba Honeymoon." You could safely say we were hot.

Backstage at the Oriental, I picked out songs and rehearsed them with Deb for follow-up records: "Oh By Jingo!," "Get Out and Get Under the Moon," and our new version of "When You and I Were Young Maggie Blues." They all hit the charts, but none had the staying power of "Honeymoon." What could? There was one song, "Didja Ever?," that I didn't care for but we had to record it, because we did as we were told. It sold like last week's news. "Maggie Blues" was jumped on and covered by a slew of others, including Bing and Gary Crosby, and we managed to outsell even them. Okay, I'll say it: Wow.

Later on I toured with my love, Jane Powell. We played more theaters, mainly in the Midwest. We did individual turns, but joined for one song at the end, "How Could You Believe Me When I Said I Loved You When You Know I've Been a Liar All My Life," the song she'd done with Astaire in *Royal Wedding*. While we were playing in Cleveland (at the Hanna Theater, I think), Judy Garland opened for the first time at the Palace in New York. We all listened backstage to the radio coverage of the event: Vaudeville was back, live onstage! It was goose-pimple time as we heard the audience screaming after that opening performance. The live reviewer in the lobby had to yell his superlatives into the mike. We all wished we were there. One little gal on the bill with us, a member of the hit vaudeville act Singer's Midgets, was dissolved in giant tears. I dropped to my knees and we consoled each other. She was three times my age and had a remarkable voice. She ended her turn on the bill with "A Good Man Is Hard to Find." It had the longest tag I've ever heard: at least a thirty-two-bar last-line ride out.

Deb couldn't make the Keenan Wynn Players' annual Christmas-New Year trip to Iceland, Greenland, and elsewhere for the troops; happily for me, Barb replaced her. Bobby Tucker, the lovable pianist who called us Barbass and Carltass, was there, along with Audrey Totter and our *pièce de résistance*, Walter Pidgeon, with his inexhaustible library of limericks. Keeno, always the emcee, would introduce Mr. P. as "the gentleman who has had the distinct pleasure of being in *Mrs. Miniver, Mrs. Parkington, Madame Curie, That Forsyte Woman* and even *The Girl of the Golden West*; here, in person, is the very tired but very happy … Mister Walter Pidgeon!" The guys loved it, and would hoot and howl as the dapper gentleman came out on whatever makeshift stage there was. He would give Wynn a withering look and bow deeply to the long applause. He was a straight-faced riot in the corny short skits we did. I especially loved dueting with Barb on "You Wonderful You."

We had a one-night-off break in Paris before we headed to the Tuscan town of Livorno (known in English as Leghorn). This was my first time in the City of Lights. We were all herded into a taxi, whereupon we headed for dinner in Montmartre. Thanks to two years with Mae Hutton's French class in high school, I asked the driver to stop, and I bounced out and explored a bit of the city alone. I ended up at a medium-fancy place called Le boeuf sur le toit, where I met a Dutch Beauty. We moved on to an after-hours place and eventually to a double bed in the Hotel California. I couldn't go back to my room, where my beloved Barb awaited me. It was another drunken though glorious night and another (shameful) blip on the non-monogamy map. We left Paris at the crack of a sparrow twit. I had maybe an hour's sleep, but I caught up on the plane. I always confessed my blips to Barb, and she always forgave me.

As I forgave her when she briefly strayed. Our tight, loving friendship forever won out. After Leghorn and Napoli, we were off on the road to Morocco, where I twin-bedded at the hotel in Rabat with Artie Loew, Jr., one of that year's volunteers. Bunking with a lady to whom you weren't espoused was verboten. In local Medina in western Saudi Arabia (walled, naturally), the stench was unforgettable. Audrey had a solid perfume stick in her purse and we all slathered the stuff on our upper lips while cutting the bizarre bazaar excursion short. I bought a red-and-white, diamond-studded leather hassock that I stuffed when I finally got back to Westwood.

We hit Tripoli in Libya before heading home, so my "short snorter" was growing by leaps and bounds. That's a long strip made up of foreign currency, with one bill, usually the lowest denomination, Scotch-taped to the next, and rolled up and secured with a rubber band. (The big, decaying wad is probably here somewhere in the house, if it hasn't completely shredded away by now.)

The following year we went to Korea. Deb was back in the group, which again included Pidgeon. On this trip he was a bit less affable, and inclined to complain about the less-than-comfy conditions we were mostly afforded. I found myself apologizing for him to some of the men, explaining that this was his way of joking, to make the unbearable bearable. We also had a country-western singer Carolina Cotton (darkly gorgeous and at that time Marlon Brando's lady); Junie, a truly remarkable accordion player; and our fearless leader, Keenan.

When we left Burbank Airfield, there were three planes lined up for press farewells. Each was destined for different parts of South Korea. One plane was ours; another held a troop headed by my buddies Jan Sterling, Dick Morris (who wrote *The Loretta Young Show* and, later on, *The Unsinkable Molly Brown* and *Thoroughly Modern Millie*), Paul Douglas, and a handsome young singer-dancer-actor named Richard Allen. The third plane carried Eddie Fisher and Dick Contino, the accordionist.

After much fuss, the three planes were airborne. On our way to South Korea we stopped in Alaska, where we were to give shows at the Army Air Force base in Fairbanks; then we went to Tokyo. Flying in an old MATS (Military Air Transport Service) two-propeller job, we hit severe weather conditions somewhere over northern Washington. Our jolly group bounced around, huddled in blankets inside the chilly aircraft, singing songs to keep our spirits high. When Keeno looked out and announced we'd just lost power in the right propeller, the studio aide on board—he was there because of Deb's age—quickly took out two Seconals and popped them. He was going to be of great help to us all if anything really bad happened. The plan was lurching around in a now-extreme blizzard.

Someone started ad-libbing a theme song for us: "The Last of the Holiday Troopers, or They All Went Down Together." Dirty. Funny. Perfect to keep us laughing. Somehow we made it to the very edge of a small airport outside of Anchorage. Though bitterly cold outside, most of us got out to happily touch frozen terra firma. The conked-out aide stayed on board while an emergency crew worked like heavenly demons to repair the dead propeller. We were too far to get to any indoor structure, but an angel in a jeep brought a huge thermos of hot coffee from somewhere. You could see but a few feet in the still-snowy night. The pilot disappeared with the coffee jeep to get in touch with the base in Fairbanks. We'd be hours late. The crew, on overdrive, worked as fast as they could. When the job was finished, the last crew kid passed us with a big grin. "We fixed everything but that guy snoring on board. Couldn't do anything for him." He waved a greasy hand and said, "Have a great trip, and thanks." We applauded, Carolina kissed him, and we climbed back aboard, yelling, as one, "No, thank *you!*"

Meanwhile, at the Fairbanks Air Base, the cocktail party to precede a dinner for the ever-hungry entertainers had started without us at the Officers Club. When we finally landed around a quarter of three a.m., it was obvious that the welcoming committee hadn't bothered with the dinner; the posh party-planners were zonked. Especially the base commander's wife. We had just made it from the bathroom and were anxious for a quick sandwich and a short snooze—the first show was slotted for nine a.m.—but The Wife was drunkenly demanding a short preview, specifically "Aba Daba Honeymoon."

The studio aide was the only one whose butt wasn't dragging; he was fresh and thoroughly rested from his Seconaled sleep. He spoke up bravely and explained to her that Deb was a minor and had to get to bed immediately. He was very official; you could hear the absolute finality in his delivery. The Wife would not be swayed, although she was swaying from her martinis. "Bullshit," she declared. "She's a midget and takes dope."

Deb and I hurried to the piano and quickly launched into the fast chorus. We'd never done it faster.

After the morning shows, we set off without any major incident for Haneda Airport in Tokyo. There we were welcomed by an incredible character, Norma Bussey, a tall, slim WAC lieutenant who would take us under her wing and brief us about everything under the rising and setting sun. Until we left the next morning I hung out with Jan and Paul and Bussey. (She would later appear with Paul in a film called "Never Wave at a WAC." She stole her brief scene with Marie Wilson.) What a hoot she was! She told us during dinner that earlier in the day at the airport, when Cardinal Spellman's plane landed, he'd spotted her among the press corps and made a beeline toward her. He raised his hand and whispered, "Kiss my ring." Nodding to the crowd, he said, "Photographers!" Bussey claims (although I doubt it) that she nodded and whispered, "Kiss my ass. Pals."

She said he was on his way to South Korea to kiss the troops. Bussey asked us when the powers that be would send over somebody she wanted. Like, oh my, yes, Veronica Lake. Bussey had a dream plan of a rehab center to be built in Tokyo. It would be five stories tall. There would be a lovely entrance on the ground floor; men and women on the first floor; all women on the second; all male on the third; and the top floor would be a hospital. Her smile widened as she mapped out the place for us.

In the morning she saw us off, holding on to our wallets and other valuables until we returned there on the way back. Once we'd reached Korea we were flown two at a time by helicopter from one outdoor show site to another. Those hot-rod pilots seemed to love scaring the bejesus out of us. We did our shows just over a hill from the constant fighting—that was our background "music" during the skits. But it was, as always, a joy for us because it was such a joy for the guys. The performances ran a little less than an hour, then the kids would put the helmets they sat on back on their heads and go back to the action. We were constantly on the move, but I never got used to those chopper pilots. Keeno, of course, loved the short flights, but our intrepid leader was as nutty as his dad, Ed Wynn, pretended to be.

Late one night (I think it was New Year's Eve), after a big show in a theater in Seoul with all three of the traveling troops combined, most of us gathered in a mess hall for sandwiches and coffee. It was there that I introduced Eddie Fisher, the kid that had come from Philly to do *Places, Please* years before, to Deb. It was nothing more than a casual, quick intro. I doubt either of them remembered it. I know that in Deb's memoir she or her cowriter, David Patrick Columbia, recalled their meeting differently. Her book was full of a lot of made-up stuff; she even misspelled "Aba Daba" all the way through. But that's okay. I haven't read Fisher's autobiography.

Flying back to the states, I switched planes and joined Jan, Paul and Dick Morris. We returned by the southern route, stopping for one night in Hono-effing-lulu, where we walked along the beach and soaked up the wonderful, warming, setting sun, followed by several head-swimmingly delicious Navy Grogs. They contained seven, count 'em, seven different kinds of rum cooled by a big cone of ice in the glass. This was a huge mistake, but again, everyone drank too much back then. The four of us had ourselves a fun-filled fourteen-hour vacation. For years to come, we roared at the memory of our farewells with Bussey when we picked up our personals back in Tokyo. She was a keeper; we'd hold her in our hearts forever.

After the war, Bussey entertained at cabarets in San Francisco. On a trip to New York she came backstage after a show I was doing on Broadway. We had a thigh-slappingly hysterical reunion over drinks. She'd dragged along a friend, young and not pretty. I thought this was a gift for me but it turned out not to be.

I arrived back in Hollywood raring to go with *The Affairs of Dobie Gillis*. Meanwhile I planned my move from Westwood to an old house on Gould Avenue that hung dangerously above Laurel Canyon. I had the two bottom floors, and the steps down from the street were steep and many. Upon arriving there for tea one afternoon, Clifton Webb claimed he hadn't been so frightened since his first trip up the Eiffel Tower in Paris, where he had to be blindfolded and led down. He was another skinny acrophobe, just like me.

There was a terrific shock awaiting me upon my return. It was headlined in Louella Parsons's column: CARP OUT OF "DOBIE" AND INTO "MARINE." I was floored. I was also fatigued, furious and unwell. Into a hospital I went. Some bug I had picked up from my Tinian time reared its temperature-raising head, and I was bedridden for several days.

The "Marine" that Parsons had told the world about was a big, Technicolor, star-studded film to be called *The Making of a Marine*. It was about basic training, and the script was duller than an empty bar. The same flick

Take the High Ground!, 1953.

had been made dozens of times before. It was filmed mostly at an army training camp in El Paso, Texas where, it's often been said, the Divine Being would, if needed, give the world an enema. The marines became army recruits, and the film was renamed *Take the High Ground!* I really hated making it. Whenever it shows on the tube, Howard Thompson's capsule review in the *New York Times* says it all: "Dull rah-rah training film."

But what did Thompson and I know? It won an Oscar for best script. The cast—including Richard Widmark and Karl Malden—was super, but wasted. It was directed by the brilliant Richard Brooks, who was also a talented writer. I remember one evening having a long talk with him over drinks about his novel *The Producer*, which I'd just read. I asked him what on earth he was doing pissing away his time on crap like *Take the High Ground!* His smile, slow and wide under his black bushy eyebrows, slid even wider as he removed his hand from the beer glass and rubbed his thumb against his middle finger. It broke my heart. But it says heaps about Hollywood.

Chapter 11 ─────────────

Whe that epic was finally in the can, I was smiling again. It's tough doing work you don't enjoy, and up to then I'd been spoiled. Now that was over, and the studio, along with the State Department, was about to send Deb, Pier Angeli, and me on an extended tour of all the Loew's Theatres in South America. But before I left, I requested a face-to-face meeting with Dore Schary, whom I liked. (Louis B. Mayer was off the lot by now and Dore was the big wheel.) I wanted to know what had prompted them to switch me from *Dobie* to *Take the High Ground!* As I settled myself into a chair opposite the chief, who sat behind a huge desk, it was as if I were somewhere up in a corner of the office, like a stealth camera watching the scene below.

When I popped the question, he smiled—he did that easily—and agreed that *Dobie* had been tailored for me, and that it had been a shame to pull me from it. I jumped in: "But I would have been better and the film would have been better. The part was so right for me. Edna Mae Oliver could have played my role in *High Ground* and no one would have known the difference." I couldn't believe I was sitting there saying that.

He actually laughed. "But I was about to say, we're going to be making fewer pictures now, concentrating on all the star power we can muster. Bigger films. *Dobie* was a small film. We needed your name on the bigger project." I wanted to say that perhaps that "small" film might have seemed bigger with the originally planned cast, but he smilingly continued on. "Your next film when you return from the South American tour will be *Sobbin' Women*. Big all-star cast, and your friend Stanley Donan directing. How about that?" (The title would later be changed to *Seven Brides for Seven Brothers*.)

156

Schary seemed to be pleased that he'd placated me, although he really hadn't. He wished me luck and said, "Have fun on the South American tour," and the brief interview—my first and last with a head of a studio—was over.

Packing judiously, for I'd learned how to keep luggage at a minimum, I was off on an incredible adventure with Pier and Deb. It was a good-will, good-neighbor effort. What a thrilling trip! Deb had taken two years of Spanish in high school, and was very helpful in translating (badly but funnily) our bits of small talk that led into the songs. It worked everywhere but Brazil, where someone helped us with the needed Portuguese. Pier's Italian made it easier to adjust, and she mostly chatted during the shows, singing a bit.

We flew first to Panama, and after an impromptu show for the servicemen stationed there we switched to an Avianca flight to (I think) Barranquilla in Colombia. It was the only air trip I ever took where there were bunks above the seats, sort of like being back in a navy hammock. We flew to so many places I can't remember the order, so I'll just list the cities and countries: Bogota (Colombia); Caracas and Maracaibo (Venezuela); Quito and Guayaquil (Ecuador); Lima (Peru); La Paz and Sucre (Bolivia); Asuncion (Paraguay); Rio and São Paulo (Brazil); Montevideo (Uruguay); Buenos Aires (Argentina); Santiago, Valparaíso and Vina del Mar (Chile). There may have been others. It was one hell of an itinerary.

A few brief scenes come to mind. I stayed at the lovely old Hotel Glória in Rio. It had a pool with the most beautiful people around it. I went up to the huge statue of Christ on Corcovado peak and gazed at it, slack-jawed with awe.

In São Paulo I was amazed to find a thriving movie industry. There were gigantic studios with product rolling out of them. I was amazed at everyone's adoration for anything Hollywood, including our little trio of performers (augmented by Junie, the pianist from the last Korea trip and a complete doll). We were really unknowns to them, but wherever we went, thousands of movie fans lined the roads from airports to hotels, screaming and shouting. It was very humbling. Who on earth deserved that kind of mass hysteria? The Pope, maybe. Certainly not three kids who happened to have been in a few movies.

In Brazilian nightclubs, I kept hearing a song I fell in love with. Once we'd reached Montevideo, I went to a music store and hummed the melody. The salesclerk beamed and brought me out a copy of the sheet music. The song was in Portuguese and, thank goodness, also in French, so I could learn it and put it into our show. The crowds loved it. When I got back to the States, I thought, I'd write English lyrics to the lovely melody and make a fortune. I was too late: A new release of "April in Portugal" by the Les Baxter orchestra and singers was already a hit.

I also loved a very popular fado called "Piel Canela." I bought a 78 of it and almost wore it out, although I still don't understand the Portuguese lyrics.

Perhaps the most exciting (and scary) part of the entire tour was in Buenos Aires. The city was in the midst of the Peron uprising, and whole sections of the city were under siege, with armed soldiers everywhere. Nevertheless, the path from the airport to downtown was heavily lined with tens of thousands of people, waving and cheering at our car. I guess we were a welcome diversion. Armed guards took us into the hotel and traveled to and from the Loew's Theatre with us. A guard was even stationed outside each of our rooms while we slept. Junie and I managed to sneak away a couple of nights to a cantina or two. The gals were non-imbibers.

It was fun seeing "Cielo del Pleno" on theater marquees. I saw part of a showing and got a kick out of hearing myself dubbed in Spanish. I wondered if anyone guessed that, in the early scenes of the film when I'm doing chores in just a tee shirt and jeans, my chest wasn't quite as it looked. When we had started shooting *Sky Full of Moon*, someone from wardrobe arrived with a vest-like thing and told me to take off the tee and put this on underneath. (I'm concave in front, just like Cart was.) As I slipped this slightly padded thing on I noticed a label on the back of the neck. J. Stewart. I was wearing Jimmy Stewart's falsies. I couldn't wait to spread that around. The garment zipped up tightly and was indetectable under my tee. Mind you, I didn't look like a potential Tarzan, but at least I didn't appear to be in the last stages of T.B.

After we'd wound up the tour, we took a two-day rest. (MGM was a tad chintzy with vacation time.) I flew to Havana and stayed one night at the Nacionale Hotel, then went to New York City for my other night. I spent it at the opening of *Can-Can*, where Gwen Verdon literally stopped the show after a Garden of Eden number. She had to come back on—no one would quit applauding until she did—and when she did, she was clutching her costume (which she'd already taken off) in front of her. What an exciting moment, to watch a star being born onstage in front of you.

When I returned to my usual room at the Wellington after the show, a message awaited me. Gramma Bessie had died. I went to the Loew's office on Broadway, saw Howard Dietz, the head of MGM publicity as well as Arthur Schwartz's fantastic lyricist, and I got permission to go up to Bennington for the funeral. That meant I had three extra days in New York before I headed back west. I saw *Hazel Flagg* that evening. An old buddy, Helen Gallagher, was the star, and was, as usual, terrific.

Then I headed to Vermont, where the dreaded funeral awaited. All kinds of wonderful stories about Gram whirled around in my head. How she'd call Jeanne on the phone and ask her, "Wouldn't you love to have some lovely ears of golden bantam corn right now?" Jeanne would say, "How very thoughtful. I'd love a few ears. Thank you, Bess."

"So would I," Gram would say. "Know where we can get any? Well, be good.

Goodbye." Then she'd hang up.

The day of her funeral I was sick as the proverbial pup. That Tinian-tainted bug, apparently stirred up by the South American climes, floored me again. I managed to call Mr. Dietz, who offered condolences for my Gram's death and my health. A true gent, that man. He told me that although he had tried to talk the studio out of it, the West Coast office had seen fit to put me on suspension until rehearsals began on *Sobbin' Women* in three weeks' time. That news didn't help my high fever to subside in the least. But a few days later it did, and I returned to New York City.

Murray Anderson was preparing a new revue, produced by a character named Harry Rigby. (Murray named him "Triple de Vediera." Don't ask.) Also aboard, from the *Three to Make Ready* days, were money-man Michael Grace and Stanley Gilkey, whom Murray called "Patron." The show was called *John Murray Anderson's Almanac*, and they wanted me. I was really itching, scratching and multiple other things to get back on stage. I called my New York MCA agent and said, "Please get me out of my Metro contract." He and the West Coast reps were none too pleased. There were three years (plus four suspension weeks) left, and a very healthy hunk of guaranteed loot. They tried to talk me out of it, indicating that the studio would never let me go and it would just be "strained feelings all around" if I went through with the impossible request. I said: "Just ask. Please."

I hung out with Jay Presson while two weeks of phone calls went on. I'd bought an unset rare pink sapphire gem for her while I was in

Lima. Now I had it set and presented it to her. She was very casual about the gift, which was no surprise to me. That was her style. Over the past few years, we always kept in touch, sometimes very closely. On many a morning in Manhattan during my quick weekends there, Jay would appear at my door at the Wellington Hotel with a bundle of daily papers. She'd crawl into bed beside me and read all the gossip columns aloud. She would also would help herself to whatever money I had in my trousers whenever she was short of cash. Once or twice she arrived at the L.A. airport to fly to New York—but she hadn't purchased a ticket. Jay had convinced the airline that her ticket would be paid for upon her arrival in Manhattan. Once there, she called me to fetch her, and I'd find myself doling out the dollars for her ticket. I didn't care. She was a very special friend, and oddly, one who had quite a positive influence on me.

Back when *New Faces* was running at the Plaza, Jay had hung out with that other buddy of mine, Dick Morris. Leonard Sillman did not take to Morris. One evening outside the Palm Court, he screamed at her (his normal mode of speaking) while we sat resting between shows. "You see too much of that Morris guy. He's crazy and a terrible influence on you. Give that guy the gate!"

Jay raised a regal arm covered from wrist to shoulder with taped-on silk butterflies (a gift from Dick) and shook her finger at Leonard. "Never!" she declared royally as all the butterflies fluttered under his nose. "He's the only sane influence in my life."

I also spent time with Murray and Rigby while I waited to find out if I would be a free soul again. As the days went on I wondered if maybe I was making a mistake. No, I decided. I was never cut out to be a motion picture star. Time I got back to what I loved: the boards. I was at Rigby's apartment on the afternoon I got the call that MGM was releasing me from my seven-year sentence. I was ecstatic. We celebrated that night and the following day.

I went in search of a New York apartment. Back over in my old EL (Eldorado) 5 neighborhood, I found a tiny, tidy one. The entrance was on 50th, and the apartment itself was one floor above the handy liquor store that faced Second Avenue. The dining area was just big enough for a table and four chairs, which I'd buy later; the wee kitchen had a small stove and miniature fridge; the living room had windows on the east and south sides. There was a short, narrow hall with a john off it and a decent-sized bedroom. After signing the lease, I had the phone connected and spent the first night sleeping on the floor. Unfurnished heaven.

Back I flew to L.A., where I arranged for my piano, books, records and assorted junk to be moved by van from Gould to New York. Clothes, bedding and personal needs went into the back of my Ford Convertible, and I headed East with nary a qualm nor a look back. I was halfway across the country when I realized I'd left behind the theater poster of *Three to Make Ready*, with the Hirschfeld caricature of Ray Bolger, legs in a split from bottom left to top right. It was in my MGM portable dressing room. I still haven't found a replacement, but hope springs.

I rented garage space a couple of blocks south on Second. They didn't cost an arm and a leg then. Before I could start furnishing the new pad, I had to wait a few days for the arrival of the van, which held my piano, a studio number I had bought when I moved into Manning Avenue in Westwood.

One evening I took Murray and Gilkey ("Patron") to the Village Vanguard to hear someone I'd liked enormously at the Blue Angel. They were as knocked out as I was. Just as I had planned it, they decided he belonged in the upcoming *Almanac*. Harry Belafonte. Before rehears-

Playing Ensign Pulver in *Mister Roberts*, Hinsdale, Illinois, 1953.
That's Buddy Ebsen holding a book.

als began, I whizzed off to the Salt Creek Summer Theatre in Hinsdale, Illinois., a suburb of Chicago, to play Ensign Pulver in *Mister Roberts*. Buddy Ebsen played the title role and Art Smith was Doc. Oscar Hammerstein's son Jim directed and was terrific. So was the show. What fun my part was! All you needed to do was say the words, exit, and time the laughs. It was so wonderfully written; not a wasted syllable—all of them honed, Im sure, by that theater magician Josh Logan, the cowriter. He would have been proud of our production, and of Ebsen, Smith and the entire cast. (The *Mister Roberts* company, alas, is too large to encourage many revivals in the current economy.) Our sets were spectacular, the work of a talented technician named Shel Janecek. The two of us hit it off like long-lost buddies, and we hung out together in whatever little time off one gets in a quick stock date.

Gene Raymond was starring in the play ahead of us. I stayed at the same beautiful home (called The Bunkers) as he and his wife, Jeanette MacDonald, who turned out to be a hoot and a half. Great gal. I didn't tell her one of my aunts was a near-dead ringer for her. I hadn't realized what a funny lady Jeanette was. Later, when I took another look at her old movie operettas with Nelson Eddy, I discovered what a clever comedienne she'd been all along.

Mister Roberts was a joy, and the Chicago press loved it as much as we all did. When I returned to New York, Shel decided to move in with me and give the big town a whirl. It was a happy decision for both of us and a boon for me, because he helped me lug and carry things and furnish the empty apartment. Always a loner, I suddenly found having a roommate and good friend around really great. I was away much of the time and we never got in each other's way.

Almanac got underway shortly after my Chicago stint, and a few weeks later I was on my way to Boston for out-of-town tryouts. It was a nice feeling to have someone at home watching over the new digs. The piano fitted very nicely against one wall, and I found an ottoman that fitted in the corner of the living room—one bolster on the Second Avenue side, the other on 50th. It pulled out at the bottom and flipped over, making a very comfortable bed. We built a wall unit for books, 78s, a small Emerson TV, and a desk. Shel planned and did most of the work. (Later I would move that unit around several times on both coasts.)

We drove up to Vermont and bought a dining set made by Cushman Colonial Creations at a bargain price. My Uncle Hike worked at the factory in North Bennington and the discount was more than generous.

John Murray Anderson's Almanac, 1953-1954. Above, L-R: Hermione Gingold, Billy DeWolfe, Orson Bean, Elaine Dunn, unknown (standing in back), Celia Johnson (seated), Nanci Crompton, unknown, and me. Below: the show's big swim-meet scene. That's me in the plaid shirt, crouching near the center as I hold Elaine Dunn's hand. To my left in the big black dress is Polly Bergen. Hermione Gingold stands next to Elaine in pantaloons; next to her is Billy DeWolfe.

Dar and Cart had moved a few yards down Darcie's Dead End to old Carpenter house, renting our place. Grampa Charlie, with his dear pigeon toes, had been "In Brattleboro" for a couple of years. "In Brattleboro" was a polite way of saying "In the Nut House." Grampa Charlie was suffering from what would today be called dementia or Alzheimer's. How crude and cruel things were a mere fifty years ago.

Now Bess was gone. Elizabeth and her growing family were in Spokane, Washington. Lewis was raising his kids overstreet with his wife Lestina. Cart had painted and spruced up the old house. It seemed funny sleeping there. Home was up the hill a spit away. But at the time it was a money-saver for my folks. Shel was instantly one of the family, and he and Cart spent a lot of time refinishing furniture later on. Actually he got to spend more time with my folks than I did, until he landed a job that took him on the road and overseas.

When *Almanac* opened in Boston, an unexpected thing happened. Elaine Dunn and I had a number called "You're So Much a Part of Me" that stopped the show cold, just like Gwen Verdon had in *Can-Can*. We were completely dumbfounded, but the audience wouldn't stop applauding until we came back for a bow in the set of a sketch called "My Cousin Who?" Elaine and I were as embarrassed as we were delighted. But it happened at every performance, so they were slower opening up the set of "Cousin" after that first night. It was a first for both of us, and a last for me; I don't know about Elaine.

That song was my entrance in the revue, about sixth in the running order. Orson Bean, who opened the show as a Harlequin-like compere, got things moving, but apparently not with the energy Murray was looking for. He begged me to do the opening and compere chores. I knew it was very wrong for me, but I also knew it would be better for the show. So I let Murray, Gilkey and Rigby talk me into it. The opening did zip along a bit brighter, but by the time Elaine and I came on to do "You're So Much a Part of Me," I'd been on and off three times. The edge was off. We never stopped the show after that. Walter Kerr, the longtime critic for the *New York Herald Tribune* and then for the *Times*, wrote a wonderful book called "How Not to Write a Play." I could have written one called "How Not to Stop a Show."

But we had three weeks of performances before I began my new duties.

And what a cast! It included Belafonte, Polly Bergen, Nanci Crompton and Kay Medford, and starred Hermione Gingold and Billy De Wolfe.

Shubert Theatre

Direction — *Messrs. Lee & J. J. Shubert*

MICHAEL GRACE
STANLEY GILKEY

in association with HARRY RIGBY present

JOHN MURRAY ANDERSON'S

ALMANAC

A Musical Harlequinade

Entire Production Devised and Staged by
JOHN MURRAY ANDERSON

with

BILLY DeWOLFE
HARRY BELAFONTE   POLLY BERGEN

ORSON BEAN   NANCI CROMPTON   CARLETON CARPENTER
HARRY MIMMO   CELIA LIPTON   ELAINE DUNN   HARRY SNOW

and

HERMIONE GINGOLD

Music and Lyrics by RICHARD ADLER and JERRY ROSS

and

RICHARD ADDINSELL   ARTHUR MACRAE   CY COLEMAN
JOSEPH McCARTHY   IRWIN GRAHAM   HENRY SULLIVAN   JOHN ROX
Sketches by GEORGE AXELROD   JEAN KERR   SUMNER LOCKE-ELLIOTT
HERBERT FARJEON   LAURI WYLIE

Sketches Directed by CYRIL RITCHARD
Dances and Musical Numbers Staged by DONALD SADDLER
Scenery by RAOUL PENE DU BOIS
Costumes by THOMAS BECHER

Orchestrations by Ted Royal and Hans Spialek
Musical Director John McManus
Vocal arranging by Buster Davis
Dance music arranged by Gerald Alters

JOHN MURRAY ANDERSON'S ALMANAC 1953

Prologue
HARLEQUINADE
by Richard Adler and Jerry Ross

Harlequin	Orson Bean
Puncinello	Harry Mimmo
Pierrot	Harry Snow
Pierrette	Polly Bergen
Columbine	Nanci Crompton

Pierrettes
Lee Becker, Dorothy Dushock, Greb Lober, Ilona Murai,
Margot Myers, Gwen Neilson, Gloria Smith

Pierrots
Jimmy Albright, Hank Brunjes, Ronald Cecill,
Dean Crane, Ralph McWilliams, Job Sanders

THE ALMANAC
Page 1
SHIPPING NEWS

The Passenger	HERMIONE GINGOLD
The Reception Committee	BILLY DeWOLFE

"The Raft Song": Lyrics by Hermione Gingold and Sheldon Harnick.
Music by David Baker
"True": Music and Lyrics by Richard Adler and Jerry Ross

This show was the last of the big, lavish revues. Our showgirls were bruisers: Siri, Colleen Hutchins (Miss America 1952), Monique Van Vooren and Tina Louise. We had a dozen or so gypsies, incredible sets by Raoul Pene Du Bois, music by the likes of Cy Coleman; and Richard Adler & Jerry Ross, who went on to write *Damn Yankees*; and Bart Howard, composer of "Fly Me to the Moon." We had three stage managers: Arthur Barkow, my old friend Perry Bruskin and Dennis Murray (father of Don Murray, the actor who had played opposite Marilyn Monroe in *Bus Stop*.) Talented Donald Saddler did the dances, Cyril Ritchard directed the sketches. Murray devised and directed the entire shebang.

The New York notices were fantastic for him. His picture was everywhere, accompanying the raves. Most critics, however, did mention that most of the audiences came out of the theater humming the sketches, not the music. (Some of it was by Murray himself, with music by his composer sidekick Henry "Hank" Sullivan.)

In retrospect, all the praise and fanfare for dear Murray were like advance obits. He died six weeks after the opening.

On December 10, 1953, we settled in for a six-and-a-half-month Broadway run. The news of Murray's death—he had died on a Saturday morning and the cast was told after the matinee—was devastating. We played that evening's show through tears, but in Murray's beloved memory the show went on. The audience must have thought we were all nutty, until they read about it on the front pages of all the papers the following morning. We kept our spirits up and exchanged hilarious tales about Murray. That was our way of mourning.

At Campbell's funeral chapel, we all signed the guest book with the special names he had given us. I remember smiling as I scrawled "Mascarp" under "Hamburger Mary." But the service—arranged by his brother Hugh, who managed all his business affairs—was so un-Murray-like that I expected him to rise up in the open casket and shout: "It's too terrible! Do it again!" Filing out of the funeral home, everyone said much the same thing. Everything had been wrong. What a shame his "last production" had flopped so badly. Well, Hugh may have been good at bookkeeping, but he hadn't a smidge of humor. How could two brothers be so different? Foolish question. It happens all the time.

The Imperial Theatre, where we played, was a magic funhouse backstage.

Often Monique Van Vooren would arrive by limo at the stage door swathed in a full-length ermine, naked as a plucked goose underneath

Above: The four New Englanders of *Almanac*: Me, Elaine Dunn, Nanci Crompton, and Orson Bean. Below: I was "The Song Plugger" in an *Almanac* sketch called "Tin Pan Alley." Larry Kert is second from left, back row.

the fur (which she rarely buttoned). She'd dash inside, part jaybird, part stoat, to everyone's delight.

Billy De Wolfe and I became great buddies. He'd often visit the pad on East 50th, complaining bitterly that people who stepped off the crosstown bus (directly opposite the john window) were watching him as he stood relieving himself after having downed a few of his preferred "Dewar's and branch water" drinks. He always referred to his toupee as "my friend." After he had done a TV plug for the show he would ask me how he was. A pause, and then: "And how did my friend look?"

When we were together our New England accents would become stronger and stronger. Billy was from Quincy, Massachusetts on Boston Bay, just southeast of Boston. When I visited his apartment for a libation and gab, I got to sit in his favorite armchair. It was wider than most; he called it "an ass and a half," an expression I'd never heard.

Soon after we'd opened, but before Murray died, Billy and I were invited to an afternoon show-business press party at the Essex Hotel on Central Park South. The event took up three big adjoining ballrooms, and there were two groups of musicians. It was on a Sunday, our day off. The matinee the day before had held great gossipy interest for the entire cast. Christine (née George) Jorgensen was out front. Jorgensen had recently become America's first famous transsexual. All of us were peeking out to take a gander at her when we were offstage. Whenever I got to look she was turned away or tying her shoe or something. I never got a glimpse.

Now we were at the Essex, where I met up with many old chums. At one point I was at the end of the far room talking with Nancy Andrews, the singer-comedienne. Billy and I were the only two members of *Almanac* who were invited, I suppose because we'd been in films. It was a loud and gregarious crowd of nice, out-of-town editors gathering stories from the New York showfolk.

Suddenly, both groups of music-makers stopped and a hush fell over the three rooms. The newly sex-changed Christine had arrived at the main entrance. She spotted me three rooms away. In a not-very-ladylike manner, she called out my name and pointed. "I saw your show yesterday. But I fell in love with you years ago singing 'Aba Daba'!" As she made a beeline through the crowd toward me, Nancy whispered: "How do you think she does it now?" I assured her I had no intention of finding out. Jorgensen approached and held out a gloved hand. (She had turned very ladylike, but it was too late.) I shook it, backing away a bit,

I'm ashamed to say. I did order a drink for her; then I escorted her to her designated table and held her chair. I noticed the faintest trace of a five o'clock shadow beneath the makeup.

She proceeded to tell me she was appearing at the Latin Quarter, which of course everyone knew. Jorgensen was commanding a lot of ink in the current press. She insisted I come see her performance, and said she'd reserve a ringside table for me that night. I told her I was sorry, but I was seeing an Actors Fund performance of *The Solid Gold Cadillac* that evening. She wouldn't let it go. Tomorrow night, then, she said, and I accepted. "The table will be in your name, dear." I nodded and fled back to Nancy, who was munching something on a Ritz cracker and sipping her drink.

"Well? Did you ask?"

"Don't be ridiculous," I said, laughing.

"Probably takes it up the bum, like always," said Nancy, chewing.

When I got home I called Jan and Paul Douglas, who were in town, and asked if they were free after the show Monday night. They were, and agreed to meet me at the Latin Quarter. I told them I might be a bit late since I was doing a TV interview right after the show, but that the table was in my name and I'd get there as soon as I could.

That Monday night, before and throughout *Almanac*, I was razzed by every single cast member. Murray, of course, topped them all. He told everyone that Jorgensen had said to him, "I've always been in love with you, even when I was a man." I found a huge Polish sausage under my dressing-room mirror with a note that read: "With all my love, Chris." Everybody got their licks in. It was great fun.

When I finally met up with Jan and Paul at ringside, they were giggling. Paul said: "You know who's here? Christine Jorgensen!" As I had hoped, they were surprised. I slid into the booth next to Jan and the "show" began. It was a chalk-talk type of thing with a board and pointer, and really almost embarrassing, like a sideshow exhibit that makes you feel more sorrow than shock.

At last the ordeal of her show was over, but my ordeal was just beginning. The star joined us at the booth and slipped in beside me as flashbulbs popped all over the place. When the hubbub died down and the four of us were left alone, she relaxed and was actually quite funny and charming. Jan and Paul were in seventh heaven, and put the poor thing completely at ease. After our chat, the four of us went to Lindy's and tore into some great corned beef. At last we said goodnight. Jan and Paul took a cab to their hotel and I dropped Christine off at the Astor, where she was staying. It really wasn't a bad evening after all. We had all had a fun, slightly strange time. That was the end of it. Well, not quite.

The next morning, the newspapers sported a shot of Jorgensen and me, with Jan and Paul cut out. The caption heralded our "date" at the Latin Quarter. They never mentioned that she was working there and that I was with friends in the audience. Her press agent had been working overtime. AP and UPI picked up the story and it was suddenly hot news across the country. Christine Jorgensen had "captured the heart of America's newest heartthrob." What a bunch of crud! Her press agent was pushing this "romance" like mad, figuring that to hook up their client with a clean-as-a-pickeral's-tooth young actor would make sizzling copy. Naturally she was right; almost daily there would be made-up items in syndicated columns. It was maddening, but there wasn't anything I could do about it. Then Christine began calling me on the phone (my number was listed, to my regret) and saying things like: "Did you see so-and-so's column today?" She was tickled pink.

I asked her to please stop her press rep from putting out all those untrue squibs. "Every knock is a boost," she said. I guess that's really the way she saw things. Well, I most certainly didn't. I told her as politely as I could to knock it off and please stop calling. I almost felt like hiring a hit man. She just laughed, saying she thought it was wonderful publicity and that I must be enjoying all the attention as much as she. Well, I wasn't, and I emphasized that, to no avail. The barrage went on for weeks. It took its toll on me and my future work. I had a contract with the Disney company to do a pilot for them about Davy Crockett, to be directed by Norman Foster, who I was crazy about. He'd asked me who I thought would make a good Crockett. Immediately I suggested Buddy Ebsen. I would play his sidekick, Young Russell. Norman loved the idea, and so did the powers at Disney. We'd shoot the pilot as soon as they lined up a national sponsor.

Finally they secured the American Dairy Association. But there was a hitch. All this publicity about me and Jorgensen had soured the milk folks on my participation in what was to be a family show. In the end, Disney bought off my contract. They paid me a lot of loot, but my opportunity to work with Foster again went down the drain. Many months later, they shot the pilot with a younger Crockett and changed the Russell character to Old Russell. Thank goodness, they switched Buddy to that part, so at least the Christine crud hadn't lost Ebsen a good role. (And it

Nick Kenny
═══Speaking:═══

ANN SOTHERN did an excellent job in "Lady in the Dark," the second of Max Liebman's color spectaculars on NBC-TV Saturday night, but it was Carleton Carpenter, as Russell Paxton, an effeminate photographer, who stole the show. He held it together with his drollery and was even more hilarious than was Danny Kaye in the original role when the show was produced on Broadway in 1941, with lyrics by Ira Gershwin and music by Kurt Weill. One of the highlights was a line that wasn't in the script. When the stage was darkened at the climax of a terrific scene, the voice of a stagehand came over crisp and clear asking: "Do I light this now?" It was by far the best of the tinted tele-attractions thus far.

New York *Daily Mirror*, Sept. 1954.

led to a whole new resurgence for the actor who would become bigger than ever in the '70s as the star of the TV series *Barnaby Jones*.

Something positive came out of this mess for me as well. By not having done *Davy Crockett*, I was free when Max Liebman, the producer of big-time TV musical specials, called me in to replace Jack Carter in the role of another Russell—this one named Russell Paxton—in the live, color telecast of *Lady in the Dark*. This was the first Broadway show I'd ever seen—and I'd be playing the role that Danny Kaye had originated.

Max had created the appelation "Television Spectacular," and this was the second in his monthly series. The first one, *Satins and Spurs*, an original musical with Betty Hutton, had not been well received, at least by the critics. *Lady*, however, was a smash. The wonderful Ann Sothern (the hottest lady on the tube pre-Lucy) starred in the Gertrude Lawrence role of Liza, a fashion-magazine editor who is undergoing psychoanalysis. I arrived late in rehearsals, when Max decided to make the casting change. I ended up learning the role in four days' time. I have no clue how I did it. Learning the tongue-twisting "Tschaikowsky (and Other Russians)" number alone would put me in shock today. I hardly slept and barely ate for those four days, and when we did the live show on Saturday night, September 24, 1954, in an old Brooklyn TV studio, I subsisted on tiny sips of Pepto Bismol off camera. Miss Sothern was so sweet to me; she'd pick me up each day in her limo on her way from the Plaza and give me a ride to Brooklyn. She was a joy to work with. (Later she'd fly me out to Hollywood to do her TV show a couple of times. Terrific gal.)

The rest of the cast included James Daly (dad of Tim and Tyne), Luella Gear, Paul McGrath and Shepperd Strudwick. Bambi Lynn and Rod Alexander danced as well as choreographed the musical numbers. Jeff Hayden, who later married Eva Marie Saint, did the staging. Max, like Murray, produced and directed. Our sponsor was Oldsmobile. Because a Mr. Curtis was president of General Motors at the time, the last name of Randy, a movie-star character, was changed from Curtis to Culver.

Lady in the Dark was a truly sensational experience for me. My first love, Jeanne Shelby, watched it at the 50th Street pad with Shel. He was now in basic training, having joined the army at Fort Dix, but he's gotten a weekend pass. Ann dropped me off after the show and I hurried in to get the Shelby review. She had a few reservations about my darling Ann, but who could ever replace Gertrude Lawrence? For her "Buzz"—as she called me—she had nothing but extreme praise. So, happily, did the papers, who reviewed Liebman's "spectaculars" as if they were Broadway shows. Had *Lady in the Dark* been one, we would have run several years on the raves. Fast forward: Just a couple of years ago, a kinescope of the show turned up. A print is at the Paley Center for Media on West 52nd Street in New York. A CD was released of the original soundtrack, taken off the kinescope, and the show itself is available on a DVD from VAI.

A few days after the show, Ann, the singers and I had cut an LP of the score for RCA Victor. I played the Daly and McGrath roles as well as Russell. I love that album, but there's something magical about the actual TV performance on the CD. I wish there'd been an original cast album for *John Murray Anderson's Almanac*. I guess with so many diverse writers and publishers and people with their own recording contracts, nobody could get the problems sorted out.

I left *Almanac* shortly before it closed the summer of '54. I was set to do a TV pilot in the Bahamas for a show called *Crunch and Des*, based on some *Saturday Evening Post* story. But when I found out I would have to sign a seven-year contract, I bowed out. (The pilot never got far off the ground.) So I missed the last two weeks of *Almanac*, whose cast now included Jonathan Winters. Working with him would have been a hoot.

Instead, I took the first honest-to-god vacation of my life. Shel and I packed up the car with a pup tent, a canned heat stove and fishing gear, and we drove across the country. We stopped to see his folks in Chicago for a couple of days, then headed west to California, stopping along the way to fish and hike and sightsee. Kerouac-ing cross-country with a best buddy was maybe the best, happiest, most relaxing recharge of the batteries in my life.

Stopping briefly in L.A., I got to visit Barbara Ruick and swim in the pool of the home she now shared with her mom, actress Lureen Tuttle. An update on Barb: Shortly before I'd left on my South American jaunt, she had quietly married a fellow actor at Metro. It ended even faster than the famous Ethel Merman-Ernest Borgnine coupling of 1964. She called me on the morning after the nuptuals and told me she should have asked the guy to audition first. A divorce quickly followed. Soon after, she met and fell for a terrific young man, John Williams, the composer who would write all those award-winning movie scores and even become the conductor of the Boston Pops.

I remained great friends with Barbara. She and John had a couple of kids, and I was like a part of the family. Darling Barb died from a cerebral hemorrhage in Reno, where she was on location for the shooting of Robert Altman's *California Split*. She was forty-three. Way too young. I still miss her. Johnny called me in New York to break the news. A couple of years later he phoned when he was in the city and asked me to join him for dinner and meet the new Mrs. In a sweet way he was silently asking for my approval. John is one of the most lovable men I've ever been lucky enough to know. What a dear guy. And talented? Don't even ask.

Before our vacation had ended, Shel and I spent a day or two with my old friends Bobby Tucker and Johnny Catlett Payne. (Catlett had given Barbara a nickname that stuck, "Barbass.") On the road again, we headed for San Francisco by way of the curvy, scary coast route. We were fortified by a gift bottle of Johnny's magic Old Fashioneds. They were very warming on the chilly nights in the tent.

Paul Douglas was starring in a local production of *The Caine Mutiny Court-Martial*, and naturally we went to see it. That big ol' ex-sportscaster was one fantastic Captain Queeg. Afterward we had dinner with Paul at some great restaurant, then finished off the night nineteen stories in the air at the Top of the Mark, with its breathtaking views of the city. Of course, we downed too many drinks. That was the cherry on top of the icing on that extraordinary cake of a trip.

Finally we headed back east. Home above the liquor store, I got an invitation from my friend and neighbor Alice Pearce, one of my co-stars in *Almanac*. Peeps, as I called her, and her husband John Rox, the song-writer who had written "It's a Big, Wide, Wonderful World," lived on Sutton Place; but Peeps talked me into joining her on the unemployment line. Back when I was getting out of the service, I asked a lot of guys what they were going to do. Almost without exception, they answered: "The Fifty-Two Twenty Club." The government was offering twenty bucks a week for a year to help veterans get back to normal life. I hated the idea; work was my reason for existence, and I had been fortunate to find it again so quickly.

Peeps had replaced Kay Medford in *Almanac* when Kay left to star in a play called *Lullaby*. Now Peeps, with whom I'd become great buddies, had convinced me to sign up for unemployment, making it sound like a great game. Every week she'd pick me up in a taxi and we'd set off for the office on East 42nd Street. We'd stand on line, sign up, and then go have a lavish lunch, giggling like idiots. Her nickname for me was "Lucky," and that's how I felt having her, John and their dog Roxy as friends.

While we were doing *Almanac*, we would decide with great delib-eration what sort of drink we'd share after the curtain came down. We'd always have dinner together between shows on matinee days, most often at Jim Downey's on Eighth Avenue. I think the lightweight special, a de-licious steak dinner, cost $1.75 or $2.25, something ridiculous like that. We'd chow down quickly and head back to the theater for a nap.

She, John and Roxy were frequent guests at my tiny pad. Shel and I were both nuts about rumaki, the Polynesian-style hors d'oeuvre made out of water chestnuts and chicken liver and wrapped in bacon. We also loved Navy Grogs, the rum-based drink they used to serve at the Don the Beachcomber restaurants. One night when the five of us had gathered after the show, Shel had surprised us by making us some rumaki. They really were tasty, and he'd made a carload of them. We'd planned ahead to try to duplicate the recipe for Grogs. The rum drinks might not have rivalled the Beachcomber originals, but they more than did the job. We were all a bit awash, and hardly noticed Roxy attacking the rumaki in the kitchen, toothpicks and all. The poor thing got as sick as, well, a dog, all over the place. But he survived, and felt much better in the morning, I'm certain, than the four of us.

My fun trips with Peeps to 42nd Street, followed by our tipsy lunches, lasted less than a month. The pull of the old New England work ethic was too strong, so I went off the dole and back to more TV. I hadn't immediately told MCA that I was home from my on-the-road adventure, but one call and I was back to steady bookings again. I started rehearsals for another big color special, *The Show-Off*, based on the famous 1924 comedy play by George Kelly. The TV version starred Jackie Gleason, who practically owned CBS-TV at that point due to the huge success of *The Jackie Gleason Show*. The wonderful Thelma Ritter played the mom; Alice Ghostley and I played her son and daughter.

But after the first read-through, we never saw Mr. Gleason again until the day we went on the air. He had hired a very good actor whose name I can't remember to rehearse for two weeks in his stead. It was thrilling to watch Ms. Ritter grow into that role and polish it into something really splendid. We lunched together daily at a place on 59th, across from CBS. We yacked, laughed and wondered why on earth Marty Manulis, the producer, would allow Gleason such leeway. But we both really knew. He was the breadwinner for the entire network then, and would remain so for a long time to come.

We did the final rehearsal at a theater on the west side. Gleason showed up only a bit late, with beer can in hand, to be shown the blocking. He strutted through the runthrough like an emperor in hand-tailored clothes. We broke for a bite—who could eat?—while the audience was ushered in. These color specials were events, with huge live audiences. The one for *The Show-Off* included Peeps, John Rox, and, on a pass from his army duties at Fort Dix, Shel.

The show began. Gleason's first entrance was greeted, naturally, by tremendous applause. Then he proceeded to bluster and bully his way through the entire play. Poor Thelma. That supreme performance she'd crafted so professionally was stepped on and pushed aside by the Great One, as Gleason was called (though never by me). It was heartbreaking to watch the nuances of Ritter's performance, the great comic timing, trashed by the bulldozing star. I watched off-camera as she seemed to wither, physically giving in and giving up on the great character she'd found in rehearsal. What a bloody waste, and what an insult to such a talented lady.

After the show, the Roxes, the G.I. and I went to Sardi's for some food. I was still so upset I had to force myself to eat something, but even my favorite cannelloni didn't help my disposition. I had one drink, but it that was useless. I wasn't very good company. The Roxes dropped Shel and me off from the cab, and I hit the bed. My stomach was churning and sleep was nowhere in sight. After tossing in bed for an hour or more, I thought I might feel better if I tossed my cookies in the john. Once I'd started, I couldn't stop. There was blood all over the bowl. I was scared, and yelled for Shel. I couldn't get up from the bathroom floor. Thank God he was there that night. Somehow he got me somewhat dressed and half-carried me out onto the early-morning street. It was freezing, something like eight below zero. Shel hailed a cab, stuffed me in, and got me to the emergency room of the Midtown Hospital only two blocks away.

Chapter 12

I was only semiconscious when I was hustled into an operating room and told to count backwards. I knew I was dying, but I started counting down from a hundred. Two and a half days later, I opened my eyes and saw my mother and my Aunt Nancy standing there by my bed. All sorts of paraphernalia were hanging over and out of me. Shel had called Vermont before heading back to Fort Dix. I was really surprised I was still among the quick, since I'd been certain I was headed for the alternative.

Later I was told I'd had an emergency ileostomy and had surrendered a few miles of large intestine over a period of five and a half hours on the table. I actually was on the way to offing the mortal coil. My old road buddy had saved my life.

A few days later, while still in the hospital, I learned he'd been shipped to Europe. Timing, as people often say, is everything. I remember thinking, after my first sip of hot tea, that I was going to live, and I would never say or do an unkind thing ever again. I would be a saint, a model of the perfect person. Everyone was so nice to me, how could I not be? Even dear Ann Sothern had sent two dozen American Beauties to the Midtown. Apparently my near-demise had hit the wire.

I was there for weeks and began to get itchy to go back to my home, where Dar and Nancy were staying. My vow of super-goodness hung with me—well, at least for a few months.

My mother returned home during my convalescence, as did Aunt Nan. Shortly after they were gone I received a phone call that surprised the hell out of me. It was from Cos. He had just gotten himself hitched. He told me he'd been married in a small church a couple of blocks from me in New York because, he said, "I wanted to be as close to you as possible." How he knew my address, I'll never know. And what was that "close" part about? Yet another Cos conundrum. Of course, it stirred up all sorts of remembrances and unresolved longings and regrets.

By the time I rejoined the apple-pie-order club with my new battle scar stretching the full length of a scrawny stomach alongside the smaller appendectomy award, I was aching to get back into the acting harness. Max Liebman phoned and asked me to come to his office. He was doing a TV adaptation of the college musical *Best Foot Forward*, the 1941 Broadway hit that MGM had brought to the screen with Lucille Ball and June Allyson. He shoved a script across his desk and said, "Pick out any role you want and it's yours." I took it back to 50th and read it straight through.

My dumbness genes kicked in. I decided I was finished with saddle shoes forever. That was a kid trademark; I longed to move on to older roles. I returned the script to Liebman and explained why I was turning it down. He smiled, shrugged and promised he'd find me a more mature part, while assuring me: "I want you back."

He was good to his word. His very next specacular was to be the Jerome Kern-Otto Harbach 1931 oldie *The Cat and the Fiddle*. It had a swell role for me. But in the week before rehearsals were to start, we learned that someone had neglected to secure the rights. No problem for Max. He called together his great gang of staff writers, including Neil Simon and Carl Reiner, and within that week they had fashioned a show to fit the sets that were already being built. Now the show was called *Paris in the Springtime*, and we started on schedule. Out went "She Didn't Say Yes" and "The Night Was Made for Love," and in came a pick-up score from a variety of other shows.

The cast was the same; we were just playing different roles. Our group was headed by Dan Dailey and also included Helen Gallagher, Jack Whiting (who'd costarred with her in *Hazel Flagg*, singing "Ev'ry Street's a Boulevard in Old New York"), Gale Sherwood (Nelson Eddy's new partner in club engagements), Patachou (a hot number from France), and the saddle-shoeless me singing numbers in French. It was great fun.

The singing and dancing kids rehearsed on the floor above us. They were pretty much a Liebman stock company, so I knew most of them. When they came down for the final runthrough, one of the guys wore a left-shoulder-to-right-waist sash. On it were bold letters that surely summed up the feelings of all those kids who had started working on their numbers a week before the rest of us, only to have everything change when *The Cat and the Fiddle* became *Paris in the Springtime*. The sash proclaimed: HELP STAMP OUT TV! They worked their talented butts off.

What fun it was to dance with Dan and Helen, both old friends. I'd first met Dan during *Almanac*. He was a longtime buddy of John Nonnenbacher ("Dr. Burton" to Murray), the personal manager of such acts as Singer's Midgets, the dance team of Tommy Wonder and Maggie Banks, and José Greco and his troop of Spanish dancers. Dan, Junie Lockhart, Jack and I used to hang. Dan would constantly chastise me for always wearing casual clothes, save for the rare special occasions. He was right, of course; I was no clotheshorse, and happily gagged about how I was an absolute "slave to fashion." It never failed to get a giggle, except from the always well-dressed and properly groomed Dailey. Over and over he'd tell me that I should "dress like a star," adding, "You owe it to people." I'd listen and promise to do better, but I'd never really get around to doing it—maybe because I never thought of myself that way, even when my name was above and bigger than the title of the show.

That was very nearly the case in December 1955, when I was hauled off to Hollywood by a hectic call to replace someone on a live TV show. The series was the *General Electric Theater*; the play, *Feathertop*, based on a Nathaniel Hawthorne story. The actor I replaced: Ray Bolger. I couldn't believe it either. I must have inherited his billing as well. The ads showed a tiny picture of the show's host, Ronald Reagan, and in even smaller print, the words "Ronald Reagan Presents." The picture of me was huge, accompanied by the headline, "Carleton Carpenter Starring as Feathertop." In more tiny letters underneath, the ad said: "With Natalie Wood."

Rehearsals were long and a bit uneasy. Natalie, poor darling, was still grieving after the terrible crash that had killed James Dean only a couple of months before. It was a sad time. Everyone had fallen for the young actor in *East of Eden* and *Rebel Without a Cause*. As of the time he died, *Giant* hadn't been released yet. But Nat had felt very close to Dean; I'm sure she'd had a big crush on him. Even in mourning, however, this talented lady had been a professional since her childhood, and she dug in and gave a terrific live performance. Live TV was new and nervous-making for her, so she deserves even extra credit for the work she turned in.

Also in the cast were the character actress Irene Tedrow, who had starred on radio in *Meet Corliss Archer* (maybe because she was used to reading off a script, she had a tad of trouble with her lines), the comic dwarf Billy Barty and a handsome young actor named John Carlyle. A few years later he turned out to be a neighbor of mine and we became fast friends. I saw him in a local revival of *The Crucible* and thought him the best John Proctor I'd ever seen.

During the rehearsals I stayed with Stewart Stern, who had written *Rebel Without a Cause*, so he was in mourning, too. He lived fairly close to CBS-TV, where we were working. I got to walk to and from my job. No one seems to walk in L.A. Everybody drives.

Not long after *Feathertop*, I made my debut on the summer-stock circuit. I'd be playing the title role—originated by Ray Bolger—in *Where's Charley?* Those three- to four-month tours of great Equity theaters don't exist anymore. Many of the theaters closed, others became non-union; just a tiny handful remain today. What a shame. It was such a good breeding ground for kids starting out. I had missed that opportunity; there just wasn't time amidst my constant Broadway and Hollywood work.

Now I had the time and opportunity and I grabbed it. We rehearsed in the city, and I managed to get the wonderful choreographer Donald Saddler to work out the dances and most of the staging for me. He did a super job on "Once in Love with Amy" and the other numbers. The talented twosome at the twin pianos was Jay Thompson and Gordon Connell. I can't remember where we opened or where we went from week to week, but here's an incomplete list of the theaters we played: Lakewood, Ogunquit, Kennebunkport and Camden Mills (Maine); Dennis, Somerset and Falmouth (Massachusetts); Ivoryton-Essex (Connecticut); Glen Cove, Easthampton and Corning (New York); Cincinnati (Ohio); Denver (Colorado); and some theater in Canada just above the border, where I first tasted Old Vienna beer. Ahhh! Maybe in another book (or life) I'll go into the wonders of my summer tours with shows like *King of Hearts*, *Oh Men! Oh Women!*, *Light Up the Sky*, *The Rainmaker*, *The Star-Spangled Girl* and others.

After *Where's Charley?* I did something I'd never done before. I didn't have a press agent, so I took an ad for myself on the back page of *Variety*. I did it partly because the show had gone so well, but mostly to let people know I was alive and working again. It was expensive, but paid off immediately with a call from William Castle, a film director and producer from California. Castle was known for his B-movies and thrillers; eventually he hit it big by producing *Rosemary's Baby*. Castle was intrigued by the picture I'd used in the ad. It was a head shot of me as the aunt from Brazil, a character in *Where's Charley?* There I was with bonnet, fan and turd-curls. It tickled Castle. He thought that since I'd had the guts enough to run that photo I wouldn't mind playing someone with a huge nose on his TV show, *Men of Annapolis*. The character was a naval cadet called Tecumsah, since he resembled that Indian's statue on the campus of the Naval Academy.

In Somerset, Massachusetts with Jean Kerr and Eleanor Brooke's *King of Hearts*, August 1955.

On the road in *The Rainmaker*, 1955. I wish I could remember the actress.

We came to terms on the phone, and I flew to Annapolis, Maryland to meet Castle and the cast for location shooting. We returned to Hollywood to finish at a studio there. Castle and I had a great time together. A few years later he became one of the kings of the horror flicks with films like *House on Haunted Hill, The Tingler, and Strait-Jacket*, which starred Joan Crawford. His movies had lots of scary gimmicks, designed, I figured, to attract all the people who'd been staying home due to the incredible lure of television.

Every studio was trying something; Cinerama, VistaVision, Cinema-Scope, Stereophonic Sound. Michael Todd Jr. even came up with a thing called Smell-O-Vision for a film called *Scent of Mystery*. Theaters had to be specially equipped with pipes running along the floor beneath the seats. When an actor on screen was approaching a flower shop, for instance, you'd hear a great "whoosh" from under your seat; by the time the actor arrived at the spot, the odor would seep up at you. The whole venture bombed. Stunk would be a better verb—even with Elizabeth Taylor making an unbilled cameo. It really was hilarious; when an actor pulled out a lighter to ignite a cigar the entire audience made a loud vocal "whoosh" before the pipe could do it, and everyone would howl with laughter. I can't remember a single actor in the film or even a hint of the plot, if there was one. You had to be there; and as it turned out, you had to be quick. That was a fast fader.

Castle's creepy creations were more successful, because he made no pretense of art; his films were just pure campy fun. During the *Annapolis* shoot I stayed at the Hollywood Roosevelt, and there I saw Michael Dreyfus, with whom I'd done my first two Broadway plays. We reunited for a long chat-filled afternoon by the pool. It was the last I saw of him; Michael died not long after. He was only thirty-two. I believe it was cancer that took him. I called his folks, with whom I had once lived in Bay Ridge, but the old number had been reassigned. They'd moved years before. I had no chance to share my grief with them and thank them again for being to nice to me when I was young and green. I'll always remember them, along with snaggle-toothed Mike.

Back in New York, I started working on *The Two-Revue, a Most Intimate Evening of Cabaret*, in which my costar was Eva Gabor. The idea had come from a Brit named Donnie Neville-Willing, a character to whom Murray had introduced me to during the early weeks of *Almanac*. He booked acts for the Cafe de Paris in London. (Murray called him Major Twit.) Prodded by Donnie, I wrote all the sketches and numbers. There would be a minimal set: simply a four-fold screen behind which Ms. Ga-

Donning a false nose, I played naval cadet Tecumseh in William Castle's 1956
TV series *Men of Annapolis*.

bor would change her fancy wardrobe in between skits, and a couple of elaborately decorated stools for duets and solos. I figured it would be provocatively sexy and something new. Best of all, we were assured a gig at that posh club in London.

Eva was a bit worried about her singing, and began studying with Herbert Green, a conductor and super vocal coach. An appointment was finally made for me to appear at Green's studio to hear the lady warble.

With Bert Lahr, Douglas Byng, Angela Lansbury, and Vera Pearce in *Hotel Paradiso*.
Photo by Nate Fine.

She was terrified, and never looked at me the entire time I was there; instead she turned her back and sang facing the farthest corner from us. Actually she sang quite well, and her accent was charming. I was certain we had a smash in the making. But after several weeks of intense rehearsal, Eva received an offer from MGM to appear in a film called *The Last Time I Saw Paris*. And that was the last time I saw her.

Once more, things worked out for the best. I won a terrific role on Broadway in *Hotel Paradiso*, an English translation (by Peter Glenville) of a French farce from 1894. The show—about a group of upper-crust French people running amok in a cheap Paris hotel—had been a huge hit in London with Alec Guinness. Now, in New York, we had the cream of creative comedians, Mr. Bert Lahr. Directed by Glenville, it turned out to be the most wonderful piece of work I'd ever been involved with. I still keep St. Peter G. on a pedestal at least a mile high. My favorite director. My favorite Broadway play.

What a cast Glenville had assembled! Making her Broadway debut was Angela Lansbury, who was already a movie star. She was only eight months older than I, and for me it was love at first sight. Angela was a hoot as the neighbor with whom Lahr tries to have a tryst. On her first entrance she looked like a luscious pink powder puff. She played my aunt. Her husband was portrayed out of town (more on that later) by dear Arthur Treacher, whose nickname was Pip. Sondra Lee played a maid who was determined to get my bespectabled face out of a book and make me submit to her adorable advances. Ronnie Radd, another import and a great drinking buddy, portrayed the hotel manager. Then there were Lu-

Hotel Paradiso, 1957

cille Benson, George Tyne, Horace Cooper, and the young James Coco, who was also appearing on Broadway for the first time.

The part of Lahr's wife was acted by the same boomingly hysterical gal who had played it in London, Vera Pearce. Glenville also brought over Douglas Byng to play a barrister who stammers whenever it begins to rain. Nora Stapleton was the assistant stage manager.

She handed me a letter of welcome from Kenneth Williams, the gent who'd played my role across the pond. We were mutual fans; he'd seen some flicks of mine and I was nuts about the *Carry On* films, a series of nutty English farces in which he had costarred. I wrote him back immediately, thanking him for his note. Thus began a correspondence that lasted for over twenty years. We'd exchange albums and books and keep each other up to date. We wrote at least a couple of times a year. That was a lot for this non-letter scribbler. I was in London very briefly after *Hotel Paradiso* had closed, but couldn't locate him. We didn't meet until years later when I was in town again to do *Hello, Dolly!*

Saint Peter G. transformed me completely into my naïve, studious character Maxime: the way I walked, talked, and looked. I wore a blond wig with sausage-curl bangs, and a pince-nez. What great fun to lose myself in this other peculiar person. Glenville even designed a suit for the role with a jacket whose tails stuck stick out in the back, like a duck. I practiced my new walk every spare moment.

He had a wonderful way with the cast during rehearsals. He did nothing to draw attention to himself, and hardly rose his voice at all. He never yelled at a stage manager—and we had four, Eddie Baylies, Fred Baker, Neil Laurence, and William Windom—about why something wasn't in place. Nothing, he felt, should distract the company from forging ahead. He knew exactly what he wanted and never wasted a moment of time, keeping all the diverse personalities unified. (I learned how to direct by watching him, and would put it to good and productive use later on.)

This production was one of the first to have multiple sets of producers, a common practice today, when so many shows rely on corporate cash. This would turn into a problem later on.

We opened at the National Theatre in Washington after a full month of rehearsing on the set. This was crucial to our mastering of all the comings and goings through doors and windows, typical of farces. But it was also extremely expensive, and the backers' investments were diminishing rapidly. We hadn't yet opened before most of the cash was gone.

The reviews were mixed to good, but not great, and frowns began to appear on "angel" brows. We kept rehearsing even after the opening, which ran the cost up even more. Two weeks before we headed to Broadway, the moneymen began searching for theater parties: those blocks of tickets, sold at group rates, that yielded less profit but might ensure enough of a run—if the reviews in New York were better—to give us extended time to turn an eventual profit. The trouble was, we were set to open at the Henry Miller Theatre on 43rd, a sweet house but, even with two balconies, one of the smallest on Broadway. With those two weeks left in Washington, it was decided that Pip Treacher's energy was too low, and that he should be replaced.

Pip and I were staying at the same hotel, the Willard, and we had late supper together after the show nearly every night. He was in a real state of shock, as was I, when he told me he'd been given notice. John "Ted" Emery appeared from New York and prepared to take over the role of my uncle. Pip dug into those last two weeks like an actor possessed. He played the royal hell out of that part with speed and professional comedic polish. He'd show 'em, by God. And he did. Wounded pride, I guess, drove him to give sixteen fantastic performances; it was an absolute joy to watch the droppage of jaws from the sudden passionate pacing he produced. I was saddened, but oh, so proud of my new friend when his contract concluded.

Meanwhile, Ted Emery, a talented look-and-sound-alike of John Barrymore, had tried to learn his role too quickly, and he was losing his voice. When we opened in New York on April 11, 1957, he had barely a raspy whisper; but somehow he managed to make it seem like part of the character rather than a personal affiction.

The opening was an out-and-out triumph from the moment the four-piece brass group began the curtain raiser, "It's Delightful to Be Married" (remember Luise Rainer singing it in *The Great Ziegfeld*?) right up to the final curtain call, after many standing ovations. The following morning, *Hotel Paradiso* was proclaimed a raging hit in every paper (there were eleven, I think, at the time). The company was ecstatic, and we all settled in for a nice run.

We were a socializing bunch. I remember taking Angela to the Winter Garden to see *Ziegfeld Follies of 1957* starring Beatrice Lillie and my old friends Billy De Wolfe and Harold Lang. I fell into the habit of having an aftershow nip with Vera Pearce and Ronnie Radd at the Woodstock Hotel bar across the street from the theater. To my surprise and horror,

Vera drank scotch and ginger ale. Is that a Brit thing? Ronnie and I usually had a brew. Vera would get weepy about the dog she loved so much and had had to leave in London. After a few short weeks she left the show and the country to be with her pet.

We were SRO from opening night on and the audiences were terrific. After the final certain call at each performance I'd race up the three flights to my dressing room to change. With this show, because of the delicate wig I was wearing, it took me longer to make my usual speedy switch to street clothes.

One evening I had just gotten the wig off when there was a knock on my door. I yelled, "COME IN!" as I reached for the wigblock. When I looked up I saw Cary Grant, tanned and tuxedoed and smiling, standing in my doorway. I stood up, gaping and beaming, with my wig still in my left hand. All I could think was, he'd climbed three flights! He was saying how much he'd enjoyed the show and my performance. I tried to take a step toward him but my feet wouldn't move. I muttered, "Thank you, *thank* ... you climbed three flights!" as I gestured toward the door with my left hand, my wig dangling from it. He said he would like to buy me a drink. Grinning from ear to ear, I said, "Oh, that would be absolutely wonderful! That would be terrific—something I could really use." (I caught a glimpse of my sneakers atop my baggy cords.) "But ... ahhh, you see, I sorta have a date, and maybe we could ..." He laughed and said, "A date! I see!" as he stepped outside, closing the door. He was gone.

I stood there staring at the door. When I could finally move, I managed to take one step back. I secured the wig to its block and sat down. I looked at the mirror. The guy I saw said, "*Asshole!* What the hell did I just do? I did have a date, but ...

"THAT WAS CARY GRANT, FOR GOD'S SAKE!"

When dear Vera left the show, the producers moved my billing to above the title—under Mr. Lahr, of course, but joining Angela, Ted and Dougie. That was the first and, to date, the only time I ever reached that exalted spot on a Broadway marquee. It was a surprise to me, and naturally the old camera was toted over to snap it.

Speaking of snapshots: When the Third Avenue El, which ran from south to north, was being torn down, I went to take a shot of it as it approached 50th. About to snap it from the southeast corner, I saw the marquee of the Beverly Theatre, an inexpensive second-run house. There on the marquee, big as life, was *Lost Boundaries* topping a double bill. I crossed Third and got a picture of the disappearing El and the Beverly marquee in one shot. Now if I can only find the darn thing. It's probably faded to faint sepia by now.

Every night and matinee was a joy—though if I had my druthers, I'd want six matinees and two evening performances. My old buddy Paul Douglas was in *Hole in the Head* at the time, but since our schedules were the same I never got to see him. Kay Medford was in it too, along with David Burns, with whom I'd work later. It was Paul's first time on Broadway since *Born Yesterday*, where he'd met his wife Jan Sterling. His Hollywood career began after that.

We were still selling out at the Henry Miller, but because of the discount-ticket theater parties we were barely making our weekly nut. The summer hit, and it hit us hard. Everyone thought we'd be running forever, and since there were no tickets available for the weeks after opening, people decided to wait until the fall to see the hottest new show in town. They departed for vacations, summer homes, Europe, and suddenly the theater parties had run their course. We had no reserve to fall back on. First to go was the brass quartet. Boy, how we all missed that oom-pah-pah to kick off the show. Then everyone in the cast except those receiving Equity minimum took big cuts in salaries. One set of the three producing firms was in favor of closing. They had been in on a huge hit; they'd had the champagne parties and wallowed in the glowing notices. Then, I guess, they thought, to hell with it; we've had our fun. Time for a vacation.

One group, Bowden, Barr and Bullock, wasn't that old and wealthy. They were young, tenacious and determined to keep this glory going. They did their best. So did the entire cast. But we couldn't keep that awesome ark afloat. We folded on July 13 after only 109 performances. What a sad time. With most shows, even hits, when the final curtain drops you can say, "Well, it was a ball, but on to the next." It wasn't that easy with *Hotel Paradiso*. That was a special gem. What a shame that when angels are sought and budgets are planned for new shows there aren't at least four extra weeks figured into the original investment to give the piece a bit of time to find an audience and start breaking even. This, of course, applies to years ago, when it cost so much less to put on a new show. I know. I dream on. But, believe me, I was heartsick about all the people who wanted to see *Hotel Paradiso* and didn't get a chance. Months after the show closed, I'd run into people who'd tell me they couldn't wait to see it. Jaws would drop in disbelief when I told them the show was long-shuttered and stowed away in Cain's Warehouse, where old sets were shipped.

Maybe to relieve part of the pain, I booked a passage on the old Île-de-France and headed for Europe with my big, brown, sticker-covered trunk. Yes, folks really used steamer trunks then. Since I'd made a last-minute decision to take the trip, it cost a bundle—eight hundred bucks one way, I think—for the single stateroom on the French liner. But boy, was it worth it: small but sensational, and posh as all get out. The moment I boarded the ship it was as if I'd slipped back a time zone or two, maybe to the mid-Roaring Twenties. I got into the old tuxedo every evening for the first sitting at dinner, and donned white flannels with a navy blazer during the day. What wonderful costume changes for this new "play." I loved the swanky aura. I even started growing a slim mustache. I felt it was proper for the role I'd cast myself in. My cabin was situated between those of two celebs. On one side was a film favorite of mine, Ella Raines. I had loved her in an old film noir called *Impact* with Brian Donlevy and Helen Walker. Ms. Raines was mostly in black-and-white jobs that would probably now be considered "B" pictures. In this particular film, Donlevy, on the run after having barely escaped being killed in a scheme by his wife's hired hand, walks miles, then comes to a tiny service station and garage. He spots a young mechanic in white coveralls and cap, bent under the hood of a car.

"Son," says Brian, "can I give you a hand?" The mechanic rises up and it's our Ella, properly placed smudge on cheek. Big Brian apologizes, rolls up his sleeves and goes to work while Ella watches in awe. Finally she says: "Tools just seem to come to life in your hands." A historic line, to me. (By now you know my off-crayoned mind.)

On the other side of my cabin was the wonderful writer of *Gentlemen Prefer Blondes*, Anita Loos. That really settled me smack in the mid-1920s. For the entire trip, however, I never spotted either lady. Did they spend all their time in their respective cabins? Were meals delivered by stewards? Was Anita writing another bestseller? Was Ella scared of her adoring public? I couldn't figure it out, and finally settled on an axiom: "They'll let Anita Loos when Ella Raines." I forgot about neighbor spottage for the rest of the trip.

Also on board was Raoul Pène Du Bois, the stage designer. Dubois and I palled around the ship together and became good friends. We'd known each other professionally when he worked on *Three to Make Ready* and *John Murray Anderson's Almanac*, but had never spent much time together socially. He had a quirky sense of humor, I discovered, and was surprising fun to hang with. He also had an automobile on board—an MG convertible, I think. He said I could share a ride with him from Le

Havre to Paris when we docked. And he introduced me to Pernod with water. He called it grapefruit juice. That's exactly what it looked like. It tasted like licorice, and it became my voyage drink of choice.

I hadn't had a cigarette in nearly a year. Whenever someone offered me one, I said no, just not smoking for now. I knew I'd start again sometime. What better time and place than in my tux at one of the intimate bars on the Île-de-France, a Pernod in my hand and my mustache growing daily more visible on my upper lip as I sailed to Gay Paree? All I needed was a beret. That would come later.

Finally I smoked a Gauloise from a dark blue packet. It was strong. It tasted like stable sweepings. After the first drag or two I felt high as a kite. (The Pernod had helped, I'm sure.) I've never tried cocaine, but I imagine the high must be something like that. After a while I got used to smoking again. But that first drag after all that time: Wow.

When we docked at Le Havre, Du Bois's MG was unloaded from the hold of the ship and immediately double-loaded and secured with ropes, along with his very large trunk and my not-terribly-small brown, theater-labeled job. Off we went, the low-slung car lower than ever. We stopped for the night in the heavily war-damaged *ville*, Rouen, on the Seine. It was still strangely beautiful even though much of its centuries-old Gothic architecture, like the Cathedral of Notre Dame, with its two different towers, and the Palace of Justice, had been hit hard.

Du Bois disappeared to his room after dinner, and I set off to explore a bit of Gustave Flaubert's hometown. I found several wee bars, family-run, most with only three or four stools. At each bar, the song hit of the day was sung and played over and over again—some wonderful tune, sung by the wondrous Little Sparrow, Édith Piaf. By the time I'd returned to my hotel I couldn't stop singing it. Well, I was mostly humming, but I'd learned a few of the words and the title, "La goualante du pauvre Jean." The music was by Marguerite Monnot (who later composed the score for *Irma La Douce*), and I decided to write English lyrics to it as soon as I got back to the U.S. Later in Paris I found a handkerchief printed with some of the music and lyrics by René Rouzaud, as well as a drawing of a young guy showing his girl that his pockets are empty while a sad man with a big sign passes by. The sign reads: SANS AMOUR ON N'EST RIEN DU TOUT! (Without love, we are nothing at all.) Finding the hankie, I figured, was a sign for me to get to the piano on 50th Street and get to work.

We reached the French capital. Du Bois, I believe, was staying with relatives, so I unloaded the big brown trunk and gave him many, many thanks for the great ride from port to Paris. Then I set off to find a room. After lugging the trunk around for hours, I finally latched onto a smallish place my meager budget could afford and moved in. I opened the trunk up, gave everything a bit of a shake, and hangered a couple of things. I had arrived at almost the exact same time as the American casts of two shows that would be opening at La Comedie-Française in a Salute to France celebration. *The Skin of Our Teeth* would star Helen Hayes, George Abbott and Mary Martin. Judith Anderson was playing Medea. I found myself grinning as I recalled a bit from *Almanac*. That show had introduced Hermione Gingold to the U.S., and in her first entrance she was greeted by a gang of reporters, all of whom asked questions at the same time. She waved them into silence and said, "One at a time, *please*," with a bit of a lisp through the open space in her front teeth. A reporter said, "Tell me, Miss Rheingold—" (Rheingold Beer held an annual contest that named a young woman Miss Rheingold.)

"GINGold!" said Hermione.

"Sorry. Could you tell us your impression of New York?"

"Well, first"—there went that lisp again—the skyline, then the harbour. Then, of course, that enormous statue"—with multiple lisps—"of Judith Anderson."

The showcard that advertised the Salute to France used the Statue of Liberty as background. Well, you get the picture.

When I went to the theater to purchase tickets, I discovered that Stanley Gilkey was one of the producers, and was staying at the Crillon. I called and we made a date for dinner that evening in the hotel's dining room. When I arrived, bedecked with a newly purchased beret and trimmed mustache, Patron didn't recognize Mascarp—until I pulled up the chair opposite him and sat down, saying "Bon soir, Stash." That was my nickname for him. He was quick: "Same to you, new 'stash." He laughed as he reached over to touch the thin thing on my upper lip. His face was ruddy, as usual. He'd had a few nips before my arrival.

Stanley was a fellow New Englander, and we always enjoyed each other's company. During my first week in the City of Lights I followed a daily routine. In the a.m., I would check into the Louvre as soon as it opened. I'd say hello to the enigmatic Mona and wander till lunch time; usually I spent the last half-hour seated before "The Rape of the Sabine Women." Every morning I discovered new wonders in that *musée*, but somehow I was always drawn back for another long study of the Sabines, who were fictionally abducted by the womanless followers of Romulus.

From there I'd stop by American Express, whose address I'd used for forwarding mail. I would cash a couple of Amex checks for francs and yack with a teller in my (I hoped) improving local lingo. One day there was a letter from my old buddy, Private Shel. He was now stationed in France, somewhere near Angoulême. Since his letter had been forwarded from 255 East 50th, he had no idea I was in Paris. I decided to track him down and surprise the hell out of him. After asking around, I found that the city was the capital of the southwestern French department (governing region) of Charente, home to many brandy distilleries.

I bought a small backpack, packed lightly and boarded a train. Compared to the choo-choos back home, this was like flying. The speed was so intense, I wondered how we stayed on the tracks. Everything whizzed by too quickly for me to take much in. We arrived in Angoulême in short order.

Anxious to see more of the countryside, and at a more leisurely pace, I rented a bicycle and peddled out of the city. How wonderfully different the rural folks were from the Parisians, who upon hearing my half-assed high-school French would immediately switch to their broken English. I'd plow ahead stubbornly with my very broken French. (The city swells thought I was Canadian, so they were slightly patient. I had a feeling they didn't care much for Yanks.) Everyone seemed thrilled I was trying to learn their language, and they were very helpful, and probably very amused as well. I'm sure I made many bloopers. When I couldn't find the exact word, I would use the English word with a theatrically heavy French accent, and somehow I was understood. Then I'd be told the proper French word and add one more to my slowly growing vocabulary.

The second day of peddling around, exploring and tasting bits of this new region, I discovered that there was an army camp not terribly far away, just a good, long bike ride. I asked everyone I passed if I were headed in the right direction. Eventually on one late afternoon I found myself facing a guard at the entrance of the camp. I hoped it was the right one. I honestly didn't know.

When I asked the guard if a Private Janecek was stationed here, he looked puzzled. Was he one of the Yugoslav soldiers? No, I said, he's one of the American chaps. (Here I felt a bit more British than Canadian.) I waited on some steps in front of an office where he checked out the answer. This was peacetime, and security was practically nonexistent. The guard never came back out, so I sat there until I saw Shel lumbering toward me. He didn't recognize me with the beret on my head and the mustache on my lip until we were almost nose-to-nose. "Hi," I said, casual as could be.

"*What the hell are you doing here?* How in God's name did you find me? What are you doing in France?" And on and on. I'd really thrown him for a loss. It was worth the whole trip.

He got a three- or four-day pass, and we headed back to Angoulême, taking turns peddling and cross-barring it. Then on we went to Paris, where he wanted to show me the sights. I told him I'd seen a few already, but after only a couple of months in France he felt like an old pro of a tour guide. It was great to get together again. The last time I'd seen him was the day when he'd literally saved my life. He babbled on. I babbled on. And we had a high old time in Paris.

Too high, when he insisted I see the city from the top of the Eiffel Tower. The elevator stops three times on its way up. At the second stop I dragged him out and said this was high enough. My knees were already buckling. He had his ever-present camera with him, and made me back up to the rail so he could take a snap. I flashed a phony smile as the bulb went off. That wasn't the end. He asked someone to take a shot of the two of us and joined me at the rail. Shel slung an arm around my shoulder, Cos-like, and another flash bulb went off. (I have no idea where that pic is.) I told him I'd need a blindfold to get me down on the elevator. I really wished I'd had one. He knew I had acrophobia, and it tickled him. Years ago, on our return cross-country trek, he had tricked me into getting on a ferris wheel in Chicago. That was the last time I was ever on one. The more frightened I became, the bigger his delight.

Some buddies can be real s.o.b.'s. But good friends are a rare breed, so you put up with their quirks. And from time to time you get your own licks in.

Eiffel aside, it was a great couple of days. We ate too much, and God knows we drank too much, but those Left Bank sidewalk cafés were like magnets. There's never enough time, but we sure crammed a helluva lot into those days together.

After he had returned to camp I stayed on a few more days, seeing more shows, including *Medea* and *The Skin of Our Teeth*, and feasting with Gilkey one more time. Then I flew to London, my big, brown travelling companion stowed in the belly of the plane.

Ah, London town. Near Hyde Park I found a smallish hotel whose name has slipped way from me—a very proper place. The room was nice, but the chow in the downstairs dining room was bland. Aside from breakfasts, I had maybe three meals there in the entire London jaunt.

But ah, the theaters! Unlike New York, London had matinees almost daily at different theaters, so with careful planning you could take in three shows a day: at two, at five, and at eight-thirty. I raced from curtain down to curtain up. Then I'd have a late meal, maybe the wonderful roast beef and Yorkshire pudding at Simpson's-in-the-Strand. The tickets were not that expensive and the audiences were always terrific. They were regular theatergoers, often with a bag of groceries tucked under their seats, like the folks back home had when they went to movies.

Shortly after arriving in town, I called Major Twit, John Murray Anderson's nickname for Donnie Neville-Willing. He invited me to dinner and to the Café de Paris, which he managed. Marlene Dietrich was getting ready for her opening a couple of nights later. I wrote a bit of special material for her, which she put into her act. The Major asked me to join him for her first night. She was sensational in her evening tails and top hat. I told Donnie about the mini-revue I'd put together for Eva Gabor and myself, and how it never would have worked in this room. The Café de Paris had a horseshow-shaped balcony as well as all the tables downstairs. The threefold screen that Eva would have used onstage while she changed costumes would have left her in full view of much of the house.

Opening night reminded me of MGM's old tagline: MORE STARS THAN THERE ARE IN HEAVEN. I'd heard of practically all of them and met practically none. That was about to change. La Dietrich herself invited me back to her hotel suite after the show. She stayed at the Dorchester Hotel in the famous Cecil Beaton Suite. The master theater craftsman himself had designed and decorated it. What a joint! The booze flowed like the Thames. I shook many gentlemanly hands and kissed many white-gloved ladies' hands and remembered a mess of names.

I stayed away from the ever-pouring champagne and stuck, sensibly, I thought, to whiskey and tall water. I sipped slowly and casually so as not to miss anything. Trouble was, whenever I sat my drink down for a moment to light a cigarette for someone or myself, the glass would magically be refilled. I was stunned by the number of guests who were familiar with my slim body of film work. Naturally that made this spectacular fête even more special.

In one unforgettable moment, Noël Coward held court, even grander than the white Steinway grand at which he was seated. He played and sang "Nina," his song about the señorita from Argentina. This shebang was posh to the nth degree. And I'm afraid I ended up pissed at least to the eighth. It was nearing dawn when I pulled myself away from the Dorchester and headed back to my staid stable of a hotel. I knew I'd "been to a *mah*velous party," as Bea Lillie sang.

On the way back, I passed Jermyn Street, where a few weary hookers were still holding on, awaiting a John. That infamous block was only a few streets down from the hotel I'd just left, where, I was certain, the festivities were still in flower.

I tried to contact Kenneth Williams, with no success. I believe his mother was extremely ill. I was so disappointed we didn't get a face to face after all our correspondence. But I met many new friends, and was escorted to some enchanting places. A bohemian couple took me swimming in the Serpentine, the recreational lake in Hyde Park. Both of them were painters, although he was better known than his wife, and had a hyphenated last name that is now completely unresurrectable. Pre-hippies sans the hair, beads and costumes, they squired me around to strange clubs and bars that bordered on the wonderfully weird.

But soon it became a bit *too* weird for me, and I realized they wanted to party at home. In the bedroom. When they saw the puritan purse to my lips as I declined, with thanks, they didn't pursue their pornographic point. The hippie honeymoon ended happily and quietly, and without a bang.

I did connect with Hermione Gingold, who introduced me to new restaurants, mostly actors' hangouts. Some were posh but friendly and fun, like the Ivy; others were simply friendly and fun spots, full of old chums of hers. One of them, an odd bird of a film director named Brian Desmond Hurst, invited us to tea at his flat at the back of some mews. The place was furnished with mid-Victorian overstuffed furniture. Everything was draped and fringed, like Hurst himself. Among the furnishings were two or three kilted guardsmen and a Teddy Boy or two.

Hermione explained what a Teddy Boy was: a young lad, usually pretty much of a thug, who affected Edwardian fashion, wearing nice jackets with velvet collars and cuffs. Teddy boys were very gentlemanly in appearance but more likely to steal your wallet or beat the crap out of you. They were street toughs, and traveled in gangs, too.

Hermione didn't seem to be a bit surprised by the added gentlemen in the house, and no introductions were proffered. At one point our host asked if I'd ever wondered what men wore under their kilts. I remained Buster Keaton-stonefaced but Ms. Gingold, as if on cue, said, "Of course he has!" Hurst waved a majestic hand. One of the guardsmen stood and happily heisted his kilt high. "Bravo!" cried Gingold, applauding at the generous genitalia on display. All the others joined in the applause, and the young man resumed his previous position on some armchair, obviously pleased with his performance. We left after tea and scones and, I think, tiny watercress and cream cheese sandwiches without further disrobing. The hour or so we spent in the mews was mostly a monolog by our host, who rattled off the names of dozens of films he'd directed. I had heard of a couple, notably the 1951 *A Christmas Carol.*

Not all of Gingold's pals were quite so bizarre. She got me together with a fellow songwriter, a really nice chap named Neville Phillips. We managed to turn out a pretty nice tune called "Pray with Me"—his lyric, my music. (I loved collaborating, and over the years have written with scores of people.)

Just before I flew home, I went to see Cleo Laine at some grand club or theater, and I was awestruck. I'd never heard her before. She had one of the most thrilling voices I'd ever been exposed to. At the end of her show I was absolutely weak at the knees. As I started to leave, someone grabbed my arm and said that Miss Laine wanted me to come back. Apparently someone had told her I was out front and she wanted to meet me. "Oh, I will, I promise," I said.

The man smiled. "She means now."

Very willingly, I was led to her dressing room, nervous as hell. Her with that gorgeous voice—what would I say to this heavenly diva? My mouth went all dry. As it happened, I didn't get much of a chance to say anything. She was in a robe, and gushing all over me about how she loved me in the "cinema." I couldn't believe it. She had a school-girl crush. Well, the scene between us was a hoot, with both of us raving about the other, laughing and giggling like adolescent fans, exchanging autographs and ending in several hugs and finally a huge kiss. What a way to wind up my trip to London. No wonder I'm a forever Anglophile. Talk about your cherry on the top of the cake! Cleo was the tip-top of the stem on the top of the cherry.

At last I returned home after that wonderful, slightly exotic vacation. The foreign break had been good for me. I'd been working almost nonstop for over ten years. Sometimes I did two shows at the same time. During *Hotel Paradiso* I was also appearing (on Sundays only for ten weeks) in a play called *A Box of Watercolors* by G. Wood, who had been Alice Ghostley's nightclub partner for years. Olive Dunbar and my friend Paula Bauersmith were in the cast along with G. Paula's beautiful daughter, Jennifer Warren, was an understudy, and Shel was technical director.

G. had included a few of his own tunes in the play; I particularly loved one called "Robin in a Peach Tree." Later on, G. and I collaborated on a batch of songs; I have an old demo of a tune called "Huggin' and Kissin'."

Alice, of course, had played my sister in *The Show-Off* with Jackie Gleason. By then she was a star, thanks to her performance of "Boston Beguine" in Leonard Sillman's *New Faces of 1952*. Also in the cast was Paul Lynde, who many believed had stolen his entire persona—later made famous on *The Hollywood Squares*—from Ms. Ghostley.

But as usual, I digress. Two-fifty-five East 50th Street looked like a tiny hunk of heaven when I unpacked the big ol' brown trunk. I'd barely unpacked before the phone was ringing and I was off on the road again—this time only as far as a coal-mining town called Barnsville, Pennsylvania. Barnsville was a tiny little burg with few homes, but it did have American Lakewood Park, which sported a huge amusement park and an immense theater.

Lynn Root & Harry Clork's *The Milky Way*, c.1957. L-R: unknown, me, Patsy Fay, Jake LaMotta, Carol Beery. Photo by Roy M. Ackerman.

Usually they presented popular musical acts like the Everly Brothers, but I appeared there in *The Milky Way*, a comedy by Lynn Root and Harry Clork. Harold Lloyd had starred in the film version to huge success. I was playing his role. But the real draw in this particular neck of the woods was the World Middleweight Champion of boxing, Jake LaMotta, who was making his theatrical debut. Although his role was minuscule, the posters for the play announced his appearance in bold print four times the size of the play's title. Underneath the title in small letters, the poster said: "With Carleton Carpenter." The theater owners were no fools. We were sold out for the two weeks we played. Where the hell did all those people come from? We scratched our collective heads. I mean, we were seemingly in the middle nowhere.

Also in the cast were Carol Beery (Wallace's daughter, and Noah Beery, Sr.'s niece); Patsy Fay, a true love of mine, who had been in *Paradiso*; and Tom Ellis, who played a juvenile role; and Wolfe Barzell in the part of a boxing trainer. Nice man, as was tyro Jake. I did his make-up for him, which included a big black eye that my milquetoast character gives him during a funny fight scene. For years after, whenever we ran into each other, he'd proudly introduce me to whomever he was with as the kid who had given him a black eye over and over. Then he'd laugh like hell, pounding me on the back.

Our two weeks of rehearsal were a hoot. Patsy, Tom and I all stayed at Bess and Jean's, a motel just a short walk down the road from the theater. Bess and Jean alternated between the jobs of cook and bartender, and every night after the rehearsal we headed to the bar. We'd climb aboard our stools for a cool beer, fifteen cents a glass and delicious. "Good clean pipes," Bess would boast. Every other beer, sometimes two in a row, would be a "sweet one" on Bess or Jean. It was impossible to spend a whole dollar in the place.

We'd arrive around four or five in the afternoon, and soon we'd be joined by the local regulars, all coal miners, as far as I could tell—a happy, coal-grimy, friendly gang of work-worn men. As the sun disappeared, so did many beers. The bar was lit by what seemed maybe three or four fifteen-watt bulbs. Dim doesn't begin to describe the place; it was near dark. Apparently the miners were used to it, and their continuing game of "tough darts" was the rule. But everybody got along. It was maybe the toughest-tenderest pub I've ever been in. I don't recall a single serious argument and never a fight.

Patsy and me and sometimes Tom would dine at the bar. When we took off for our rooms, which were in rows behind the bar, it felt like we'd been out on the town till two a.m. It was usually about a quarter after eight. I'd escort Pats to her room, give her a nightly kiss and depart to study lines. After we opened, we'd have a couple of sweet ones after the show.

Certainly never before. In one scene, Patsy and Tom were upstage. At the same point at every performance they'd get the giggles. I'd chastise them nightly about breaking up during a scene. Finally I threatened to crack their heads together if they did it again. Well, they did. And I did. I stopped in the middle of a speech, walked upstage, pushed their heads together none too gently, turned front and carried on as though it were part of the play. They were both shocked. But they didn't giggle onstage for the rest of the run. Sometimes you gotta do what you gotta do. I apologized after the show, but they both thanked me and said the equivalent of, "We needed that."

Patsy and I got to know a very young teenager, maybe thirteen or fourteen, who worked as an usher at the theater and who was crazy in love with show business. His name was Marle Becker, and he came from the next town, Mahanoy City. We had spotted him during rehearsals when he was dancing up and down the aisles and singing a song from *Bells Are Ringing*, a current Broadway musical with Judy Holliday. We became his surrogate parents. Marle was very short, and never seemed to age in the forty-plus years of our friendship.

The three of us would picnic together, family-like, and he'd insist that Patsy and I talk about our careers while he sat like a wee leprechaun, completely enthralled, with a smile twice too big for him, lapping up the tiniest details. We had great fun together, and it was difficult at the end of the run to say our goodbyes. We all hugged, and tears flowed freely. Pats and I felt as though we were abandoning our child. We never met his real family, but for those three and a half weeks our own little family felt much more real than pretend. The farewells to Bess and Jean were almost as sloppily sentimental as Patsy and I climbed into my car to head home. I drove, and she kept me in stitches the entire trip. She's one really funny Irish gal.

Back on the corner of 50th and Second, I hardly had time to change my clothes before hitting the road again. This time I went to Indianapolis for two back-to-back shows at the city's huge, outdoor Starlight Theatre. In the Frank Loesser musical *How to Succeed in Business Without Really Trying*, I played Bud Frump, the fawning nephew of J.B. Biggley, president of the World Wide Wicket Company. Starring as the ambitious young J. Pierrepont Finch was my old Metro pal, Van Johnson. In *Oklahoma!* I was Will Parker, who discovers that everything's up to date in Kansas City. The star was my old Broadway pal, Gordon MacRae. The choreographer, whose name has slipped away, had me dancing way better than I had ever thought possible. All the aches and pains of those heavy rehearsals really paid off. Bless his demanding heart.

I stayed at a slightly crummy motel with no restaurant, and with the money I saved I took my dinners in the dining room of a pricey hotel nearby. As for breakfast, during the first week of *Oklahoma!* I found myself joining the gentleman who was currently starring at Starlight, and staying at the hotel. Jack Benny. (Wayne Newton, who I'd thought was a girl when I first heard him, opened the Benny show. I never met him.)

Ah, Mr. Benny. What a gentle, sweet soul. He never cracked jokes or brought attention to himself. He was a wonderful meal companion, interested in everything, asking all sorts of questions and really listening to the answers. No ego. Never "on." Which proves the old adage: The bigger the star, the nicer they are. I cherish those mealtimes with one of the true greats of show business. Talk about being in the right place at the right time.

As *Oklahoma!* was winding down, Forrest Tucker was getting ready to open in the same space as charming shyster Professor Harold Hill, the title character of *The Music Man*. Tucker was a fine and hearty fellow, but after watching a really rough pre-opening runthrough, I thought him a bit lead-footed for the role. I'm sure he had lightened up by his first night under the stars. My double-header there had been fun but exhausting, what with rehearsing one show while playing the other. After the round of goodbye hugs and kisses with cast and crew (a happy ritual), I took off and drove straight home. I made it to the garage on Second Avenue at about 4:30 a.m., dragged myself and my suitcase up the two blocks to 50th, crawled into bed and barely moved for two days.

Chapter 13 ⎯⎯⎯⎯⎯⎯⎯

I n the late '50s I lived briefly in L.A., mainly because I was getting so many TV offers. I'd found a small place on Sweetzer in West Hollywood; it was one in a series of little stone cottages in a horseshoe shape. Mine faced the street at one prong; the film actress Kathleen Freeman lived in the opposite one. In the rear of the folksy enclave was a lovable grump named Sam Rosen, who instantly became a cowriter and lifelong pal.

I think I was only there a couple of months, busy with TV, when I got a call from Cyril Ritchard, the Australian actor who had directed the sketches in *Almanac*. He and his wife Madge had become great and lasting friends of mine. On numerous theater trips to New York I'd stayed at Cyril's apartment on Central Park West while he was working out of town. This was fun, because his "man" took care of everything; he cooked, cleaned and served me breakfast and lunch too, if I was there midday. For the first and only time, I had a servant.

Now here was Cyril on the phone, giving me the sad news that his wife had died a few weeks earlier. Nothing had been written of it in any of the Los Angeles papers, so it was a terrible shock. Now, sensibly, Cyril was getting back to work as an actor-director with a show called *Lock Up Your Daughters*. He wanted me to play one of the leads and tour with him. Naturally he was starring. Rehearsals were to begin soon in New York. Back east I headed, trading the promise of steady, well-paying tube jobs for the fairly meager Equity salary the show would pay. There's no choice, however, when one's heart is onstage.

I called an old agent friend, Francie Hidden, and had her handle the already set deal. She was going through rough times, and I wanted her to have the weekly commission for the protracted run. We did the southern circuit: Coral Gables, Coconut Grove, Palm Beach, Atlanta, and so on.

The show had a really fun company, and we partied as well as performed. The singer-dancer Johnny Downs, a regular in the *Our Gang* shorts in the 1920s, did our dances, and they were really foolish. It wasn't choreography; I don't know what it was. I do know it wasn't good, and it became a great source of amusement for all the company—behind Johnny's back, of course, but we were about as subtle as a bus wreck. It bonded the cast completely together. Cyril's performance suffered a bit because of his double duties. Our star's dialogue didn't exactly stick to the farcical script, but when the words wouldn't come his ad-libs were something to behold. Often they had nothing to do with what was happening at the moment, which led to stifled onstage giggles.

I wish I could remember the names of all the talented cast members. I recall Stephen Everett, Ronnie Cunningham, Pert-something (a hysterically funny and unpredictable redhead, and a true one, as she proved later when she greeted me naked at her apartment door) and Rudy Tronto, who played a manservant. Rudy was a funny gent with a great face; he went on to become a well-respected director and choreographer as well as a good friend with whom I worked many times.

After we had finished *Lock Up Your Daughters*, Shel returned from Europe. He was suddenly out of the service, having served his two years. Shel got a job with my old friend John (Jack) Nonnenbacher, the showbiz manager, as a general assistant and errand-runner. Soon Shel would be running the entire enterprise as John shifted more and more of his work onto his ex-G.I. right-hand man.

Dr. Burton, as John Murray Anderson had called Jack, was now working solely for the José Greco dance troupe as manager. They were constantly on tour, so I hardly saw Shel, which was just as well given the tininess of our flat. I plunged back into a round of TV, and began writing songs on a regular basis, hoping for a pop hit again. Lead sheet after lead sheet piled up on top of the piano. I began going to the apartment/studio of Dick Charles (his apartment), a songwriter who lived about four blocks away. Charles had cowritten several hits, including "Along the Navajo Trail" (Bing Crosby & the Andrews Sisters) and "May You Always" (the McGuire Sisters). He'd round up a trio for me and we'd cut an acetate demo or two per session. It was a small investment for possible great returns. I did manage to get a few songs placed with publishers, and one song, "Cabin in the Woods," got recorded. (All these years later, I'm thinking of doing a CD called *Acetate Dreams*. I have no idea whether there would be a market for all those '50s-style tunes; probably not. But I'll probably go right ahead and try. Who knows? Maybe that retro stuff could click with a hunk of audience. I live in hope. My half-a-glass-of-water runneth over.)

Years later, Dick Charles Recording opened on Seventh Avenue and 49th. It was a big professional place with all the latest tape equipment. G. Wood and I recorded several of our songs there. So did David Baker and I. One Baker-Carpenter number, "Come Away," was recorded twice on Imperial Records, by Grady Chapman and by Jules Farmer with Henri René's Orchestra and Chorus. They both got a lot of play and made the charts, but neither got into the top twenty. I also made demos with Bob Cobert (who went on to write the music for *The Winds of War*) and Alice Pearce's husband, John Rox.

Another old friend, Dion McGregor, wrote lyrics for me once in a while. Dion never had much success as a songwriter; he was best known for talking in his sleep—a proclivity later made famous on an album called *The Dream World of Dion McGregor (He Talks in His Sleep)*. Dion only wrote with me under pressure; he really just wanted to hang out, talk hilariously about old movies, cadge a meal here and there and generally be wonderful company. He moved from friend to friend to find free room and board. We all loved him. He was an absolute wild riot. When it was my turn to take him in, I happily did, for a while. I kept after him to work and squeezed out a few good lyrics from him, almost like a barter for the place to crash. But it was difficult to sleep with him in the other room, making strange, indistinguishable noises, sometimes loud shrieks, most of the night. I'd keep yelling at him from the bedroom to knock it off. Sometimes it worked, most often not.

Finally I introduced him to the songwriter Mike Barr, whom I'd met at Northwestern University when I was sixteen. He lived just a few blocks away. Dion happily moved in on Mike. That stay lasted quite a spell, and turned out to be a good move for them both. With Mike, Dion wrote his biggest song, "Where Is the Wonder," which Streisand recorded. Meanwhile, clever Mike began taping Dion on the sly Dion as he slept. The tapes piled up and were fascinating to listen to. Dion would dream whole stories out loud, becoming several different people. Barr and McGregor were determined to make a musical from the collected tapes, but it never happened. Transcriptions of them did, however, become a book, then the aforementioned LP. Much later, several CDs of the Mike Barr tapes were released, including *Dion McGregor Dreams Again*, produced by Phil Milstein. A slight bio by Milstein was included with the CD, but it was almost as confusing as the dream talker himself.

Suddenly, it seemed, Shel was back from his long tour of the U.S. and Europe. As he unpacked tons of gear, our apartment at 255 East 50th Street began to seem terribly cramped. We agreed to find a bigger place and share the rent. So East 88th between First and York became our home base. We had a good-sized apartment in a new building, and it wasn't back-breakingly expensive.

The trouble was, neither of us got to see much of it. Shortly after the big uptown move, Shel was off again with the Greco company and I flew west to meet with Carlo Ponti at Paramount. He was coproducing a picture for his bride, Sophia Loren, called *That Kind of Woman*, and there was a good role for me. I'd given up the place on Sweetzer, so I rented an apartment at a building called the Montecito on Franklin Avenue, just above Hollywood and Vine. The place was inhabited mostly by New York actors who had come out to work or, between shows, to look for jobs. One and all called the Montecito "the poor man's Chateau Marmont," referring to the posh, star-filled residence on Sunset Boulevard. I paid a month's rent in advance, certain that my interview with Ponti would go well. It did. But I didn't get the part. In California, one doesn't read for a role. One "meets." I guess my meet wasn't as hot-diggity as I'd thought.

But I'd plunked down the loot for a month, so I stayed. The pool down by the garage, where the telephone could bring good or not-so-hot news from your agent, was fun; and the guests, like Sidney Poitier, the Australian actor Murray Matheson, and Jonathan Harris (who later played Dr. Zachary Smith on *Lost in Space*) were great company. Percy Kilbride (Pa Kettle in all those *Ma and Pa Kettle* films) and I would meet at the elevator most every day, and after saying "Mornin'" we'd head down the hill to Dupar's on Vine for blueberry pancakes.

Like everyone else I brought the *Hollywood Reporter* and *Daily Variety* each day—the Trades, as they were called. A day or two after I'd heard from Paramount that Ponti was "going in different direction" (read: "They've hired another guy"), I read that Tab Hunter had been signed for the film. Previously I'd read that he was scheduled to do a World War II navy picture at Warner Bros., where he was under contract, called *Up Periscope!* The producer assigned to the flick was Howard Koch, who'd been an assistant director on my old stamping grounds, MGM.

So, I did something I'd never before done. I called him at Warner's, never really thinking I could get him on the phone. To my shock, I was put straight on to him. I said: "What about me replacing Tab in *Periscope* since he's doing a replacement gig on me at Paramount?"

Answered Koch: "Sounds like a good idea to me. Come on out and meet the director." It was as simple as that. I drove out to the valley, met Gordon Douglas, and the part was mine. Sometimes you just have to take the bull by the proverbials and ask.

The film was scheduled to begin shooting in San Diego in a month. My contract had a seven-week-minimum clause, and it paid seventeen-fifty per. That sounded like a fortune to me at that juncture. I'd gotten used again to the fairly meager wages of the stage and live TV.

So the Montecito would be home for a spell. The place must have been somewhat grand in the distant past, but the years and inattention to up-keep had taken a toll on the joint. My apartment was in the back corner on the lobby floor—number 108, I think. The furniture was huge, clunky, red, frayed as hell and uniquely uncomfortable. The kitchen was a barely work-able mess. I had maybe the very first gas stove ever made and, for sure, the original refrigerator hot off the beginnings of an assembly line.

Still, I thought the place was heaven. It overlooked the pool as well as Hollywood Boulevard down the hill. So I giggled at the condition of the pad and put up with it. The bed, which was quite busy *de temps en temps*, was comfortable. And, God knows, congenial.

Right after I'd arrived in L.A. I sought out and finally found my old chum, Patsy Kelly. Unhappily, she was going through a rough time of it, due to little loot and way too much booze. But I loved the old gal, and eventually moved her into a small apartment at the Montecito where I could keep a better eye on her and, sneakily, keep her off the sauce as best I could. I had the room added to my bill, but told her the apartment was on the house because the management were such fans. Otherwise she would never have moved in. No charity for Pats.

Though a wonderfully funny, talented lady, she could twist you out of shape if you didn't watch yourself. It was frustrating for me. I could not get her even to want to work. There was a tremendous opportunity for her to play the dowager Mrs. Paroo, the mother of Marian the Librarian, in the road company of *The Music Man*. It would star Shirley Jones and begin in Los Angeles. All Patsy had to do was show up at the Los Angeles Philharmonic downtown and the part would be hers. I begged, cajoled, tried every trick in the book to get her down to the theater. I couldn't budge her. She was impossible. Of course I knew she was scared and had lost confidence. The bottle, naturally, hadn't helped. It never does. She had all sorts of excuses. I tried to explain that she wouldn't even have to read. They wanted her. Just let me drive you down there, I said. No luck. She flatly refused, and got angry at me for pushing. The part went to Pert Kelton, who wound up in the film as well. That role could have been Patsy's. (Years later, when I finally managed to talk her into doing a show, she told me she should have given in to me with *The Music Man*.)

During her Montecito stay, Patsy held almost nightly poker sessions. She won most of them, usually deviously. Patsy would almost invariably be drinking, and the tighter she became the more obvious it was that she was fussing around with the deck. Nobody ever cared, or called her on her shenanigans. She was a hoot to play with, and worth more than what one might be losing.

A while back in New York, I'd done the commercials for a live telecast of Mary Martin in *Annie Get Your Gun*, performed onstage in San Francisco, where she was starring in the road company. They were for Buick or some big automobile company, and staged by John Butler, who was mainly a ballet choreographer and had his own dance company. I believe there were only three spots: before, during the interval and at the close. The network switched from California to New York, where I was in some giant studio. I remember the final commercial. Singing slightly altered lyrics to "My Defenses Are Down," I was all over that car, petting and stroking and doing everything short of "going all the way" with it—kissing the hood, fondly caressing the leather interiors, tickling the fenders and finally, at the end of the song, climbing into the trunk and, with a sly smile, slowly lowering the door. It was original and funny and even got mentioned in reviews. It also created quite a stir. The ad agency received thousands of letters from parents, saying that their kids were imitating me and crawling into the trunk. The car company had to run a special spot warning of the dangers of not keeping the trunk locked.

Now the same agency called again, booking me for the commercials for the upcoming Emmy Awards, to be telecast live from the Cocoanut Grove. The timing was perfect, and the money really neat, since I was waiting for *Up Periscope!* to start filming. On location we shot several spots in the style of a western series, all comical and with a lot of familiar faces from westerns, such as like Jack Elam.

On the night of the event at the Grove I wore a tux, and my date Olive Deering, a pal who was staying at the Montecito, was all tarted up in an evening gown. We sat at a ringside table. When one of the auto commercials was about to be shown Jack Benny, who was emceeing, would say: "And now a word from Carleton Carpenter." The cameras would pick me up at the table and I'd introduce the spot. It was fun to be "working" with

Mr. Benny after our breakfasts in Indianapolis. The car company shared sponsorship with some line of ladies' products, so Mr. Benny would sometimes say: "And now a word from Laraine Day." She sat fairly close to me and did her introductions from her table. Olive, bless her heart, looked terrific and stayed relatively sober for the entire thing. We celebrated back at the Montecito.

Just before going on location for *Up Periscope!*, Richard Derr, an actor-realtor, showed me a house in West Hollywood. Dick had starred on Broadway in *Plain and Fancy* and several other shows, but now he was strictly West Coast. The house was on Norma (named after Norma Talmadge) Place, a couple of blocks above Santa Monica Boulevard off of Hilldale. The place was great and the price was right: $23,000. The problem was, I had no credit rating, since I was strongly the "cash on the barrelhead" type. I did, however, have a contract with Warner Bros. That did it. The bank, Great Western Savings, never asked how long it would run, so they never knew—and I certainly didn't put forth that bit of info—that the contract had a life expectancy of a mere seven weeks.

I got a big first mortgage and a small second one. Then I entered that twilight stage known as escrow. I called New York to tell Shel about the house. He was still on tour. I did reach him a couple of weeks later, and I don't think the news that I was buying a house and had decided to stay in California for a spell went over very well with him. He and I decided to give up the apartment, since we would both be away most of the time. Poor guy. He'd uprooted himself from Chicago and was finally adjusting to working in and out of New York. He wasn't interested in changing coasts as a base for his work. I didn't blame him. We were great friends and sometime roommates, but we had our own lives. I, no doubt selfishly, wanted to be where the best paying work was.

So now the Montecito was home. I couldn't move into the house on Norma until after escrow. I finished the film before I actually got to move into the place. But I made my payments to the bank and the previous owner on time. And I couldn't move my junk from 88th Street to West Hollywood until I got into the place. All things considered, it made escrow seem spookier than ever. I never really understood the whole thing, except that several diverse people were collecting a bunch of fees for whatever it was they were doing.

After wardrobe fittings at the San Fernando Valley studios of Jack Warner's fiefdom, I and the rest of the cast headed down to San Diego, where we were put up in some brand-new elite hotel with exposed, glass-walled elevators. Due to my height phobia, they brought on instant terror. The rest of the cast seemed to find them very nifty. And a great company they were, headed by James Garner, Edward O'Brien, Alan Hale, Jr. and a new gal, Andra Martin. She wasn't in San Diego with the rest of the submarine crew; her scenes were shot mostly at the studio. The entire bunch of actors were fun and friendly and, over a very short few days, we all became a really unified crew, hanging out together and enjoying one another.

Up Periscope!, 1959.

I played Lt. Phil Carney. In a small role was a nice guy named Frank Gifford, the football star. Edward Byrnes, before he became the Edd "Kookie" Byrnes of *77 Sunset Strip*, played a member of the crew. Most of the scenes were shot in the harbor or a bit out from port in the Pacific; we submerged a few times but not for long. The interior shots were filmed in Burbank. Gordon Douglas was an affable director and a pleasure to work with. We had a fine time for the weeks we were there.

After dinner at the hotel, Jim, Eddie, Alan, Frank and myself would head for that dreaded elevator, which whizzed us up to the top floor where the bar was. I always faced the door and they always kidded me. We'd have a couple of rounds, and before heading down to our rooms we'd kiss one another goodnight in a manly, buddy-buddy fashion. This habit began because of Jim Garner. The first time we were leaving the bar he said to me: "Carp, I never thanked you for coming all the way over to Korea just to perform for me." Laughing, he gave me a big smack, full on the lips. That started our "tradition." Our nightcaps from then on ended with kisses exchanged all around.

In a key scene of the film, an air attack is raging above the submarine. My character bravely sends what crew is left topside down to the bottom, as alarms shriek and "DIVE! DIVE" is the shouted order. I man the gun to take down the enemy plane while yelling at the guys, "GET BELOW! CLOSE THE HATCH!" One last gob tries to get me to follow but again I scream, "CLOSE THE HATCH!" I'm hit, and the water rushes over me. I die.

In fact, I almost did. Back in Burbank, they shot the closeups of me in a water tank rigged with wires that created an explosion effect, simulating the bullets from the plane. I didn't drown, but I was damned near executed in that churning, crackling tank. But we got it in one helluva take. When my poor mother saw the film, she was furious with me that I hadn't warned her about my onscreen death. "It looked so real. How could you do that to me?"

The flick was fun to make, but not so hot to see. I refer to it as *Up Your Periscope*, just as I call my MGM Korean War film *Take the High Ground and Shove It*. Two stinkers. Unfortunately, they both show up too often on the tube. You can't win 'em all.

Now it was time to attend to the new and very peculiar door that had opened for me: the house in West Hollywood. I took a quick flight east, hustled my stuff together and hired yet another moving van to lug it west. Now I was planted on Norma Place in a nice, smallish, stucco-covered house with a patch of succulents (mostly cacti) in front. I painted the good-sized living room my favorite wall color, light tan with a hint of pink. Very relaxing. The kitchen, sans appliances when I attacked it, sported a long half-circle table against one wall. Sliding glass doors looked out onto a wee backyard going wild with bamboo. I'd get to that job later. There was a small bedroom; my piano, wall unit and Castro Convertible fit perfectly. I tore out a window and installed more sliding glass doors. The bath, thank God, had a tub with a shower; I love a good laid-back soak before bed.

Every time I purchased something for my new home, this terrifying thought popped into my head: "How the hell am I going to get rid of all this stuff when I move?" I never felt very "permanent." As it turned out I was more permanent there than I'd ever been before. Happily, the reason was work.

Television was going nuts just then, and since a T had been added to the radio union, turning AFRA to AFTRA, there was lots of loot hanging around for the taking. I guest starred in series after series: *The Rifleman*, and *Wanted: Dead or Alive*, *Perry Mason*, *The Alcoa Hour*, *The Alaskans*. I did an episode of the *General Electric Theater* with Fay Wray of *King Kong* fame, and sang a song I'd written, "A Little Love." With Audrey Totter, one of my old buddies from the Keenan Wynn Players, I appeared on *Lux Video Theatre* and *Cimarron City*; for the latter show I wrote and sang another song, "Mi Corazón."

One particular TV stint of mine from those days turned out to be unforgettable. Shirley Temple was hosting a children's anthology series, *Shirley Temple's Storybook*. Her marriage to John Agar was far behind her; when I met her she was married to one of the wealthiest men in California, Charles Alden Black. For the last episode of the first season, *The Shirley Temple Show* switched from black-and-white to color, which was still rare. Alvin Cooperman, one of the producers, cast me as Jack (who was nimble and inclined to jump over candlesticks) in "Mother Goose." The title role was played by Elsa Lanchester. Shirley would play Polly Baker (who put the kettle on), and an old buddy of mine, the songwriter and future poet laureate of America, gravel-voiced Rod McKuen, would play opposite Shirley as Tom (the piper's son). Another dear, dear friend, Patricia (Patsy) Fay, had been cast as Miss Muffet. Patsy and I had had a brief fling in Hollywood before I returned east. I happily signed on.

Two days into rehearsals, Mr. Cooperman decided that Rod and I should switch roles. I was delighted to be elevated to Shirley's costar,

I played a callow young wanderer in "The Coward," an episode of *The Rifleman*, 1959.

but worried about Rod taking on the lesser part. No problem—he toothily and happily agreed. I picked him up every morning at the house he shared with his mom and dropped him off after rehearsal. The renowned film director, Mitch Leisen, put us through our paces. The musical had an original score that we pre-recorded with just a piano; the orchestrations hadn't been finished yet so the music was mixed and added later. It was fun doing the duets with Shirley, and when we were filming on the set later, and lipsyncing to playbacks, she stood there with the same apple-cheeked grin and wide eyes she'd displayed at seven or eight. She held her hands the same way as she had in *Curly Top*—fingers sticking out.

When the episode aired late in 1958, the cast all went to the NBC studios so we could see it in color. The company had recently begun producing the long-running color western *Bonanza* to promote the sale of color sets. So it really was a hunk of history, and now I have a copy of it.

During its last full season of original shows, I appeared on *Father Knows Best*. After eleven successful years—first on radio, then on TV starting in 1954—the star, Robert Young, had decided he didn't want to play that role anymore. I'd never imagined that he had a serious drinking problem. I guested as the new boyfriend of daughter Betty, played by Elinor Donahue. The role of Bud, her younger brother, was played by Billy Gray, who had played Debbie's kid brother in *Two Weeks with Love*. Dear Jane Wyatt was the wife, of course. It was a fun set.

But Elinor and I hit it off best—away from the set as well. We started dating after my appearance, and things got very hot and heavy for quite a long spell. She had been through an early and unpleasant marriage, and had a very young child who was adorable. I was crazy about them both, but I think Elie was even more smitten than I and had long-term commitment in mind. She approached the subject of wedlock on a few brief occasions, watching me closely. When she didn't get the responsiveness she was expecting from me, the relationship cooled back to plain old friendship. I really wasn't ready for a wife and baby at that juncture. Maybe I missed out on a terrific thing. I'll never know for sure. But I think not.

Chapter 14 ⸻

My new home, West Hollywood, was like a small, comfy village. Short blocks connected and shot off from one another, and most of the residents were "in the biz." Living to my right was Dorothy Dandridge, so beautiful and talented; she had starred in *Carmen Jones* in 1954 and was about to begin *Porgy and Bess*. A very few years later she made heavy investments in some get-rich-quick scheme involving oil, went bankrupt, lost her house and, just before she was set to open at a posh club in New York, was found dead in her apartment due to an overdose of antidepressants. So terribly sad.

On my left lived a wild, cat-loving, hard-drinking female screenwriter, aptly named Hagar Wilde. Her screen credits included *Bringing Up Baby* and *I Was a Male War Bride*, both of which had starred Cary Grant. Three houses up from me was Alan Campbell, soon to be joined by his wife, Dorothy Parker. Also close by was an apartment building owned by a friend of mine from New York, Paul Marlin. The remarkable British stage and film actress Estelle Winwood (whom I had first met at the naked pool party thrown by Tallulah) was ensconced next to Paul; and near her lived Tuesday Weld's mother, who was known as Wednesday. (I always thought it should have been Monday, because she happened first.) Another neighbor was the Baltimore-born, darkly handsome actor John Carlyle, with whom I'd worked in *Feathertop*. Almost next door to this group on Lloyd Place was Nina Foch, with whom I'd acted on early TV. Across from Nina were two more actors, Clement Brace (who had mostly retired after a string of Broadway bombs) and John Dall, who was still going strong.

So there were connections galore. We all mixed and mingled like mad. I really felt at home. Even with all the television I was doing, I managed to keep working in the theater, though it wasn't exactly a thriving industry in L.A. At the Century, a small bandbox-type theater with boxes on La Cienega just south of Santa Monica Boulevard, I did a farce called *French Postcards*. My costars were Lynn Bari (whom I had once watched on a big, outdoor movie screen singing "I'm Making Believe") and Wanda Hendrix, the B-movie leading lady of the '40s and '50s. She was just out of rehab, and often her mother escorted her to rehearsals, assuring the cast, "She hasn't been drinking!" At one point in the show she had to pass herself off as a boy, but she had gained a touch of weight, and was a bit too curvy to be credible. An actor name Allen "Boomie" DeWitt played a fop and nearly stole the show from the rest of us.

The run was fairly short, but it was all great fun. We laughed a lot, maybe more than the audiences. Lynn and I would regularly toss back a few after the show. I loved that lady. I was heartsick when she told me she'd been dubbed for "I'm Making Believe," but that didn't dim my admiration for her.

My home on Norma Place was a continual project. It had a tiny garage out back that was too short for my Ford convertible, so the driveway became its home. I decided to convert the garage into a wee guesthouse, and invited my parents up in Vermont to help. I had the backyard in almost garden shape by the time they pulled up in an old car. The front wheels had barely touched the highways because of Cart's heavy tool chest in the trunk. He happily got to work. Cart dug up the garden to connect plumbing from the house to the garage, rewired the place, put in a sink and teeny shower. Everything was sort of miniature, and illegal, since I never knew about the need for permits. We installed a window high up on the garage door and put sliding glass ones on the side that faced my future garden. Tan and white square tiles were laid on the floor and smaller ones on the kitchen counter. The place had started to look really neat.

All the time my father was working, Alan Campbell would stop by to see how my "wetback" was getting along. After my folks had gone home, he continued to ask: "How's the Wetback? Say hello from me when you write."

Dar, Cart and I had had fun together. I took them on tours around town and showed them the old MGM lot. Since I often played bridge, I could gather a third and fourth partner any time Dar wanted a game. Debbie, bless her heart, had the three of us over for dinner one Sunday. She was then married to Eddie Fisher, but he wasn't around when we visited. Deb was a terrific hostess, and impressed the hell out of my parents. When we came home, Dar mentioned how sad Deb had seemed to her underneath all the smiles and charm. She never missed a thing.

I hated having them leave, but I was looking forward to moving from the Castro Convertible back to my bedroom. No one ever found about all the construction work my dad had done without a permit. Alan constantly threatened in villainous tones to "report both of you rascals to the legal authorities," as he curled an invisible mustache.

Our "tiny tinsel town" included a post office just around the bend on Hilldale; a Bank of America almost next door on the corner of Santa Monica; and just a couple of doors to the left, our local hangout, the 4 Star, a bar, grill and café with a candlepin bowling lane. Directly across the Boulevard was a do-it-yourself laundromat and our unique grocery store, Shermart, an oddball market that locals called the Queermart. It was a well-stocked, friendly—sometimes overfriendly—place that was a part-shopping, part-pickup cruising joint. It had a bulletin board with bits of news, ads, places to rent or share, and barely disguised offers for bodies in those same categories. There seemed to be an unwritten law in our neighborhood that bras and underpants were verboten. I once picked up a cauliflower and discovered on the stem a local phone number, written in ink. I was intrigued, but I never called it, although I giggled a lot and couldn't wait to pass on the news at our pub.

A wonderfully dimpled and smiling grandmother-type was our favorite checkout gal. She seemed like a throwback to an older and more proper age. She must have been aware of some of our more outrageous antics, but she never showed it; she kept smiling her genuine smile and making homespun conversation with all who passed by her register.

During wash cycle at the launderette you could grab a twenty-five-cent glass of beer at the 4 Star before putting the wash in the dryer. Then you could force down at least a couple more and maybe have a turn at the bowling machine. Everything in the area was handy and, best of all, walkable. Unless I was driving to and from whatever studio I might be working in, my yellow convertible stayed mostly in the driveway. The neighbors traveled back and forth across Norma and around Lloyd, dining at one another's homes and exchanging whatever TV, film or sex gossip there was. And usually there was an abundance. Even the most discreet goings-on were invariably spotted, caught or instinctively known about by someone. No one was absolutely safe. We were a wise and wise-assed group. Consequently most of us shared our shenanigans at once, making a rousing, comical story out of any misbehavior.

By now our in-group had grown. Mrs. Alan Campbell had arrived from the East bearing books and one-liners. I couldn't believe that the author who had written the very first Pocket Book (with its tiny kangaroo logo) that I had saved my magazine-route pennies to buy as a kid in Vermont was living three houses up the street. That quiet, petite lady who could smilingly swear like a sailor and make it sound like poetry became a good buddy. She often stopped by unexpectedly for tea, a drink, or a game of Jotto, which we both adored.

We were the oddest of couples—she barely five feet tall, I gangling at over six-foot-three—as we shopped together at the Qmart. I never stooped and Dottie never stretched. We were completely unaware of the height difference and chatted away as if we were cheek to cheek. I was mad for the lady and she, incredibly, had taken quite a shine to me. Her place was stacked with books, most of them piled on the coffee table in front of the worn and sagging couch. Though rarely meeting deadlines, she was often writing reviews for *Esquire*. She'd be hard to spot when you entered the house; she sat hidden behind the stacks and her spectacles.

On the other side of my home, next to Hagar Wilde, was Diana Booth, the lady who, years before, had provided me with my first sexual "engagement" following my late-in-life bris. She had promised to be gentle, but got carried away while I was pumping cautiously, and she busted the whole thing open. I had to race back to the doctor for quick repairs before leaving on one of my Christmas trips to Korea. Now she was an unapologetic neighbor, and our friendship was happily renewed.

Another house away was a wonderful portrait artist named Richard McKenzie, who became a protégé of Raymond Burr when he owned a gallery in Beverly Hills. Richard had a daughter, I think, but was amicably divorced from his wife. We shared many good times together. An oil painting that he gave me as a gift hangs near the foot of my bed to this day. It shows a young figure that could be a boy or girl—making it a very apt image for my bedroom.

Those were swinging times. Anything went. Other pals lived close by: Chuck Williamson and Fleming Tucker; the painter Paul Jasmine; a character we called Clara Van Cluck; and Archie Keener, who seemed to own the corner stool at the 4 Star. He'd worked in the film industry for years, and was a wit and a half and an all-around great buddy. My darling Patsy Kelly soon moved close, sharing a small house (I'm sure as guest) with Richard Hanley and John Lee, who worked for the Burtons, Richard and Elizabeth.

My friend Jim Smith, whom I had met by accident on the beach in Santa Monica, lived nearby as well. We're still very close. He's very bright, with a terrific sense of humor, a must for me. At the time he was working in television as a cue-card guy. He rose to the position of assistant director for *The Danny Kaye Show*, *The Carol Burnett Show*, and other programs. I'll always remember one special Christmas present he gave me. Knowing how nuts I was about Kurt Weill, he found a recording of *Rise and Fall of the City of Mahagonny*, which I hadn't known about. I cherish it still, and think of dear Jim every Christmas Eve.

My big project at the time was a show I worked on with my cheerfully grumpy curmudgeon friend, Sam Rosen. It was a musical version of *Oliver Twist* called *Dear Boy*, and we spent nearly three years writing it. Sam did the book and lyrics and I wrote the music. It was a super time of really inspirational work that even now surprises and delights me. We envisioned Cyril Ritchard as the villain Fagin. I thought this would intrigue him, for as far as I knew he'd never done that kind of role before. Well, it did. He had come to star with Cornelia Otis Skinner in a production of *The Pleasure of His Company*, and he came to Norma Place to hear Sam and me perform the whole thing for him.

He was delighted with it and we were delighted with him—especially when he arranged for the two of us to fly to New York City and audition it for Jule Styne.

Off we tore, with visions of Broadway success swimming in our collaborating heads. We arrived in his apartment at the designated time, and introduced ourselves to the great composer and producer with nary a qualm. He waved at the grand piano in his living room and stretched out on a sofa, hands behind his head and eyes closed. Mr. Styne said something to the effect of, "Okay, guys, let 'er rip." We ripped away with everything we had, racing from one song to the next, with Sam giving brief intros.

Mr. Styne listened to the entire score, which took maybe fifty minutes. He rose from the sofa, thanked us, and was completely noncommittal as we returned his thanks (with added emphasis) and headed out. In the hall we looked at each other and said, almost together: "What do you think? Did he like it?" We both shrugged and headed for the elevator with our briefcases.

We never did find out what he thought of our work. At the airport, I bought a copy of *Variety* and read it on the plane. Toward the back of the legit section was a tiny one-line squib. It reported that someone in England named Lionel Bart was peddling a musical called *Oliver*. (Bart had written *Lock Up Your Daughters*.) Our jaws dropped to the cabin floor. When we'd started work on *Dear Boy*, no one had ever tried to musicalize any of Dickens's works. We had felt very innovative. We couldn't believe it. We guessed that Mr. Styne had read that week's *Variety* ahead of us.

For months we scratched our heads. How had someone else come up with our idea? Had Bart started three years ago? We doubted that. Sam finally came up with a possible answer. He was a good friend of Elsa Lanchester and her husband, Charles Laughton, who, being British, spent much time in London. Perhaps at some party where theater people were discussing unlikely possible West End projects, Laughton had scoffed: "You think that's a stupid idea? I have a friend in Hollywood who's trying to make a musical out of *Oliver Twist*!" It could have been that simple—a dropped remark at a party or pub. At any rate, the work we did on *Dear Boy* was a joy to us both, and maybe one day that delicious material will find its way to some audience.

Back on Norma, I took a job to do for two shows back-to-back at Lewis and Young's Sacramento Music Circus. In Rodgers & Hammerstein's *Cinderella* I played one of the wicked stepsisters; the other was Sterling Holloway, who had introduced "Mountain Greenery" in Rodgers & Hart's first hit show, *The Garrick Gaieties*. Marie Santell, a talented soprano, played Cinderella. She worked opposite me in the other show, *The Boy Friend*, which we rehearsed during the run of *Cinderella*. By day I was was making love to Marie; at night I was screeching at her. It was a weirdly fun mixture, but exhausting. We couldn't do matinees under the tent; it was too hot. Even at five in the afternoon it was be about one hundred and twenty-five degrees.

We'd head inside the VFW (Veterans of Foreign Wars) hall nearby for the air conditioning and a cool refreshment after rehearsals, which were held mainly in the morning when the temperature was almost bearable. Thank God for the pool and the VFW. After closing I swore I'd never do back-to-back again. But I probably would.

I'd hitched a ride to Sacramento with the terrific lady stage manager and returned to West Hollywood with her as well, since these were the last two shows of the season. The rides were memorable for me because she wore a seat belt. It was the first time I'd ever seen one. I wanted to know if they were a hindrance, but she said, "Not at all. I just do it automatically now." That was some time before they became standard equipment. At the time I could hear Dar's voice in my head: "Another of those darned modern inconveniences."

Shortly after I'd returned home, Shel showed up. He'd had some run-in with Nonnenbacher and the Greco company and had decided to quit and give California a try. It was a bit before the Christmas holidays. He had hardly settled in when, true to form, I was called to get myself on the double to Palm Beach, Florida to do *The Beachcombers*, a new comedy by Paul Crabtree. Off I flew, leaving poor Shel with the house, the car, and a few brand-new people he'd barely met. He must have gone through six weeks of lonely hell.

The play was described as "A Cocktail of Tropical Nonsense." I costarred with my old pal Pip, Arthur Treacher, and a gorgeous creature named Fernanda Mantel. Also featured were Enid Markey (who had played Jane in the first two Tarzan movies ever made, opposite Elmo Lincoln); Larry Fletcher and the 1920s and '30s movie star, adorable Nancy Carroll. The spanking-new theater was the Royal Poinciana Playhouse, where on opening night there were so many bejeweled ladies in the audience that the glitter and reflection from their diamonds was almost blinding from the sandy set on stage. It was a "world premiere" that never saw any more of the world than that one beautiful theater.

I stayed at a boarding house a short walk from the Playhouse. My good friend G. Wood was a fellow guest. It was a fun place, with a huge pitcher of freshly squeezed temple orange juice every morning on the big breakfast table. I've loved temples ever since. They're only in season for a short time—late January and February, I think—and it's worth picking out all the seeds that come with that variety of orange. With G. in rehearsals for the play to follow us, we managed to get in many good bridge games. He was a shrewd "bridger" and a comic joy to play with as partner or adversary. The poor guy suffered (mostly in silence) from gout, and some days walking was unbearable for him. But he gimped ahead, and never seemed to be out of work in the theater for long. What a talented actor, writer and composer he was.

By the time I'd arrived back in West Hollywood, Shel had had it with his West Coast experiment and had decided to return to the José Greco dance company. He had fallen in love with one of the dancers in the Greco group, probably the main reason California didn't take. They married and moved to Chicago, where they were happy as clams at high tide. Shel kept the Greco job for several more years, then joined a company that sent out touring companies of Broadway shows: what we used to call buck-and-truss (bus-and-truck) companies. Shel was very successful at everything he put his hand to, and to this day we're still the closest of buddies. He's more sensible than I am: He finally retired, but I'm too dumb to quit.

Meanwhile, back at the raunch (of West Hollywood, that is), work and play rolled on in almost equal measure. I did lots more TV and a

West Coast run of the hit musical *Little Mary Sunshine*, which was still running off Broadway at that time. We played at the Legrand Theatre on Sunset near Vine. It was on the old location for the Hollywood Canteen during World War II. Shirley Knight, slim as a rail then, was Mary; Peter Walker was her singing love; the incredible Sylvia Lewis (who had danced in *Singin' in the Rain*) and I were the other singing, dancing, comical pair. What a wonderful satire Rick Besoyan had concocted, a hoot to play.

We did a week of previews before opening on that small but adorable stage. The front formed a perfect half-circle, like my kitchen table. Trouble was, there were no wings to speak of, there was only about a foot of space on both sides. I kept telling the stage manager to get some glo-tape down so one of the gypsies wouldn't break a neck during blackouts. At least the curved front of the stage had little hooded lights like old-fashioned footlights, spaced about two or three feet apart, which added to the period flavor of the sets.

The night of the last preview, Corporal Billy (me) was singing "Colorado Love Call" (a takeoff on "Indian Love Call") center stage at the end of Act I. Big finish, blackout, big applause—and big slip in the corner as I tried to find that one-foot space in the dark. (Obviously there was still no tape.) It wasn't a big fall, but one of my RCMP (Royal Canadian Mounted Police) boots hit the floor a bit askew. I felt my ankle crack a tad, but not much, and scurried around to get backstage. During the interval, the drummer came to the dressing room and said, "If you're planning on doing that tomorrow night, I'll pick it up with the drum and cymbal." We both laughed, and I assured him I didn't aim to do that slip-off at every performance. The ankle hurt a little but I didn't pay any attention to it. It's funny; when you're onstage you can cut yourself on something or knock something out of whack and never feel it. You can even come offstage bleeding and think, "What the hell is this?," and never know when or how the thing had happened.

The opening night was a complete success. Reviews were great, and we settled in for a long run—happily, with glo-tape in the wings. About five weeks or so into our run, I arrived a half-hour before showtime and squeezed into the dressing room I shared with the other guys. (Backstage space was sparce.) I got into makeup and my costume, but couldn't pull on one boot. I'd realized my ankle had swollen a bit over time, but I hadn't given it much mind. The stage manager tried to help, pulling and pushing to no avail. I felt as if I were back in *Cinderella* trying to squeeze into my stepsister's tiny slipper. Finally he called a doctor and made an appointment for me that very evening. He put my understudy into my outfit and shooed me off to have the doctor take a gander.

The doc looked at my swollen ankle, poked it gently and X-rayed the thing at once. A few moments later he had the still-wet X-ray in one hand and a phone in the other. He was calling Cedars of Lebanon Hospital. After obtaining directions, I drove myself there and was rolled into a small room. I undressed and, as ordered, put on that backwards, too-short gown that ties in the back. They gave me a shot. I was faintly aware of being shuttled onto something that moved me to an operating room, then told to count backwards from a hundred. I vaguely remember murmuring "95," then … blackout. End of sketch.

When I came to, the sun was shining. I was back in my tiny room, and my right leg, from calf to toe, was in a cast hanging from a pull of some kind at about a thirty degree angle up in the air. When the surgeon came in, he told me he had made an incision in my ankle, and forty or forty-five small pieces of bone had sprung out—like popcorn, he said with a smile. Like an idiot, I grinned too. Then he told me I'd be off my foot for at least a month, maybe more. My grin vanished at once, unlike that of the Cheshire Cat. But I could go home, with help, in a couple of days. That helped perk me up a bit, but I was anxious about the show and wanted to know how long before I could resume my role. "Don't rush it, son, and you'll be fine," he said. That was great for him. For me, it seemed like the end of the world. *Little Mary Sunshine* was doing sell-out business and I wanted back in as quickly as possible. He left me in a state I rarely ever visited: depression.

It vanished that afternoon, when Sylvia Lewis and a gang from the show arrived with flowers, fruit, candy, jokes and a photographer. They joined me on all sides and in bed for pictures that would hit the press the following day. Pals are pals and publicity is publicity; sometime they go hand in hand, maybe neck and neck. Friends came to rescue me from Cedars of Lebanon, one of them driving my Ford, and got me settled back in on Norma. Sooner than I'd expected, I was able to hobble about with a cane by myself.

I heal quickly, and in short order the operation was just another scar on the ever-increasing road map that covers most of the ol' body. By the time I rejoined *Little Mary Sunshine* the show had moved to a larger theater, the Music Box at Hollywood Boulevard and La Brea, and two of my co-stars had been replaced: Jackie Joseph had taken over for Shirley, her husband Ken Berry for Peter. My love Sylvia was still with it, thank heavens.

She was a joy to partner with, but our happy reunion turned out to be rather short-lived. Less than two weeks back in the role of Corporal Billy,

I received a pleading phone call from Paul Crabtree in New York. Paul had acted on Broadway since his teens, notably in Oklahoma! In 1950 he had written, directed and starred in a show called *A Story for a Sunday Evening*. Its Broadway run had only lasted a week, but now it was being revived off Broadway at the Cherry Lane Theatre. This time Paul was just directing, and he insisted I was the only actor he knew who could "make sense out of my crazy dialogue." They were deep in rehearsals, and the guy chosen for the lead wasn't giving Crabtree what he wanted. I told him I'd just started back in a local hit here. He begged. He cajoled.

And I caved. When someone wants you that much it's hard to resist. I finished out the week, left Corporal Billy in the capable hands of Larry Billman, the standby, and raced back east. There were only three days until opening, and that role was long. I was only offstage once, for a twenty-second costume change, during the entire play. A beautiful actress named Louise King played opposite me; the lovable character actor Tom Pedi (who had acted in Jules Dassin's famous film noir, *Naked City*) was among the smallish cast. A man name Barry Tuttle did the scenery and lighting; a few years later I would work for him when he was a producer and running a summer theater in, I think, Rochester.

How I learned all those lines, I shall never know. I do know we ran for only eight performances. Talk about shooting yourself in the foot! Still it was a challenge, and I liked working with Crabtree again. But the play was just—let's be kind—a tad dated.

Back to L.A. I flew. Where were the frequent-flyer miles in those days? I'd have piled up a ton. But it felt good to be home, and one of the ways I celebrated was by throwing a helluva Halloween party. "Halloween, Halloween, all other holidays fall between": So went a lyric by Ralph Blane (with music by Harold Arlen), written for the Fox musical *My Blue Heaven* with Dan Dailey, Betty Grable and David Wayne. With me, Halloween runs a close second to Valentine's Day.

For this particular Halloween, I set the stage properly by exchanging all the light bulbs in the house to five-watt orange ones. I set up the bar in Cart's Cottage (my former garage) and invited all the neighbors and practically everybody else I knew, and their friends. All in all, probably two hundred bodies drifted in and out during the evening. Many came early, and a handful were still there the next morning.

While I was bartending out back, an exact, I mean, exact replica of Frankenstein's monster lumbered in for a drink. I looked up and said, "Hi, Stewie." The monster softly murmured, "Fuck," and seemed to shrink a bit. Stewart Stern took his drink and hunkered out. Troy Donahue, whom I'd met when he first arrived in town—he was Merle Johnson then—arrived in full, fairly attractive drag, fooling none of the guests. Tom Royal, with whom I'd written a couple of songs, arrived dressed as a Hell's Angel. He had a buddy with him, as well as a kid whom they had "discovered" on their way to the shindig. He was pumping gas at a station, and they asked him if he wanted to go to a party. The kid said sure. He hung up the hose, quit on the spot and jumped in their car. At one point fairly late into the night, the young guy spotted an old actor friend of mine dressed very properly as a nun (tall and lean, with wimple and rosary beads) and drinking beer from a bottle. The kid, who wasn't exactly sober, took umbrage at the sight and began screaming obscenities. He threw a punch at the nun, who was leaning against the sink. She dodged the blow and hit the attacker delicately on the top of his head with her beer bottle. The surprised kid took off. Said the nun: "Sacrilegious bitch!"

Maila Nurmi, who played a character named Vampira on TV and in the Ed Wood movie *Plan 9 from Outer Space*, lived nearby, and she was there too; although she spent most of the evening curled up under the desk in my den. She was a strange, fascinating lady, difficult (for me, at least) to get to know. Errol Flynn's very young girlfriend, Beverly Aadland, managed to throw up in the middle of my bed. Another guest, Patsy Kelly, kept yelling at me to turn up the lights. I told her about how I'd changed all the bulbs. "Jesus," she complained, "I've been trying for over an hour to pick up this chick and it turns out she's my roommate, for God's sake." Later I heard her lecturing (if you could call it that) a bunch of guys who'd been taking turns running drinks for her. "I don't get it with you boys," she said. "When you have an argument with your trick or lover or whatever, you talk and talk and analyze and talk and analyze and talk and talk. I don't get it. When a couple of gals have an argument, there's blood all over the walls and that's the end of it!"

Toward dawn, John Dall passed out in the bedrooom with a lit cigarette dangling. Happily there wasn't much damage, just a bit of burned rug. By then the place had pretty much cleared out. The medicine cabinet in the bathroom had likewise been emptied. Every sort of pill, prescription or not, had disappeared along with the guests. I awoke (late, of course) to find Jimmy Kirkwood asleep on the couch and a few other bodies curled up on the floor. The place in daylight was a disaster zone. Gunk was everywhere, even on the ceiling. It took a week to clean up and repaint in a few places. There was no blood on the wall, but almost everything else was there: grease, hair, makeup, stains from drinks, you name it.

It was worth it. Even today, those who are still here to remember talk about *the* Halloween party. I've only recounted a few printable incidents. You wouldn't believe some of the others.

Then there was Thanksgiving. I remember one monster dinner party I gave: two turkeys, a ham and all the fixings, fixed by me. I turned the living room into a dining room by adding a rented table that seated twenty. The meal took me two days to prepare, but everything turned out so tasty it was all worth it. I enjoy cooking, as you can guess. Thanksgiving meals, to me, aren't complete without mashed rutabagas (yellow turnips), and several of the local diners seated at the long industrial-sized table hadn't associated that veggie with that holiday. I made believers of the lot.

I had taken up oil painting in my off-minutes, and had done a portrait of Estelle Winwood in costume for *The Madwoman of Chaillot*. That Thanksgiving was to be the unveiling. I'd had it framed and hung on the wall. Estelle listed in, saw it, staggered back a few steps and said, "Give it me. Give it me. Give it me!" I was thrilled. But I wouldn't part with it for the world. It hangs in my bedroom still. I probably should have given it her. I adored the lady. She tickled me so. She informed me one morning that "that man upstairs [John Carlyle] was dragging a dead body up his stairs last night!" I could picture her lying in her bed, cigarette dangling from her lips, deep into one of the mysteries she loved to read nightly. She went on: "Something should be done about this, my dear! The authorities should be notified! It was around three-thirty or four in the morning. I heard it. I'll testify!" I told her she must be mistaken. It had to be something else he was lugging up the stairs.

"Nonsense!" she cried. "I know a dead body when I hear it!" It turned out Carlyle was tipsily hauling in a large bag of chips for his tiny patio. I had nicknamed John "Black Starr" from the posh jewelry firm Black, Starr & Gorham, simply because he was inherently elegant. He quite often overcame that trait, however, with the help of scotch. I remember the pre-dawn appearance he made, jaybird-naked, on his patio, where he preceded to relieve himself of way too many beers. It must have been a record-breaking length of time for taking a leak.

The following morning, Estelle told me that the sudden cloudburst of a few hours before must have been enjoyed by my succulents. She never heard the truth. I had witnessed it from across the street, and thwarted the urge to applaud at the finish of Black Starr's incredible pee.

Not long after that, a fairly new friend, Polly Adler, visited me for dinner. Polly had long since given up her infamous career as a madam and written her book, *A House Is Not a Home*. Hours later on her way out, she had hauled up her skirt and relieved herself in my succulent bed. I missed it, but the neighbors didn't. When they told me, I could only hope that she hadn't been scratched in delicate places by the cacti.

At some point, prodded, I suppose, by the constant barrage of advertisements by wild and wacky car salesmen on the tube, I decided it was time to turn in the Ford. Having caught a glimpse of a sports car called Caravelle, made by Renault of France, I couldn't resist the itch to own one. I headed down one of the main, ever-crowded and crisscrossing throughways that clog the daily life of L.A. I walked into a dealership, and there it was, sleek, gold and glorious: a low two-seater with a hunk of canvas from door to door, a zipper down the middle. It came with a removable tonneau cover, which protected the unoccupied passenger seat. I rarely used that. A deal was struck. I left behind the ol' Ford convertible and a check, and gingerly pulled out of the place in my Caravelle and drove back to West Hollywood.

As I edged into the main stream of traffic, my head was about even with the hubcaps of passing trucks. It was the scariest drive I'd ever taken. I felt as if I were lying down in the new gold treasure; it was very comfortable, with lots of leg room, but I felt spookily tiny in traffic. It took quite a while to get used to being so close to the ground. When I finally did, I felt as if I were the coolest cat to ever hit the highway. "René," as I called my new vehicle, and I were an admired couple, and all sorts of adventures awaited.

About that time I began to realize how much my personal life had changed. It had just evolved out of the times and places I had lived and out of sheer instinct.

West Hollywood was often referred to as Boystown. It all seemed perfectly natural to me and I guess to everyone else. Sexes were mixing and mating and swinging. So I swung. Happily. My golden "Ren" and I made almost weekly trips way down on Vermont Avenue to a mostly black bar. It was maybe the happiest, most fun bar in the world that I ever quaffed a few in. There was a great jukebox, and I played the Lloyd Price record "Personality" over and over. I never saw a fight or even a serious argument in that wonderful joint. Selfishly, I always went alone. I wanted to keep the experience unchanged.

Sometime in the early '60s I got a call from a man in New York named Hugh Fordin, who years later would start a company called DRG Records. He wanted me for a tour he was producing of *Bye Bye Birdie*, the Broadway smash of 1960. I would play Albert Peterson, the role originated by Dick Van Dyke. I agreed. We would rehearse and kick off a long tour—sixteen weeks, I think—in Lakewood, Maine. This was Ren's first trip, and the Caravelle took to the road like an old pro. When I pulled into the resort with its beautiful theater—the oldest summer theater in America, they claimed—a surprise greeted me. An old friend from New York, Ruth Manning, an actress about my age, was playing my mother in the musical, the part Kay Medford had done on Broadway. What a great reunion! Pat Finley was terrific in the role of Rosie, whom Chita Rivera had played. Jim Nichols did the Paul Lynde "father" part and Ann Collins was the mother. James Karr directed and wonderful Johnny Coyle did the dances.

It was a company to die for, and all the kids were incredible actors, singers and dancers. We became a big family immediately and gathered super reviews and sold-out houses wherever we played, from Maine to a huge domed theater in Detroit, Michigan.

On August 5, 1962, we were playing at the John Drew Theater in East Hampton when we got word that Marilyn Monroe had died. It hit me particularly hard, since by that time in the tour I was feeling a bit ill and weak, from what I didn't know. I remember feverishly crying myself to sleep that night. I'd never met the lady, but I knew she was only one month older than I. Being unwell, I began to think about how tenuous life is. I'm sure I wouldn't have done that if I'd been my usual hardy self. (Operations don't count. They keep you feeling hardy.)

I rested a lot on that tour and kept partying with "the family" to a minimum. I was almost always tired by the end of the performance, which was odd for me. A couple of theaters later, something besides my energy level came crashing down.

I'll explain.

The opening of *Birdie* finds me onstage, my back to the audience, on the phone to my mother in a music office. On opening night at the Grist Mill Playhouse in Andover, New Jersey, an apprentice in the wings mistakenly untied the wrong rope after the overture. He was supposed to have taken the curtain up; instead he released the front light rail directly over where I was standing on the raised office set, which was on wheels. The lights were spaced maybe eighteen inches apart on the rail, which came crashing.

Luck was with me. I was struck on the shoulder by a hunk of rail and knocked off the set-piece. Had a light hit me, it could have sliced off my arm. Pat Finley, waiting to enter from the wings, let out a terrifying scream, thinking I had been killed. The set took most of the blow. I hurt like hell but didn't lose consciousness. I vaguely heard someone yelling from in front of the curtain, "Is there a doctor in the house?" That tickled me. Some dear man showed, and they hoisted the light rail off of me. I said I was fine which of course I wasn't, but "the show must go on" should always follow the doctor line. The stage manager insisted, as did the doctor, that I go for an X-ray. Nothing was busted, and forty-five minutes or so later I was back onstage. The sold-out house had stayed, and when the curtain finally rose there was a standing ovation before I got a line out. What a terrific audience. We gave that particular show everything we had. I couldn't believe that not a single theatergoer had left before I got back.

I felt so sorry for the apprentice. The poor kid must have felt terrible. I told the stage manager to be sure and tell whoever had made the slip-up that mistakes happen and that I was fine. But I really wasn't fine. I ached all over, and soaked in a hot tub before I took a sleeping pill. The next morning I really hurt, but we finished out the run to record business. That Sunday was moving day, and one of the gypsies drove me to the next theater.

Whatever was the matter with me before had been multiplied by the accident. By the time we'd reached Detroit, our last gig, I was hanging on by a thread, using the show as a nightly pickup. We were in for a three-week stint. (The previous theater, Pocono Playhouse in Mountainhome, Pennsylvania, had added an additional matinee on Thursday, making the week even tougher. All nine shows were SRO.) In the middle of the second week my gas tank went dry after the first act. I rushed to an emergency room, got a shot of something and raced back to finish the show. But that was the end. The doctor told me I had mononucleosis, and ordered me to stay in bed in my rented apartment in downtown Detroit. The Dome was in a big shopping center on the edge of town, and we bused back and forth during the run. I was heartsick not to be able to finish the last performances with that loving cast.

They trooped by to say goodbye, then departed for their homes. I had to stay on for two weeks after the show until I was well enough to travel. Even then, I needed to fly a friend in from California to drive Ren and me home. On the way we stopped every night in motels on the way to rest up for the next day's drive. It seemed to take forever to reach Norma Place and my own bed.

And that is where I stayed for most of the next three months till I could kiss off the frigging disease. Those months turned out to be a welcome, needed time of introspection, something I hadn't had since the brief days following my lifesaving operation of 1955. My reflections on my wild lifestyle were somehow cleansing, without becoming too "spiritual." Sometimes they were comical. It was fun to think back about the giant juggling act I'd been performing, carousing and constantly working at the same time.

But the shenanigans continued all around me. Shortly after I'd converted my garage to a guesthouse, my next-door neighbor, Hagar Wilde, turned hers into what she called Cat House. It was filled with dozens of them. Thank God I like cats, although my pleasure with them was diminished greatly by the vast number next door. More worrisome was a late-night human incident that Hagar alleged. On a particular evening, she claimed, she was set upon by an unknown intruder who blindfolded her while in bed. He took off his clothes, piled them neatly on a chair and stood naked at the foot of her bed. One wonders how she could have divined all that without peeking, but she swore she hadn't.

Before the rapist attacked her, explained Hagar, she told him, "The lubricant is in the top drawer of the bureau." She claimed she'd said it for self-protection because of the size of his equipment. She'd divined that as well? It was a bit difficult to figure out just who was the rapist and who was the rapee. Of course the tale spread like a brush fire, due largely to the lady herself. The laughable story lasted for weeks. She later told us that the intruder turned out to be someone she knew, the son-in-law of a very famous writer-producer. She'd identified by his cologne, she insisted. No charges were ever filed, of course, and the tale got Hagar lots of attention.

There were further hijinks at the 4 Star, which had opened a back room to hold the nightly crowds. It had an old upright piano at which I sat from time to time, blasting out evergreens for singalongs like "Shine On Harvest Moon" and "For Me and My Gal." One night I was sitting at the packed bar. A young pool hustler had managed to pick up (or get picked up by) a very drunken Montgomery Clift at some joint in downtown Hollywood. From there he'd taken Monty to the 4 Star. The super actor was in terrible shape physically—he died two or three years later—and he was sagging over the bar a couple of stools from me. Most of his time he was on his knees grabbing at a couple of the regulars. It was really sad. Everybody adored him and paid no attention. There was no smirking or tittering, just unbearable sadness. We eventually got him out to the street and into a cab. I could have killed that stick-hustling kid, the only one who thought it was all a huge joke.

Whenever a new theater workshop was being organized I couldn't wait to be in on it. And joining Theater East was one of the best decisions I ever made. It was composed of a carefully selected bunch of writers, directors and actors, all of them working pros. A special carrot on the stick was the participation of my old friend Bobo Lewis. We rented a space in Hollywood and went to work doing scenes, one-acts, sometimes entire plays. There was never an audience, not even relatives or roomies, and the pieces were critiqued only by us, after they'd been worked on for a time.

It was a great atmosphere in which to polish, improve and often fail, but sometimes to achieve incredible success. Everyone was of the same mind, and the process kept us oiled and busy even as we earned our livings in film or TV. I made many close and cherished chums in that group. A bunch of us hung out together across the street after a long evening, relaxing, having a drink or two, and playing the occasional game of bumper pool. Anyone with an early call the next morning would have a quickie and head out; the rest stayed on into the wee hours. I remember directing a new one-act by a member. After a few weeks of work on the piece, we did it at the regular weekly gathering. Everyone loved it. The current chair of the group yelled after the applause, "No critiques needed tonight. It was super!" I was as pleased as the cast. I gave the actors all the credit; they gave me all the credit. A love fest.

One of our longer projects was Bertolt Brecht's *Mother Courage and Her Children*. I played the cook, a part I would never have been cast in commercially. What great fun to be able to stretch out like that. The dear TV actress and nightclub performer Connie Sawyer played Mother. At some point, several members of our group did a benefit for our workshop at a theater in San Fernando Valley. They chose Dylan Thomas's *Under Milk Wood*. I had a rough time wrapping my tongue around all the Welsh words, which don't look anything like they should be pronounced—all those double or triple l's. But the benefit did swell our coffers a bit and helped keep us a step or two ahead of the rental agency.

One mid-morning in 1963 I ran into Dottie Parker at Shermart. We walked back to Norma Place together. When I asked how her "groom" (Alan) was, she giggled, as I knew she would. When she had first arrived in West Hollywood to join Alan, who was already my neighbor, I told her in our first meeting that I'd known her groom for some time and was so thrilled to finally meet the bride. It had tickled her then and it still did.

On this particular morning, she said, "Groom fine. Bride divine." When she reached my house she asked if I had time for coffee and a game of Jotto; Alan was still sleeping. In she came, parking her groceries by the front door and heading for her usual end of my couch. I joined her with mugs and the green pads and we were off on another round of word stumpers.

It was later revealed that the groom wasn't fine at all. Alan had had some success as Dorothy's screenwriting partner in the '30s; the two of them had scored an Oscar nomination for Best Adapted Screenplay for the 1937 *A Star Is Born*. But all that was far behind Alan when I met him; he'd been Mr. Dorothy Parker for years. While Dorothy and I sat cozily three houses away trying to outwit each other with our hidden words, Alan had gotten drunk on Bloody Marys, then had swallowed a fistful of Seconal and asphyxiated himself with a plastic bag. Dorothy went home and found him dead.

She called me. "Groom gone," she said, "no more among the quick."

Poor old sot. I had the idea that I'd miss old Alan more than his bride. Through the whole time that followed she remained tearless, as far as I could tell. She wore dark glasses during the funeral, so no one knew for sure.

Chapter 15 —————

'Twas the time of the Hully Gully and the Twist. A gang of us, most often two carloads, would race wildly out to Santa Monica Pier on Friday and Saturday nights—not to the pier itself but across the Pacific Coast Highway to an old deserted-looking building. We would find the unlit door around the side of the place and head down a flight of steep stairs to heaven in hell's location.

It led us to a crowded, barely lit room with a generous (in every way) dance floor and a gang of people who were sweating away to the just-loud-enough-not-to-reach-the-highway jukebox. They were mainly youngish, with a few wrinkle-room types sprinkled here and there. Male with male and female with female comprised the majority of the couplage. Those were the dancing days when partners didn't touch; they simply squirmed and twisted sort of at one another.

Nevertheless, every so often a red bulb would suddenly flash above the fray. That signaled that the cops were on the way down the stairs to check the joint out, making sure everything was perfectly normal. They cruised by almost every night at least once. When that red bulb flashed, guys would grab the nearest gal and start dancing with lovely enraptured looks. All beer cans, which we toted there with us, magically disappeared from view. The place, of course, had no liquor license. I can't remember anyone actually being dragged out of the place, although I heard about arrests that were made outside in the wee hours when someone had brought too many six-packs and had left no can unconsumed. The police were no doubt paid off anyway; that's the way things usually worked.

A frequent member of our group was a handsome kid with a baby face, a friend of Black Starr. Everyone called "Coca-Cola" since almost nothing stronger ever passed those innocent lips. Years later he met and married the talented and terrific actress Marsha Mason. It didn't last long, but it was a loving, friendly roommate arrangement while it did. Marsha later married Neil Simon.

Back home on Norma, my guest cottage had a long string of renters. I think I charged fifty or seventy-five a month for the converted garage. It was rarely unoccupied, and the tab changed according to someone's ability to pay; sometimes I charged nothing. Shirley Knight's husband stayed there. I think they were separated. He was a quiet soul whom I rarely saw; he slipped in and out and never asked for anything. Not really unsociable; just a loner, I guess.

I remember coming home fairly early one night from a bridge game, maybe at eleven-thirty, to find my front door locked. This was back when no one locked doors. I wondered if I'd done it by mistake. I went around to the back and saw a hole in the screen door and the sliding door slightly ajar. The den was a wreck: books pushed in and all askew in the cases, desk ransacked. Several residual checks were missing, along with an old out-of-date driver's license and I don't know what else. Apparently the first thing the burglar had done was to lock the front door from the inside before he or she went to work. I called the police and they arrived shortly. I tried to make a list of things were missing.

It was so creepy, worse than being mugged. I felt unclean, as if I'd been raped or something. So invaded. I called my agent the next morning to put a stop-payment on the checks he'd sent. It wasn't until a day later that I discovered that all the stamps that I'd collected since I was a kid—and sheets of commemoratives I'd acquired over the last ten or twelve years—were gone. At face value alone they were worth in the thousands. No one even knew I'd collected them. I guess when the robber found that cache, he just took off. When I called the police about the stamps, they told me they'd do their best but that stamps, like cash, were almost impossible to ever catch up with. They held out little hope. I was devastated—not about the value but about all those hours of lovingly mounting the collection over a lifetime, carefully arranging the mint blocks in albums I had designed. Writing about it now still hurts. Except for coins, I never collected anything else again.

My tenant at the time, Wyatt Cooper, an aspiring screenwriter, had been away the night of the burglary. When he appeared at my back door the next morning he told me he'd been hit too. Most of his splendid wardrobe had vanished. When I said that no clothes of mine that I knew of were missing. "Of course not," Cooper said. "You have no taste." He made me laugh. It was true; I don't. I'm no slave to fashion. Consoling me, Wyatt added: "Well, Carp, at least we were burgled by a gentleman of good taste."

Wyatt was really was a joy. Sometime later he met Gloria Vanderbilt while she was on the West Coast, and he returned with her to New York. A short time later he came back, and she followed him. He hid from her for a bit. I knew where he was staying and promised not to tell. She came by and checked out old digs in the back. I kept mum about his whereabouts. I gathered she was determined to get him to the altar; I don't know what his hide-and tease game was all about. Finally he surfaced, and they were married soon after in New York. It was a pure case of a girl who chases a man until she catches him. I miss Wyatt.

Now that the horse had been swiped from the barn, I quickly had a strong wooden fence built from the edge of the house to the side of the guest cottage. Another new fence protected the back of the cottage and reached to the existing fence that marked the boundary line of my property. The gate from the driveway into our shared "garden" was secured with a strong lock. And I began locking my front door. The thief was never caught, even though I learned that several other break-ins in the area had been going on for about a month.

I continued to rent out the cottage. The tenant who stayed the longest was a young actor named James Secrest, an old friend of Robert Osborne, who now does all those super lead-ins as a host on Turner Classic Movies. He was a budding actor then. I remember a trip Jimmy planed for a bunch of us. We motored north to Santa Barbara to catch Osborne at the old Lobero Theatre in a play with Joe E. Brown. I think it was *Harvey*, the Pulitzer Prize-winner by Mary Chase. The highlight of the evening was Brown's famous clowning after the bows. He threw in all his vaudeville schtick, even his old baseball routine. It was wonderfully funny, but it did go on for what seemed like forever—and we had a long drive home awaiting us. Bob was fine, but I believe he really found his niche as a columnist for the *Hollywood Reporter* and, of course, as a TV host.

Secrest remained my renter for as long as I kept the house on Norma Place. At some point in the early '60s, Dick Derr, the realtor who had sold me my Norma nest, talked me into what he called "trading up." I had no clue what that was. He explained: "The more you owe, the more you'll be able to get for a new mortgage." That made no sense to me, with my New England "cash on the barrelhead" mentality; I was thrilled that I had nearly paid off the Norma mortgage. But Dick persisted. He had found a terrific investment opportunity for me, he said: ten rental units on some property on Harper at the east end of West Hollywood.

Dick was a charmer, so I said I'd take a look. Clever agent that he was, he knew the place he proposed was right up my New Englander's alley. He showed me two adjacent buildings: one of them an old home with honest-to-God wooden clapboards and a huge tree in front; the other, a two-story match to the big house. Not a palm tree or hunk of pink stucco in sight. It was like a tiny Vermont island in the middle of all the lookalike apartment houses on Harper. I was sunk. Derr told me that the main house held four apartments, the two-story job had two, and in the back of the property was a four-car garage with an equal number of apartments above. These were brand-new and two were already rented. One would be for me and I'd have but one to rent; all the rest out front were occupied.

The monthly income, said Derr, would more than take care of the mortgage and leave plenty for any repairs or maintenance. Plus I'd get to live rent-free above the first garage. When I looked at it, it seemed so tiny after the house on Norma, and I wondered how I'd get everything in. Still, it was so sparkling-clean and inviting. There was a sort-of Alpine ceiling in the living room, a kitchen with a broad counter, a fair-sized bedroom in the back and a good bath. The place was bigger, I guessed, than my old pad on 50th in New York.

Before I knew what had happened, I was back in that terrible place called escrow. My old friend Jim Smith immediately wanted the one remaining apartment, so I never had to worry about finding a tenant. I started giving things away. An out-of-work director from Theater East took dishes, silverware, pots and pans and several pieces of furniture I would no longer need. I had put my whole collection of 78 records on reel-to-reel tape—those recorders were the hot new gadget then—and given all my records to Theater East. The tapes were much more compact and less weighty. Unhappily, I later lost many of those invaluable tapes to a basement flood.

When it was time to move, I had nothing left but the bed, Shel's bookcase and desk unit, my piano (which fit snugly in the bedroom), the ottoman-bed, piles of books and my unstylish wardrobe. Wonder of wonders, the new place had a stove and fridge, so I could leave mine, which increased the value of the house on Norma. A buddy with a truck helped me make the great move. To be honest, it felt rather good being in the smaller space. I was still a New Yorker at heart, and the Alpine apartment seemed more like a place in the Big Apple—more like home, more familiar, almost like a return to the roots I'd been ripping out for the last few years here in California.

I made two new purchases for the new digs, one small, one big. Both seemed like miracles. When I bought a non-stick frying pan, I couldn't get over how easy it was to fry an egg. How did that work? My other magical buy was a *color* television set. An RCA, I think. After I'd hooked it up I sat in awe at the lifelike hues; I would call my neighbors in to share the wonder of it all. Jim Smith, who was working on *The Danny Kaye Show* at CBS, would stop in often to watch the tube. I think he was amazed at my childlike fascination with my expensive new toy. He was used to seeing things in color at the studio. I remember him telling me one day how Danny reminded him of me: not performance-wise (God knows I'd never put myself in that rarified level of comic genius) but just in the way he acted around the set; the way he moved and his sense of humor. Still, it was flattering. I later learned about Kaye's bouts of temperament and wasn't so flattered. Jim insisted that I didn't share that trait. I can't remember ever being temperamental at work; certainly not when I did Kaye's role in the TV version of *Lady in the Dark*. I was just trying to hang on to all the words and keep my Pepto-Bismol down.

At some point Debbie called and asked if I'd pose for some book called *If I Knew Then*. I believe Bob Thomas was writing it for her. It was a guide to teenage dating. I agreed, and we had great fun doing a series of photographs of assorted types of male dates. I kept changing clothes, hairstyles, and makeup; I looked wild, leering (with a mustache for that one), nerdy, innocent, wiseguyish, whatever. Deb was always sweet and cute. I have no idea if the book sold well, but it must have; she was very popular (still is, bless her) and I had a few fans myself. Whatever. The two-day shoot was gratis and of course I didn't share in any royalties. She did send me a bottle of vodka as thanks. That was fine by me.

There was a bar/restaurant on the corner of Santa Monica and Crescent Heights, only a few blocks from my apartment. I loved going there in the afternoon and gabbing with a bunch of regulars, mostly writers. I had discovered the place some time ago while still on Norma and I used to bike over. Now it was a very short stroll, which was much better, since I'd overdrunk on one of the bicycling days and had a terrible time peddling back to the house. I fell often and finally arrived battered and bruised just before the sun was about to go down. A small gang had watched me depart from the back door of that special joint, and they'd laughed at my attempts to get my stupid self onto the bicycle. Why they let me take off in that condition, I'll never know. At any rate, that wobbly departure yielded great merriment among those semi-sadistic s.o.b.s for months. What an asshole I was. But I loved the place, the shuffleboard bowling machine, and even those bastards who gave me such a ribbing.

Across the avenue and a couple of blocks down was another great bar where the game of preference was darts. Young Clint Eastwood hung there on off-hours from playing Rowdy Yates in the hit TV western *Rawhide*. He was beginning to get a name and a great following. I liked the place, though I thought it a bit clanish.

An extremely popular commercial had been running for some time. It featured a very proper English character called Manners, the Butler, who hawked a paper napkin by the makers of Kleenex tissues. The dinner-sized serviette would be proffered to diners by a miniaturized Manners; the napkin looked like a tablecloth in his hands. The product was a smashing success. Now they had a brilliant new idea: a smaller napkin to be introduced by a new character called Cousin Casual. I'd been doing a lot of commercials, and was called to audition for the role. It would be a blockbuster national with tons of residuals; I could see the checks piling up. But unlike most other auditions where you had one callback or maybe two before being signed, this job entailed one reading, four callbacks, several interviews and finally two, count-'em, two screentests. Wild.

But it might be very lucrative, so I went through the whole megillah. It was the hardest and longest I'd ever had to work for any role, but I finally got it. The shooting was great fun. This was long before special effects and computer tricks; the soundstage had giant furniture, making Cousin Casual about as tall as the backrest of a dining-room chair. Altogether we shot maybe a half-dozen spots. They ran the bejesus out of them, and the checks did indeed begin to flow steadily in. My shrunken bank account began to swell up again. But after less than a year the spots were pulled. The smaller napkin wasn't catching on with buyers. Well, it was a windfall while it lasted. It would be several years before I landed a five-year gig with a product. Commercials are the annuity that keeps many, many actors afloat between theater jobs. Those lovely residuals checks seem almost like stealing after awhile, but you have to do about a hundred auditions and shoot four or five commercials before one really pays off.

I flew back to New York for some off-Broadway play, temporarily leaving my golden Ren to my friend Lewis Freedman, who now lived in L.A., and the apartment to Blossom Dearie. At a reading of the play, a British director asked me if I'd join a show he was about to do. It was called *Boeing-Boeing*, and the director, Jack Minster, wanted me to stand by for the star, Ian Carmichael. Since the comedy was headed for Broadway I jumped at the opportunity. Good thing: The off-Broadway effort had several more readings but never went beyond that.

After *Boeing-Boeing* had finished rehearsals we headed to New Haven, then to the Wilbur Theatre in Boston for the pre-New York tryouts. I went a couple of times to a musical that was running across the street at the Shubert. *Kelly* had a score by Moose Charlap, direction by the wonderful Herbie Ross and a cast that included Anita Gillette, Jesse White and Wilfrid Brambell. The star was a Canadian actor-singer named Don Francks. *Kelly* opened a couple of days after us in New York and closed after one performance. Now when I say I saw the infamous *Kelly* twice I'm usually asked, "How?"

In New Haven and Boston I loved rehearsing *Boeing-Boeing* with a great gal, Nelle Nugent, one of the stage managers but a really good actress too. We had fun together. (She later became part of a very successful producing team with Liz McCann.) In anticipation of a long run on Broadway, I resituated myself in New York. Kay Medford lived at the Parc Vendome on West 57th Street, and she managed to snare me a former servant's quarters on the ground floor. It was very cheap—I think just seventy-five bucks a months—and had a phone (the switchboard took messages), a bathroom with a big bathtub and a tiny room facing the court. Jim Nichols from the *Bye Bye Birdie* tour lugged over a long, skinny mattress for me from his apartment around the corner.

But I wasn't there very much, especially when the Second New York World's Fair came to town. I'd attended the 1939-1940 edition in Flushing Meadows-Corona Park, Queens. I was in such awe of everything, and my twelve-year-old arms grabbed up all the free stuff I could find. I took it home and pored over everything. Even today I have a scrapbook with the fair's old Trylon and Perisphere logo on the cover.

Twenty-five years later the fair was back. I drank everything in, almost literally; I loved all the ethnic bars and pubs from around the globe. My companion was Harry Rigby, my chum since 1953, when he had produced *John Murray Anderson's Almanac*. Harry and I spent several days in Flushing taking in campy sponsored shows whose casts included several of my fellow actors. "Triple" (Murray's name for Harry) always wanted to stay for the fireworks, but they bored the bejesus out of me. If I watched them I'd miss the start of the Mets game, which I used to hear on the radio in my tiny room at the Parc Vendome. The New York Metropolitans, as they were originally known, were my new love. They had just joined the National League in 1961, and I was now their number-one fan. But begrudgingly, I stuck with Harry and watched the fireworks.

Jim Nichols had concocted a TV game-show idea, and I did a number of backers' auditions for him. It was a good game, with ad-libbing a prerequisite for the panelists, one of whom was Jo Anne Worley. The show never sold, but I had a much bigger disappointment in store. One day a call came from a complete stranger, who gave me some bad news. Jeanne Shelby, my darling first love, mentor, cheerleader and inspiration for being an actor, had passed away. The sudden guilt I felt was unbearable. I'd been in California for so long, and back and forth to the East Coast east so many times in the past few years, that I had been very neglectful of wonderful Jeanne. I hadn't kept in touch; I didn't even know she'd become ill. Now there was a funeral to attend on Lexington Avenue. It took place at some smallish place where the assembled friends of Jeanne's were total unknowns to me. I was asked to speak, and of course I did. It was a tearful performance; I'd been in love with the lady since 1928.

Later a group of us went to someone's apartment and toasted and talked for hours. They were terrific show folk. I missed her old roommate Minette Barrett, who had predeceased Jeanne; she was the only close friend of Jeanne's that I'd known.

A couple of days later there was a knock on my door at the Parc Vendome. A messenger stood in the hallway and handed me a package. It was Jeanne—or rather, her ashes. I hadn't expected that. I guess I was supposed to bury her. I piled into my VW Bug—I'd traded off the Caravelle just prior to this trip—and put Jeanne beside me in the other seat. I headed for Bennington and Park Lawn Cemetery, where her mother, Auntie Shelby, was interred. My young nieces and nephews were shocked when I described the journey. I told them how I had talked to Jeanne all the way up and sometimes sung to her. We actually had a lovely time, just the two of us.

My sister's kids thought I was weird, spooky and nuts. So did B.J. But Dar and my Aunt Pat took it all in wonderful stride. I hadn't obtained permission to bury Jeanne, but they abetted my unlawful act by standing guard while I dug a deep hole in the near-frozen autumn ground and planted my darling next to her mother. We three lawbreakers gathered at the spot when the crime was completed and had a nutty ceremony recalling funny stuff about the departed. B.J.'s kids would have thought it pure science fiction or horror, maybe both.

Jeanne had been a favorite of the director Hazzard "Bobby" Short, who cast her in many musicals in her later years. After his death, the roles for Jeanne seemed to wither away. But she had a long if unsung career, both on Broadway and the road. In these days of instant celebrity, hundreds or perhaps thousands of devoted working actors plug away unnoticed and unheralded at the profession that obsesses them. So it was with Jeanne. She had introduced me to the glories of Shakespeare as a kid. I'll be crude, rude and probably booed, but I'll plow ahead and add a bit to one of the master's lines: "The good is oft interred with their bones" … the inspirational spirit with the ashes.

Before *Boeing-Boeing* opened, I'd moved into a new building, Lincoln Terrace, at 66th Street off of Broadway. But I was in Beantown when I received a phone call from my buddy, Helen Livingston Nicholson. She told me that David Merrick and Gower Champion wanted me for the role of Cornelius in the international company of *Hello, Dolly!* I had seen the musical in New York with Helen and told her, "I'll play that part." She said, "It wouldn't surprise me at all." (Funnily enough I'd said the same thing in London when I saw the nonmusical basis of *Dolly!*, Thornton Wilder's *The Merchant of Yonkers*.) I auditioned for Gower. Now, stretched out on my bed at the Avery Hotel in Boston, I heard it was going to happen. I was ecstatic.

Boeing-Boeing opened at the Cort Theatre on February 2, 1965. I sat with Mr. Minster opening night—the only time I appeared at the theater since, as the standby, I could call in, and if I wasn't needed, I didn't have to come down from 66th to 48th. The show ran twenty-three times longer than *Kelly* and folded on February 20.

No matter. With *Hello, Dolly!* I was on the verge of one of the great adventures of my life, and I had much to attend to before the whole thing began—notably moving out of the apartment I'd just rented. Cart and my Uncle Hike rolled down from Vermont with the truck. Into it we piled what little furniture I'd acquired for Lincoln Terrace and carted it off to Bennington. The baby grand stayed. I found someone in the city who wanted it and would keep it while I was on tour.

I had found someone to take over my New York lease, but at the last possible moment she changed her mind, and I was stuck for a couple of months rent. The lady, Elaine Kaufman, was planning to open a restaurant on the Upper East Side, and wanted to be closer to the spot she'd picked out. I couldn't blame her. I wished her well before I headed for a quick trip West. She never needed my good-luck wishes; almost instantly her restaurant, Elaine's, became one of the hottest in-spots in town.

In California I arranged for someone to manage the Hilldale property: an out-of-work TV producer who'd been recommended to me. With that, I left for New York to begin rehearsals.

Hello, Dolly! had opened on Broadway on January 16, 1964, just over a year before. It was nominated for eleven Tony Awards and won ten of them. The only one it had lost was for Best Supporting Actor in a Musical: the role I was about to play. I had attended the Tonys that year with Helen, who worked for Merrick, so I sat at the *Hello, Dolly!* table.

Now here I was, rehearsing for the show. Gower attacking the entire thing as if it had never been done before: bliss. He changed many things, including the second-act opener; Gower substituted a polka for the original butterfly number. (It was later changed in the New York company, too.) More important for my purposes, he exchanged the personalities of the two clerks at Vandergelder's Hay & Feed Store. Now the younger Barnaby was the bespectacled, more sober character and Cornelius the devil-may-care, wilder one. The switch suited both me and Johnny Beecher, the actor chosen to play Barnaby. I loved the courtroom scene that including my number, "It Only Takes A Moment," such a lovely ballad. I was a bit frightened of it, and told the composer, Jerry Herman, that I thought it was a little high. Bless his professional heart, he would have none of it. "It'll be fine when you're on stage," he said. "You'll hit the high F with no problem." Of course he was right. Everything seems too high in a rehearsal hall.

Our Dolly, Mary Martin, was a dream to work with, and a hoot to boot. This was the first time she'd ever come into a show without knowing her whole part beforehand. She learned the numbers right along with us. Mary never played just to the audience. When we got on stage she was always right there with us, making great eye contact, really listening, playing off of us, going along with any odd readings, adjusting and having fun, constantly in character. Loring Smith, who played Horace Vandergelder, was a joy, too. So was the entire cast. And those dancing guys and gals! Gower had chosen a bunch of real champions. Please excuse the long list, but we became such a close-knit family that I have to mention them all: Judith Drake, Mark Alden, Eileen Barbaris, Debra Lyman, Beverlee Weir, Coco Ramirez, Charlise Mallory, Skedge Miller and my incomparable Mrs. Malloy, Marilynn Lovell, a Kay Kendall-like presence with a glorious voice.

We opened on April 19, 1965 at the Orpheum Theatre in Minneapolis to an SRO crowd and a standing ovation. That became the norm everywhere we played. This wasn't the national tour; that would come later. We

were officially called the international company since we were headed to
Japan and, thanks to a Cultural Exchange Program with the U.S.S.R., then
to Saint Petersburg in Russia and on to London. But before going overseas
the show was booked into several U.S. cities, where we played the biggest
theaters and arenas available. The weekly grosses listed by *Variety* were
phenomenal—the highest of any touring Broadway show up to then. The
sold-out houses in New York for the original had remained record-breaking, but the capacity of the St. James Theatre couldn't come close to the
business we were doing. In New Orleans we played in one half of a sports
arena while a basketball game was going on in the other. We did the same
in Cleveland, minus the competing event. In Toronto we christened an
enormous new theater, the O'Keefe Center.

A sort of unspoken rivalry surfaced between the two leading ladies,
Carol Channing and Mary Martin. It tickled all of us in the international
company. Gower showed up practically everyplace we played. He was enthralled with our version, but his presence helped keep us on our toes.
We all loved that musical so much, though, that we didn't need much
brushing up.

In Toronto, Dar, Carto, Uncle Burt and Aunt Pat arrived to catch
the show and celebrate my thirty-ninth birthday, the one Jack Benny had
ruined for everyone.

People who knew I had a birthday coming up on July 10 would say,
"What are you, twenty-seven or twenty-right?" I'd say, thirty-eight. After
my birthday, anyone who knew I'd turned thirty-nine was likely to say:
"C'mon, what are you, forty-five?" Thank you, Mr. Benny.

At one point in the show, a lady seated behind my mother told her
friend that she'd loved me in films, but this was even better. Dar turned
around and whispered proudly, "That's my son." The woman said, "Are
you joking?" Answered Dar: "It was no joke washing all his dirty under-
wear this morning." The lady and Dar had a whole conversation during
the intermission; my mother told me later that she was basking in my
reflected glory. I told her she didn't have to talk about my dirty skivvies.

Gordon MacRae also caught the show in Toronto. Afterwards he
came backstage and told me he was going to call Mike Douglas in Cleveland, where we were set to play next, and tell him to book me on his show,
which was based there. MacRae had just done it recently. I guess he was
true to his word; shortly after we opened in Cleveland, a call came to appear on the show. Herb Alpert and the Tijuana Brass were also guests. I
sang "It Only Takes a Moment" and a medley of "Row, Row, Row" and

A presidential moment in Kansas City during the 1965 tour of *Hello, Dolly!*
L-R: Harry S. Truman, Loring Smith (who played Horace Vandergelder), me,
Bess Truman, Marilynn Lovell, Mary Martin.

"Aba Daba Honeymoon." Unbeknownst to me, a big guy in a gorilla suit was sneaking up behind me as I sang the medley; he grabbed me at the finish. The audience was screaming when we broke for commercials. I yelled out a request to the prop guy. When the show resumed I was lying flat on the stage with my eyes closed and arms crossed on my stomach, holding a lily sticking straight up. Mike, the crew and the audience broke into loud applause. The improv made the local papers and was picked up by the Associated Press. What good ink for me and the international company of *Hello, Dolly!*

There were many other memorable moments on that tour. I remember our moonlight riverboat trip after playing one night in Memphis. We met Bess and Harry Truman in Kansas City. In Dallas we got to know Larry Hagman, Mary Martin's son; he was a nice guy and a big TV star thanks to *I Dream of Jeannie*. In Seattle we saw the Space Needle from my hotel-room window (that was as close as I got to it!), and a gang of us from the cast saw the Beatles' movie *Help!* We loved the beautiful sights (and nights) in Vancouver, B.C. I'd never seen much of the Pacific Northwest before—spectacular. We had too many joyful moments to conjure up in a single session at the typewriter.

Before heading overseas we stopped at a wonderfully restored theater in Portland, making time to visit a terrific nearby pub that had a huge selection of home brews. We also got all the necessary shots—a slew of them—before we headed overseas. It was an agonizing adventure. I felt sorriest for the male dancers, whose arms were killing them. Eight times a week they had to perform the intricate and exhausting "Waiter's Gallop" as devised by Gower. The poor guys had to hold up trays with arms that had been stuck by all those needles. I took no chances. When I was told to roll up my sleeve, I simply turned my back, pulled down my pants and shorts and offered a flatish cheek up to the needle gods. Okay, so it was uncomfortable to sit, but you rarely sit in a fast-paced musical. And I've always hated needles; doesn't everybody?

In Tokyo we played at the Takarazuka Theatre, which was across the street from the Imperial Hotel, designed by Frank Lloyd Wright. That's where most of us stayed. I had to watch my head because of the fairly low doorways and ceilings. Most of us were doubling or tripling up on rooms in order to cut costs, and practically all the time I doubled with a super dancer named Lou Zeldis, who was as tall as I. He loved shopping during the day and Frug-ing with the other kids at whatever dance joint they found after the show. I saw little of him except at the theater, which made him a really good road roommate.

The Japanese had constructed the most beautifully intricate, delicate set, with incredible detail. The theater offered headsets for instant translation. Well, almost instant. We had to alter our timing a tad on stage because the titters—the audience was too polite to guffaw—would come a touch later after a laugh line. The applause sounded more like gentle rainfall, but everyone adored the show and the theater was jammed to the gills at every performance.

Lou and I decided to grow long sideburns; they'd be in keeping with the musical's era, and Lou had often said that there was little to do on the road except work, shop and play with your hair. That sounded pretty good to me. I even joined him on many shopping trips. We caused quite a stir on the Ginza as a tall, fair-haired duo loping along, our long hair growing longer by the day and waving in the breeze. Shorter heads would gape up and giggle at the odd pair. We loved the effect we were having, but pretended not to notice any of it.

At the Imperial bar I met Shirley MacLaine's husband Steve Parker, a businessman. He introduced himself by reminding me that we'd worked together on some early TV show in N.Y. I didn't remember him, but found his company interesting as we shared a couple of Kirin beers.

There was a Japanese fan who repeatedly came to see the show, always bringing some sort of gift, a kimono or a little box of sandwiches or whatever. He finally asked me if I would dine with him and his family. Of course I happily accepted, and the date was set. When I arrived at his home I learned I was the first American to set foot in their house. He had persuaded his folks to allow me to visit. They were extremely polite and reserved but very gracious, and the shoeless, floor-sitting meal was delicious and fun. They spoke no English and I'd only learned the barest bit of Japanese, so my new fan and now friend, Katutoshi Toyoda (nicknamed Suzumo), translated all night. When I left, his parents presented me with a beautifully wrapped gift, a super kimono, and we smiled and bowed. I felt I'd presented myself (and my country) in a respectable manner. Later, Suzumo told me his grandparents had been killed in Hiroshima by the bombing during World War II.

You can imagine how I felt, with my links to Tinian and the Enola Gay runway, which my battalion had built. I was inconsolable and cried openly when Suzumo told me how much his parents had liked me after so many years of hating all Americans. I never told him about my time with the Seabees. He couldn't understand why I wept so at what he considered exceptionally happy news. What a sweet guy he was. We corresponded for many years before losing contact. At that special dinner, he had asked his dad take a snap of us at the low table. He gave me a copy. I still have it in my passport wallet.

Marilynn Lovell and I did several forums at schools, most of them places where the kids were learning about theater. We probably learned more at these sessions than the pupils. That's the way it usually works; the teacher is also taught by the pupil. Except for a moment in the second grade when I thought I wanted to be a doctor, the only thing I ever imagined myself doing as a life's work aside from performing was teaching. But of course I hadn't the credentials, and knew that I was in no way qualified. Still I keep on learning, and sometimes I get the opportunity to have a positive effect on someone's life.

Toward the end of our six-week run in Tokyo, Russia suddenly cancelled the cultural exchange program because of our country's involvement in Vietnam. Merrick and Gower flew right in from the States and called a meeting of the entire company. We were faced with an alternative plan: to go to Vietnam and entertain our troops instead.

Some of the performers weren't so hot for the idea. But me and my pal Edmond Dante were immediately up for the adventure. He had come in as a replacement for a cast member who had declined the overseas gig. Edmund, formerly Ed Belson, was a great singer who'd been in the *Bye Bye Birdie* tour with me. (I remember him singing at a cast party in someone's cabin in Lakewood, Maine. He'd chosen "Lonely House" from *Street Scene* by Kurt Weill and Langston Hughes. I'd never heard it sung more beautifully.) Now, in *Hello, Dolly!*, we'd picked up our acquaintance and turned it into a lifetime friendship.

Merrick told the cast that we'd vote the following day on the Vietnam idea. He stated that it had to be one-hundred percent or nothing. Some of the kids were scared, some just a wee bit nervous; all of us were sorry we wouldn't get to see Russia. We'd had extra-painful and now-unecessary injections for the USSR.

Ed and I, being older than most of the kids, did a bit of campaigning. I offered tales of World War II and Korea and how wonderful it had felt to entertain such enthusiastic audiences. Whether or not the two of us made any difference I'll never know, but the following day there wasn't (as I recall) a single "nay" vote.

During the time left in Japan we crammed in as much of Tokyo as possible: seeing other shows; meeting Japanese actors; watching at least part of the six-hour traditional Noh drama at some theater; going to local movies, mostly action-filled with little story to follow; dancing at various clubs; saying goodbyes to favorite bars; stuffing ourselves with everything Japanese.

Meanwhile, the local artisans who'd produced the incredible set were busy constructing a spare, portable version of the delicate work of art we were performing with at the Takarazuka Theater. The orchestra was recording the score on tape since we'd only be carrying the drummer, banjoist, lead trumpeter, pianist, and the conductor, Jay Blackton.

The goodbyes from the cast to all our new Japanese friends were sad indeed, but underneath there was this knot in our bellies of excited expectation for the adventure awaiting us all in battle zone. We arrived in Saigon and were billeted in a partially finished new building—workmen were still busy at it all day—that would be an R&R (Rest and Recreation) place for rotating troops when completed. It was almost directly across the street from the American Embassy where Ambassador Henry Cabot

Singing "Elegance" with three of my *Hello, Dolly!* colleagues. L-R: Johnny Beecher, Coco Ramirez, myself, and Marilynn Lovell.

Lodge, Jr. was ensconced. The first three floors, I think, were habitable but the upper three or four still needed weeks of construction. We gathered on the roof most nights to look beyond Saigon into places where nightly skirmishes lit up the uneasy darkness.

Now that I was older, I wasn't as awestruck as I'd been on Tinian watching the airraids on Saipan. Now I couldn't believe I'd ever thought of those sights as if they were fireworks. Still, some of the youngsters in the company felt the way I had at their age—thrilled and terrified at once. The performances themselves were full of surprise. We never knew when we'd be crowded onto a bus that rumbled off to some huge plane hangar in a locale we didn't know. Most often it would be around noon and the places would be jammed with soldiers crammed onto sandbags and stretching out far beyond the confines of the hanger. Everyone except Miss Martin traveled by bus. She helicoptered. Although we loved her, we began calling her (behind her back, of course) Foxhole Mary because of the special treatment. We even started singing "Bloody Mary" from *South Pacific* (a show she had starred in), substituting her new nickname. Even her stand-by Ann Russell, a terrific gal and great sport, joined in.

The sets may have been sparse, but the staircase down into the Harmonia Gardens was there for Dolly's triumphant return to her old haunt and her singing of the famous title song. The Freddy Witt-designed costumes were there in all their heavy glory. We never knew exactly what the temperature was, but man, it was hot and sweat-producing every single time. We smiled. danced, sang and sweltered.

However, with the orchestral tape and the main musicians and wonderful Jay, and of course ol' Foxhole herself, it was one helluva great Broadway show for the guys. And they let us know it, screaming, hooting and whistling in all the right places. We had absolutely no audience like those bunches of G.I.s., particularly after the gentleness of the Tokyo patrons.

After each show we'd mix and mingle with them, joking and singing, with the banjo player from the pit helping out. We stayed with them until we were herded back onto the bus and the troops were redeployed to the front once more, clinging to their cameras and autographs and waving and grinning like mad. So much love had radiated back and forth.

Since almost all the shows were in the daytime, we had evenings free to roam around Saigon, shop and try some new food. I even got to brush up my French a bit in a few places downtown. And there were military social duties to perform, notably dinner with General William Westmoreland, who famously led the U.S. forces in Vietnam. Miss Martin and I were invited. I guess I was included because of those MGM flicks. I asked Marilyn Lovell to join me, and she turned out to be the most charming person at the reception and dinner. She was a big hit with all the brass and their wives. Another big affair, held at the embassy, was great fun—though marred a bit by Miss Martin, who insisted that Ambassador Lodge join her in a chorus of "Some Enchanted Evening." He very obviously wanted no part of it, but finally succumbed to her pleas. He was embarrassed, as was I, and it took a bit of the enchantment out of the evening.

The night before we were to leave, we played for the locals in a partially bombed-out downtown theater. Word must have leaked out about the performance, and we rushed through the second act since we were beginning to be shelled. We kept going so the South Vietnamese wouldn't panic, but some of them did anyway and the thing ended in a scattered mess. We were hustled out and rushed back to the R&R place. We left it just before dawn and boarded a plane for Korea. Once airborne, we saw the place where we had stayed being shelled by bombs. We'd escaped just in time, and even then were dogged in the air and actually fired at by some dogfighters. It was scary, but we were all together and safe; those poor guys on the ground were anything but.

When we landed at Seoul, all seemed peaceful and thriving. It was a great relief. We were put up in a nice, modern hotel; on the top floor was a bar with a piano player. Heaven. It became our oasis almost nightly after the shows we gave in a theater for the Koreans and the U.S. military stationed there. We met a tailor who would run up a suit to measure overnight, very inexpensively. Most of the guys took advantage of the bargains.

Sensational news leaked out. Since the stop after our canceled Russian tour was an extended stay in London, Merrick and Champion were secretly but vigorously negotiating with British Equity to allow us to bring the entire company to the Theatre Royal. That meant all the dancers as well. It would be an unprecedented first. Gower argued that the robust American style of our wonderful gypsies, particularly the strong athletic quality of the male dancers, was essential for performing his difficult choreography. (At that time British male dancers were a tad more balletic than they are today.)

Just before our last stop in Southern Asia, Okinawa, the rumors about London were confirmed. Our company was elated: We wouldn't have the break up the family. So we were bursting with joy as we played our five performances at the Stilwell Field House in Okinawa. It was October of 1965. Just before our closing matinee show, we learned that British Equity had ultimately backed down on the proposition. All the principals would go on to England and the rest of the cast would return to the States to start another company of *Dolly* with Betty Grable.

We were heartbroken throughout that performance, knowing it was the last we'd all play together. It was a mess of a show; all of us tried to smile through tears but were barely able to control our emotions. Thank God the Field House was so huge and the audience (all G.I.s) so big. What a sad, sad day for all of us.

Chapter 16 ———————

A pretty young gal with a camera had been touring with us since Tokyo. Her name was Shana Alexander, and we later learned that she was on assignment from *Life* magazine. Months later there we all were, spread out in color across the two-page centerfold, with Miss Martin on the cover. I'm sure this heightened the competition between Carol and Mary, although I'm not sure why; Carol had certainly been covered earlier. Musical leading ladies were (and are) a strange breed.

The next year, NBC telecast a special called *Hello, Dolly! Round the World*, with footage from Japan, Korea, Vietnam, Okinawa and England. Years later a friend of mine somehow obtained a copy, so I now have a treasured keepsake of those glorious times.

The company flew together to Haneda Airport, where the actual family breakup took place. The tears flowed like Kirin beer at our last get-together in a joint in Shinjuku. The next morning we boarded separate planes; the kids flew back

East, while the rest of us kept going west, landing in Hong Kong and Cairo before winding up in London. So we really did go "round the world."

Anglophile that I am, I was thrilled to be "home" again in England and to find such a wild buzz of anticipation for our show. The window cards were everywhere and the advance tremendous. I loved my billing: last, centered and in a lavender box.

Our contracts ran for different lengths of time. Mine was actually the longest (probably because of the flicks); Mary's was second; the others were shorter. I found myself a tiny bed-sit on Fleet Street and settled in, cozy as a cat. I bought milk by the liter, fixed sautéed mushrooms and tea for breakfast with the occasional banger, and visited the small shops and cafés in the neighborhood on evenings when I 'et' out. I loved the town.

I sorely missed my old "family" from the show, but I loved the new dancers and singers. The principals had quite a bit of free time since Gower and his assistant, Lucia Victor, put the local newbies through their paces. We had, I believe, three weeks of rehearsal in Limehouse before we moved to Drury Lane and the Theatre Royal, right next to the flower stalls (remember *My Fair Lady*?). The Royal was now under the management of H.M. Tennent, Ltd. and Hugh "Binky" Beaumont, who were British theatrical giants. What a beauty of a theater! She'd opened in 1812, and kept herself in fabulous shape. The dressing rooms looked like ancient set pieces; they were overly furnished and set on odd angles. Mine was a few steps from the stage and around a little corner. It had heavy draperies and an overstuffed loveseat. I felt I'd been in the theater for centuries, not at all like a young man making his debut in London.

The stage was raked rather sharply from upstage to downstage, a fact I didn't discover until our first tech rehearsal. Things were rolling along fairly smoothly until the beginning of "Put On Your Sunday Clothes," when I yelled the lead-in, "Let's get dressed, Barnaby—we're going to New York!" and raced stage right to the center-stage ramp to lead the entire chorus, hands to hats and high-stepping, into the song. Since this was my first trip from the feed store upstage to the ramp downstage, I leapt off at my usual clip, a tad too quick for the rake. I hit the ramp a little off-balance, and my foot slipped off the edge. It was only about four and a half feet to the pit floor, but before I hit it, I heard something crack on my left side, which had collided with the sharp edge of a steel beam. I was hauled up, God knows in pain, by a couple of guys and laid out on the ramp. My body weight had been enough to do the damage. I'd broken my pelvis.

Gower, rushing down to the front, tried to lighten things up. 'You couldn't do it center-stage, Carp, you had to do center-ramp!' I smiled up into his dear, worried face. "I'm a ham," I said.

A stretcher was brought from somewhere and I was carted straight to a nearby hospital. I had indeed broken my pelvis. I hurt like hell, but was determined to return to the show before opening, which was two weeks away. I wouldn't let them operate on me or do anything that would take long too heal. I wanted to start physical therapy immediately. I asked if that would damage anything or make the break worse, and was told no, but that I wouldn't be able to endure the pain. I told them that was no problem. They gawked and asked if I was a Christian Scientist. I said I wasn't; I just wanted to be mobile again as soon as possible. I think they considered me nuts. Maybe I was.

But a nurse was assigned to help me in my impossible task. She was a dilly. Two days in bed was enough for me. We started gradually on the third day. She was a wonder and worked me carefully, every day letting me put more and more weight on my left foot. When I hurt a little too much, I'd lie down for a few minutes and go at it again. We'd work out in the hall, using stairs, and I grew more and more determined to make the opening night. I could jump if I landed on my right foot. At night, in bed, I'd go through the entire show in my head to figure out how I could manage everything. I knew I could jump from the feed store to the stage, but getting back up was a problem. I finally solved it. There was a barrel at the side of the feed store for a bunch of brooms, used by the guys early in the show for a number called "It Takes a Woman." I figured if one of those broom handles were fastened securely to the back of the barrel, I could grab it to swing up to the platform where the trapdoor was and be able to land on my right foot.

Perfect. Everything solved. I'd be a bit gimpy but it'd work. The big "Dancing" song, where Dolly teaches Cornelius to dance, would only be enhanced by a tad more awkwardness before I ran across the stage and said, "Look! I'm dancing!"

During my brief time of infirmity, who should appear at my bed-side with a lavender-colored bound book in hand but my old pen-pal, Kenneth Williams, in person at last. He passed the gift over to me with elaborate ceremony. It was *Harriette Wilson's Memoirs* in the lavish Folio Society edition. My three ward mates and all the nurses applauded loudly and laughed wildly at seeing one of their favorite comedic personalities there at the hospital to visit me. I was overwhelmed, and wondered how on earth he'd found me. "My dear, you are everywhere in the hated press," he said, and proceeded to do at least a half-hour's-worth of a one-man show. Absolutely hysterical. He had the place rocking with laughter, which brought even more people into the ward. Kenneth, whom Nora Stapleton had told me was really rather shy, seemed to be having the time of his life. I certainly was. What wonderous medication he was. We did have a few quiet moments to giggle about *Hotel Paradiso* and our shared experiences in the role of Maxime. We promised to meet after the opening of *Dolly!*, and he wished me well in the show.

I checked out of the hospital in ten days. The day I left, a gent across the room from me was helped out of bed for the first time and sat happily in a chair beside it. He too, had a broken pelvis, and he'd been in bed for five weeks. He shouted goodbye and waved in wonderment that I was taking off so quickly. The nurses gave me flowers and I kissed and hugged them all. My special gal who'd helped so much had tears in her eyes as she wished me luck with the show. I was happier than the little train that finally made it to the top of the steep hill: "I knew I could! I knew I could!"

Soon I was sitting with Merrick and Champion on some steps in the back of the Theatre Royal. Binkie Beaumont had rejected the idea of my returning to the role—*my* role—even after I'd shown him onstage how I could maneuver everything I had planned by using the one permanent broom. Gower agreed with me and thought it a great idea. Binkie agreed that everything would work fine, but he but was afraid I might somehow injure myself again. The theater owner was worried about possible litigation. I told him I'd sign anything, *anything*, to guarantee that he and the theater would not be held responsible. He wouldn't budge. He said he didn't want to feel personally responsible if I injured myself permanently. He couldn't bear the thought of that. Terrific.

So there I sat on those old steps with David and Gower, the three of us spilling tears—yes, even the supposedly curmudgeonly Merrick. (I had always thought him a hoot; the more he glowered, the funnier he seemed. He was a wicked old fake, or a faker of wickedness.)

They both asked me what I wanted to do: stay in London on salary until I was allowed to join the cast again, or return to the U.S. and go into the Broadway version, which now starred Ginger Rogers. I was so heartbroken, I didn't know what to do. I was set on opening in London. It was a dream I'd had for years. And I felt the show needed me. We were such a well-oiled, smooth-running bunch, used to each other's timing and family-like love onstage and off. I felt completely orphaned. It was the saddest moment of my acting life. It still is.

Since I couldn't open, I opted to return home. I sat with Gower and his wife, Marge Champion, in a box on opening night, December 2, 1965, and flew with them the following day to New York. All I could bring back from that wonderful city was a window poster, my busted pelvis and that lavender book inscribed "For Carleton, from Kenneth," dated 22/11/65. The "hated" press wasn't all that kind to the preceding evening's opening. It was the first time our show had received anything less than glowing raves. At the curtain call, Miss Martin had sung, "Hello, London. Well, hello, London. It's so nice to be back home in Drury [she made it sound like "dreary"] Lane..." I thought it a mistake. It was. Some of the hated mentioned it less than kindly. I, however, hit the press as if it had been my night; a full-size, front-page picture of me in the *Daily Mirror*, with the banner "GOODBYE, DOLLY!" What a sad sendoff. It was probably David M. working overtime on promotion, as usual.

The show wasn't selling out, and in May 1966 Miss Martin was replaced by Dora Bryan, a great British favorite. She had a substantial run as Dolly. After staying for a couple of days at the New York pad of one of Gower's assistants, Lowell Purvis, I began to stop feeling sorry for myself. Grabbing my bootstraps, I headed out to Omaha, Nebraska, where the original gypsies from our "family" were now backing Betty Grable as Dolly. It was a joyful reunion. That evening I sat in the back row watching those wonderful kids and the gal with the glamorous gams. She was a beaut and a hoot. At the interval, someone tapped my shoulder and said I had a phone call in the box office. It was Gower. He told me to get my broken ass back to New York to replace the understudy who was on with Miss Rogers. After a late-ish gathering after the show, too much to drink and too little sleep, I flew east the next morning.

Rehearsals at the St. James Theatre were brief. Pat Finley (with whom I'd toured for ages in *Birdie*) was now playing Mrs. Molloy. Sondra Lee, my castmate from *Paradiso*, was Minnie Fay. Jerry Dodge, my castmate in *How to Succeed*, was Barnaby. We ran a bit of the hat-shop scene. It was like old home week. We knew what we were doing.

Miss Rogers didn't rehearse with us. Gower had told me about his first bit of corrective direction to Ginger. Toward the end of the show, Dolly walks up the stairs, looks up and to the right, and says something like, "I'll repaper the room blue, I think." Ginger was backing up the stairs carefully and daintily, turning her head slightly over her shoulder for a brief glimpse, then facing front and delivering the line.

Gower said, "Just walk up the stairs, Ginger."

She replied grandly: "Miss Rogers does not turn her back on her audience."

As he told me later with a laugh, he knew then that he was in trouble. (Ginger had also brought her personal coach along to rehearsals.) None of it really mattered. The show was a smash, with lots of repeat ticket buyers who wanted to see Fred Astaire's famous movie partner, and that's what they got. The musical rolled along merrily on its glorious own.

I enjoyed telling cronies that the only rehearsal I'd gotten was with David Burns, who played Horace Vandergelder. A wondrously funny, wicked and deliciously dirty old man, he would knock on my dressing room door at the fifteen-minute call and lean in leeringly, saying: "You want your joint copped or anything before you go on?"

My first performance was going smoothly and the kids were terrific; gypsies adore any change in a long-running gig. Then we got to "Dancing." I was accustomed to Dolly teaching me how to dance, so at first I was hesitant and a bit clumsy, as always; then when I got the step I burst out and ran across the stage shouting, "Look! I'm dancing!"

I could tell that Miss Rogers was confused. She obviously had a neat little step that I was supposed to fall into immediately. I was hard to move, which forced her to really show me. (In other words, I wanted to actually play the moment. In one word: *act*.) After the curtain came down, the stage manager called me over. "Miss Rogers would like to see you here tomorrow at two." No surprise.

We met. From now on I would do exactly what she wanted: two steps right, two steps left and a little twirl. So be it. In performance I'd screw it up a bit then suddenly get it, and burst joyously across the stage. It still worked for Cornelius.

In the curtain calls, Miss Rogers would say the damnedest thing ever. After the final bow she'd hold her hands up to quiet the audience; and then, straight-faced, she'd add: "While I have your attention ..." Where on earth did she think they'd been looking for the whole show? Then she'd launch into a long curtain speech, always introducing her mother (who attended every performance) and going over what seemed like her entire movie career. The patrons probably adored it, but the cast would stand there shifting from one tired foot to the other while secretly unfastening the back of their costumes. The musicians, lucky stiffs, had filed out of the pit after the last note. Why is it that some leading ladies of a certain age feel obliged to give career résumés at the end of shows?

That period in my Manhattan life was very warm and friendly. Once a week, I and the other bowling fans from *Dolly* gathered at the Roxy Bowling Center, across the street from the old Roxy Theatre. We were a great gang. There was much laughter, much beer, much horsing-around, and lots of gossipy talk. The weekly bowl-off shifted later to a place on Seventh Avenue between 42nd and 43rd on the second floor. At the time Nancy Sinatra had a hit single on the charts, and one of the male gypsies, whose rented shoes were a bit too big, sang out gleefully as he guttered a ball: "These shoes were made for waltzing, and that's just what they'll do/ One of these days these shoes are gonna waltz all over you."

After too short a time, Merrick wanted me to join the touring Carol Channing company so I could open in the show's Chicago premiere. He presented me with a contract and said, "Sign it." I told him I already had a contract. He said, "Sign it." Equity said, no way. I couldn't have two at the same time. It was all very friendly (and flattering) when his lawyers and that union's lawyers met in his office above the St. James Theatre.

Merrick sat in one corner. I sat diagonally across in another. We kept our eyes on each other. He tried to glower under his heavy black brows, but he was secretly smiling. My eyes were open, and I had a full smile on my lips. I couldn't help it. Merrick always made me crack up. After insisting to the union lawyers that I was the best of all possible Corneliuses and that he wanted the best for the Chicago opening, everything was sorted out and a lovely new contract was agreed on. I really had no say in it, but it was financially a boon and a half for me.

Soon I was on the road again, something I wasn't exactly nuts about. I loved New York, even though I didn't have an actual home there at the moment. Before the packing and departing, Gower passed on some pertinent advice. Ms. Channing, he said, was like a "tape machine" that turned on at eight-forty and wound to the end of its reel at eleven-ten. Pat, the stage manager, would show me the exact spots on which I should plant myself for various scenes. Even four or five inches off-mark and the lady would play to that spot, with or without Cornelius precisely there. If she should go up on a line, he added, I shouldn't try to help her; she wouldn't hear it, and would just keep repeating a few words over and over until the machine would kick in and she'd roll ahead. As always, he was correct. It happened many times during performances, and it was astounding to stand on stage and watch.

To get into the rhythm of the new company, I joined it for the last two performances in St. Louis. On my first night, scrunched beneath the feed store before the curtain rose, I heard the stage manager announce to the audience that the role of Cornelius would be played by me: "fresh from the fabled Vietnam company tour." Through the curtain I heard muffled but sustained applause, and the overture started. Then when I popped up for my first words, I got terrific applause. The announcement was never made again. I guess the old Martin-Channing competition was still going strong. On occasion, however, my entrance was greeted by applause. What a lovely feeling.

We played a ten-show gig in Oklahoma City before moving to the grand opening in Chicago. I wasn't very happy there; perhaps I'd been spoiled by the Martin version and the wonderful family love we'd all shared. The actress who played Mrs. Molloy had a pretty voice—her sister was a star at the Metropolitan Opera—but she was no comedienne,

I thought; certainly no Marilynn Lovell. I think my new love interest was in the throes of another love affair, with herself. But I stayed on and finished out my contract—and that was the end of me and *Hello, Dolly!*

Shortly before I'd finished my long, three-lady-stars run, Dottie Lamour came backstage after the show to say hello to me. She said, "Oh, honey, how I'd love to play that role!" I said, "You will, Dottie!" Later she did, in New York. As for me, since I was now back in the Apple, I set about finding a new home. I landed a great floor-through apartment at 28 Bank Street in the West Village—a top-floor, good-sized back deck for $225 a month. That was the most I'd ever paid, and I wondered how I'd ever be able to afford it. Would I ever work again? It's a syndrome I suffer each time a show is over.

I shouldn't have worried. I plunged into my longest, steadiest period of work ever. Maybe some of the shows are out of order, but here goes.

First I took a standby job—something I had sworn I would never do again—to get immediately to work. It was a shorty, and I probably should have been arrested for stealing the producers' money. The play (which was on Broadway) was called *A Minor Adjustment*, and it should have had a major revision. I read the thing as a favor to the director, Henry Kaplan, and took the job. I never opened the script again. Shame on me, but it was a clunker. During rehearsals, while I watched the mess try to assemble itself, Henry would join me at the back of the theater from time to time and always ask me: "Is this as bad as I think it is?" I'd nod my head sadly in agreement.

I stood by, totally unprepared, for the wonderful William Redfield. Poor Bill. But thank heavens he remained in good health physically. Mentally, I'm not sure. At any rate, the show, a two-act job from Canada, opened on a Friday night. At the interval on opening night I went out the stage door for a smoke and was joined by an understudy, Evelyn Paeper. I had the ol' tux on and she was dressed to the nines, too, for the opening-night party. It promised to be a lavish affair, since the Mirvish brothers had loot galore.

Ev, very optimistic, asked: "How do you think it's going?" I took a huge drag on my butt and said: "I think we're about halfway through the run." I was almost right; we closed the following night after three performances. The party, though, was a smashing success. It was at a new rooftop place, 666 Madison. Kate Reid, a buddy of mine (and the ex-wife of Austin Willis from the show), managed to get happily high or actually roaring drunk on the Brothers M. I think they saw a flop coming and felt happy for the tax loss. I was happy to add the ill-gotten gains to my bank account, but felt guilty as hell for my unprofessional conduct. I swore I'd never, ever do something like that again. And I haven't.

Before Robert Ludlum became the best-selling author of novelist of twenty-seven suspense novels, he was an actor in minor roles on Broadway, early TV and lots of radio. In 1960 he became a producer, and opened Playhouse on the Mall in Paramus, New Jersey. Now, in 1967, he wanted me for a Neil Simon play, *The Star-Spangled Girl*, that had recently closed on Broadway. It was a nice theater and an easy driving commute. I costarred with Joe Ponazecki; we played two radical friends who publish a struggling anti-establishment magazine. It had the all-too-familiar short run, although business was terrific, as it was with anything that had the Simon name on it. Later I heard that *The Star-Spangled Girl* was maybe his own least-favorite work. Joe and I worked together a few other times. Lovely guy. I was destined to return to Playhouse on the Mall as well.

After that I did a Southern tour (my second) of *Lock Up Your Daughters* with Cyril Ritchard. We played Atlanta, Palm Beach, Miami and elsewhere. The show, of course, had been written by Lionel Bart, the Brit who beat Sam Rosen and me to a musical version of *Oliver Twist*; that was still a bit of grit in my gizzard. But the cast was fun, and included my love Ronnie Cunningham, that delicious all-over redhead who had done the show with me previously.

Cyril had some trouble learning his lines, since he was directing the piece, but the old Aussie pro managed both things fairly well, and he was great fun to hang out with. I knew he missed dear Madge, his late wife, and I spent most of my offtime with him so he'd feel less lonely. We made a trip on a free night to the understated but obviously expensive Florida home of Louisa Carpenter, the du Pont heiress. She was an out lesbian who dressed so mannishly that some people actually mistook her for a man. Tamara Geva, the ex-wife of the actor John Emery (Arthur Treacher's replacement in *Hotel Paradiso*), was now in residence. She had been an exceptional dancer on Broadway, she and Ray Bolger had introduced the George Balanchine ballet "Slaughter on Tenth Avenue" in the Rodgers & Hart musical *On Your Toes*.

Cyril was driving as we approached the residence. He leaned toward me and in a conspiratorial tone he informed me: "You know, dear boy, Geva has ... well, crossed over to the other side of the street." How discreet can you be about dropping the news that someone is a switch-hitter? Though Australian, Cyril was a proper English gentleman to the epicenter.

Dinner was a delight, with Geva in wonderful hairtossing form. The staff would quietly vanish and reappear, bearing goodies. I had stone crabs for the first time. I guess "WOW!" sums it up. (I've eaten them since, but you know how firsts are.)

After *Lock Up Your Daughters*, I moved on to other fun roles. At the Paper Mill Playhouse in Millburn, New Jersey I played Lucentio opposite Karen Arthur's Bianca in *Kiss Me, Kate*. Enzo Stuarti and Patricia Marand did the leads. I thought, and still do, that it's Cole Porter's best score. Who else would rhyme Bianca with Sanka? Three weeks after opening I had to leave to fulfill a previous contract. David Evans played the last week for me as I raced into rehearsals for a summer-long tour of *The Star-Spangled Girl*. This time I played the other lead, Norman. Edd "Kookie" Byrnes and Diane McBain were my co-stars. Both were young TV stars, and their lack of stage experience showed a little at first; but they kept improving from theater to theater. The show did extremely well for four months, but Norman, I immodestly confess, ran away with the reviews.

With Diane McBain and Edd "Kookie" Byrnes in Neil Simon's *The Star-Spangled Girl*, Cape Playhouse, Dennis, Massachusetts, 1968. Photo by Jerry Overman.

On a Sunday off, I drove home to New York from Maine to pay some bills and sort out some mail. I parked my VW Beetle on the street overnight. We were opening in Connecticut the following evening, so I didn't haul my wardrobe and makeup case up the three flights to my apartment. On Monday morning I discovered that the Bug had been broken into, and everything, shoes included, was gone. I had to hustle up a whole new set of costumes (we supplied our own in those days). Among the missing items were the corduroy jacket I'd had hand-tailored in Korea and my steel makeup box, which held little makeup but lots of photos and mementos. Irreplaceable stuff. I searched the trash baskets for blocks. Who would have wanted that stuff? The box probably looked like it might have money in it, but I figured anybody who opened it—it wasn't locked—would have given it a heave.

Sadly I gave up my search. With new duds for the play, I headed to Connecticut for that evening's performance. A bunch of cousins came for the opening night and gave me a loud and sustained welcome when I made my appearance. That sort of frosted my co-stars, and it took a hunk of schmoozing them up during the show to get on an even keel again. I truly wished we weren't getting reviewed at every stop along the tour. Reviews are fun to read after a show closes. Good or bad, like personal publicity, they should never be taken seriously. And God knows, not believed.

Back I went to New York to finish putting together the 28 Bank Street flat, a process I'd abandoned to go on tour with *Lock Up Your Daughters*. The apartment was three winding flights up from street level, where the owner and landlord's apartment was. I watched in terror as three moving guys guided my recently reclaimed baby grand up and around the narrow stairs. Somehow, after considerable swearing and sweating, they managed to get the ole Schumer in, re-legged and ensconced in the front room facing the street. I don't know how they did it. Neither did they. As I paid them, they said, almost in chorus: "If you ever move out of here, call another company."

A new cat, Blue, became my roommate and closest companion. I loved all my cats, but Blue was really something else. Whenever nature called, he'd go to the door leading out to the deck and, with perfect manners, would use a box outside. When he'd finished and wanted in, he'd knock, not scratch. Well, it sounded like a knock; exactly how he made the rap I never discovered. I just imagined Blue sitting out there and politely knocking with his paw. Sometimes a guest of mine would hear it and wonder who was at the back door. When I opened the door and Blue came bouncing in, guests would be agape.

Right across the street lived the popular lawyer and politician Bella Abzug, known on the block as "The Hat." Other neighbors of mine joined me in two game gangs that moved from place to place, one for poker, one for charades. Among the poker-playing regulars were my friends Jimmy Coco, Bobby Dreifus and Dena Dietrich (Mother Nature from the Chiffon margarine commercials). Usually there were five or six of us, along with a big plate of sliced meats, hunked cheeses, and libations of all types. The charades bunch included Michael McKenna, theater owner Bunny Waldman, Merv Nelson (a guy John Murray Anderson had called the English Walnetto) and many others; the group ranged from ten to fourteen or more, enough for two good tough teams.

I miss those days when people made time for games on a regular basis. Now it would be nearly impossible to gather enough folks willing to tear themselves away from the tube for an entire evening, or from their computers, video games, and cell phones. Something's wrong here. People don't seem to connect in the flesh much anymore. One exception comes to mind: On the road with a show, the cast still plays games and connects with one another. All the younger ones, of course, still have cell phones glued to their hands.

Throughout my Manhattan days, many of us relied on *Cue* magazine to guide us as to how to spend our nights. I miss *Cue*—not only for its going-out information but because of its wonderful back page, full of games and puzzles and tricky things to tackle every week. "The Puzzler," who devised them, demanded utmost concentration from her readers. Who was she? The wonderful Marilyn Stasio, the longtime crime-book columnist for the *New York Times Book Review*. I still have a crush on her. I read her reviews, and they make me smile. I like to think I made her smile from time to time. In *Cue*, one of her challenges to readers was to write a limerick in some particular style, maybe one based on a well-known children's story. Here's what I submitted:

> *A wolf hanging out in the wood*
> *Spied the kid with the basket and hood*
> *He raced on ahead*
> *Got in drag, then in bed*
> *The rest isn't really that good.*

Well, Marilyn loved it. It won first prize that week. I hope she remembers it.

Chapter 17 ⸻⸻⸻

S ince I'd settled into the Bank Street apartment, I had begun doing quite a few commercials. Rule of thumb: One must go on about a hundred go-sees before getting a job; then you have to shoot four or five before you make any real money. Often I'd read over copy I thought was exactly right for me, but would seldom get the spot. Conversely, if the copy seemed as though it would fit anyone, and the casting crew wasn't even needed—those jobs I'd get. Go figure.

After the Neil Simon tour, I got an invitation from Richard Barr, the producer of Mart Crowley's groundbreaking off-Broadway gay play *The Boys in the Band*. The show had gotten rave reviews and had been playing to overflow houses for months at Theatre Four on West 55th Street. The original company had departed for a London run, and Dick called for me to take over the lead role of Michael.

I had seen the show its first two-weekend, off-off Broadway experimental run. It had caused a sensation. I found it fascinating. Now, faced with the prospect of playing that long and emotionally exhausting role, I was a bit unsure. I didn't want to be "put into" a part that Kenneth Nelson had played to perfection. I told Barr that if he'd get Robert Moore, the original director, to guide me I'd give it a go. I was in luck. Moore had two weeks free before he was due on Broadway to direct Neil Simon's *Last of the Red Hot Lovers*, starring Jimmy Coco.

In *Boys*, Michael is celebrating his thirtieth birthday. Feeling apprehensive and too old for the role, I showed up at the theater. The entire cast was there; the stage manager had gathered them, and they, too, wanted to work with Bobby Moore. That first day was a very hectic, nervous-making seven hours. I couldn't wait to hit the bathtub at 28 Bank and soak. I felt really inadequate. I crawled from the tub, grabbed the phone and called Dick Barr.

Jill Choder and I in the national tour of *Your Own Thing*, the rock musical based on Shakespeare's *Twelfth Night*. December 1968, Wilbur Theatre, Boston.

"Dick, I'm sorry. I'll never be able to learn it, much less do Michael justice. I'm really sorry."

"Calm down, Carp," Dick said. "Just give it one more day. Okay?"

"Well …"

"Well, nothing. This was your first day. You'll be wonderful. I know it, and Bob thinks so too. Give it one more day. If you still feel as shaky as you do now, I won't hold you to the contract. Get some sleep, Carp, take a pill and give me tomorrow. Okay?"

I hated to let him down; we'd done a lot of work together starting with *Hotel Paradiso*. I hated to let me down, as well. I said okay, took two Seconals and went to bed. The next day I was at the theater early, walking through the play with script in hand. By the time the cast showed up I was feeling much more like Michael, and I forged ahead with the rehearsal.

The opening was great and the jam-packed house ecstatic; they wouldn't stop yelling and applauding. At the end they were rushing up steps to paw us. Mayor Lindsey grabbed me with both hands and slobbered a kiss on my neck. He was a much better kisser than he was a mayor.

It was a difficult gig. Michael's breakdown at the end was a killer. The four weekend performances (Friday evening, Saturday matinee and evening and Sunday matinee) were grueling. On Sunday nights I cuddled with Blue. Monday we were closed, and I had Tuesday off. But I spent most of my free time doing backer's auditions for my next gig, *Lyle*, a musical about a crocodile. When my six-month contract with *Boys* was finally finished, I did something I hadn't done since my cross-country fishing trip with my old friend Shel: I decided to take an entire week off. I booked a hotel in Puerto Rico, left Blue with my friend Ray, and flew off with a bathing suit and almost nothing else.

Upon arriving at the hotel I learned that the pool was being repaired. I grabbed a local phone book and found what turned out to be a terrific tiny place smack on the ocean, with maybe six rooms total. Perfect. I started on my daily routine: I swam in the morning, snoozed and read the rest of day, ate and went to bed early. It was the complete opposite of my usual timetable in Puerto Rico, where places opened late and closed at daybreak.

What a heavenly week. I did no sightseeing except for one afternoon when I ventured out and bused around for an hour or so. Nothing was going on. I preferred to be alone in my tiny room.

I came home and began rehearsals for *Lyle*, and heaven turned into hell.

The show had a charming score, written by Eddie Cantor's youngest daughter, Janet Gari. An older Cantor daughter, Marilyn, was the lead producer. They didn't get along. I'll leave that alone. In fact I'll leave the next several weeks alone. Janet and her cowriter, Toby Garson, had based the show on a children's book called *The House on East 88th Street*, a sweet tale of a crocodile adopted by a nice couple and their young son. It would be too grim to describe all the changes of lines, cast, directors, opening dates, costumes, sets, etc. It was unending. My agent, a patient gent, finally insisted I leave the wreck. I did, not without tears. I had wanted *Lyle* to work and gone along with all the changes. I loved the show. It opened on March 22, 1970 with my understudy, Steve Harmon, and folded two days later after four performances.

For whatever reason I suddenly got a bunch of commercials, and happily several of them were very long runners. The one for Purina Dog

Chow worked out so well that I became the on-camera spokesman for almost five years, doing new spots every couple of months. Another long one was for Frito-Lay. It was shot in New York, and it was a takeoff on "Aba Daba Honeymoon": "Muncha buncha muncha buncha, muncha buncha muncha buncha/Fritos go with lunch."

They wanted Debbie, too, but she was in California shooting a sewing-machine commercial at the same time, so they hired another gal, who was fine. We were in the studio for less than fifteen minutes. We went over it a couple of times, and someone in the booth called out: "Can you sound a little more like Debbie?" I quickly yelled back, "I'm doing my damnedest!" They cracked up and saved the gal any embarrassment. She kissed me. That spot ran for over a year. I also got lucky with Stroh's Beer and Cousin Casual napkins.

But come on! That isn't acting. I missed the stage. I missed working evenings and matinees. That other stuff was just gigs. I got a call to report for rehearsals of a play by Sidney Michaels called *Dylan*, about the final

The cast of the 1970 national tour of Moss Hart's *Light Up the Sky*. Among my fellow cast members were (standing, far right) Peter Adams and (seated, starting second from left) Peggy Winslow, Kay Medford, Kitty Carlisle Hart, Jan Sterling, Sam Levene.

years of Dylan Thomas. The producer, Marty Richards, had worked with me before, and he knew I'd be right for the part of John Malcolm Brinnin, Thomas's biographer. I didn't have to read for it; I was hired instantly for the role, and it was a good one. Will Hare played Thomas and Rue McClanahan was his wife. All three of us were terrific, and got wonderful notices from all the critics—except John Simon, who hated all three of us. That rotten review got me so many congratulatory notes and calls. What a hoot!

We had a nice run, so Rue and I grew fairly close. We usually had a drink together after the show. I remember her asking me if she should take an offer for a television series in Los Angeles. She didn't know much about it, and worried about moving west. I asked her who had contacted her. She said it was someone named Lear. I asked what his first name was. She said, I think, Norm. I told her to grab it. Norman Lear had already changed TV with *All in the Family*, and if he was doing a new show, it would no doubt be something special. It turned out to be *Maude*.

After *Dylan* closed, Rue headed west. I had already started a new routine at 28 Bank: I got up early, fed Blue and me, then scrunched down at my desk with my Royal typewriter. The object was to move a stack of paper, one sheet at a time, from a pile on my left through this hated machine, then to the smaller pile on my right.

I would read what I'd done the morning before, judge it, change it or not, then roll in a new sheet. I'd write until about four (except on matinee days) then quit, feeling happy or so-so. Then I'd meet up with a local pal, Dudley Perkins Fraiser, and his buddy for a restorative beer. Perkins was a New Hampshire guy, very bright and witty. He was in the book biz. I never let on what I was doing. If he'd known I was working on a mystery novel, he would have razzed the hell out of me: "How dare you? You didn't even finish all your senior English in *high* school, for God's sake! You, a writer? The world is crashing to an end." I'm glad I kept my trap shut.

Perkins was very picky about the beer bars we quaffed at. If the place got too packed or the jukebox too loud, we'd move on. I shouldn't make him sound like a creep. He was really funny and well-educated, and I loved his New England dialect. He was sort of an older brother to me, and I learned lots of terrific stuff from him. Without knowing it, he was helping me with my writing. When I didn't show up at whatever bar we were currently patrons of, he'd glare at me and scold: "Doing another show in the theater?" I'd nod. "It's a wonder you have the strength to lift a brew. Why do you work so much?" He'd gaze at the ceiling while I told him, again, that

On tour with the revue *Curse You, Spread Eagle*, Washington Theatre Club, Washington, D.C., 1971. Marcia Lewis's head is on my shoulder. Below, L-R: Marshall Borden, unknown, Donna Liggitt Forbes, Josh Mostel.

I loved what I did. One gig after another: That's been the case all my life.

My newest theatrical turn was called *The Greatest Fairy Story Ever Told*. It was about a bunch of Chinese characters, and it was funny, I guess; audiences laughed a lot. The greatest thing about it for me was the short three-week run and working yet again with the wonderful actress Alix Elias. She's a forever love. Then I did a short run, twenty shows only, of the Cole Porter musical *Something for the Boys*. Patricia Carr, Virginia Martin and I were the stars. The incredible Bruce Kirle was the conductor.

My third off-Broadway play in a row was called *Miss Stanwyck Is Still in Hiding*. It was a really, really funny show. The authors, Larry Puchall and Reigh Hagen, had dreamed up a great premise and very good set-ups for laughs, which poured out steadily out from curtain up to final bow. What a pleasure! I would have loved playing it for longer than its four-week limited run.

Throughout all these shows, I'd stayed busy at my typewriter. I noticed one morning that my right-hand pile was a bit higher than the left. I was at a scene I really enjoyed and my fingers were flying; the Royal hummed happily along while this long section played itself out. I was a happy guy. For the first time I thought, I'm gonna finish this thing after all.

Two weeks later, I groggily yanked out the last page of my novel, *Games Murderers Play*. I slept that night and a hunk of the following morning.

Heaven.

Two days later, loins girded, I met with Perkins at a new beer bar. I plumped my grocery bag, wrapped and taped, beside his drink.

"Gift for your elder?" he snorted. "What are you calling it?"

I sank like a puppet on my stool. "How the hell did you know?"

"You mean, about the book?"

"Of course, you A-hole."

"I knew about it weeks and weeks ago."

"How? Did Patrick say anything?" Patrick O'Connor was a friend whom Perkins had introduced me to some time back. A good bridge partner—we'd played a couple of times—and a wonderful gentleman. I'd never told him that I was writing anything, however.

"He never said a word," confirmed Perkins. "But, my dear Vermonter, I work with writers every day. They give themselves away in so many ways. I can smell a writer within ten minutes of meeting him. Maybe five. *So?* You want me to read it?"

I didn't know where to look. "You mean you'll read it?"

"Have some pity on an easterner," he sang, quoting an Ira Gershwin line that Mickey Rooney had sung to Judy Garland in *Girl Crazy*. "Hand it over," demanded Perkins. I drank my brew in a long guzzle.

Three days passed. Perkins never mentioned the book. On day four, over beer, he said, "Get rid of all that mandarin prose and you might have something. It's a mystery. Stick with the plot."

The best advice I'd ever received. I read the thing over. I cut, and cut.

A few days later I made a bridge date with the nice Patrick O'Connor. "Oh," he said, "bring along your *Games Murderers Play*. Anxious to read it."

Huuuhh?

Patrick O. turned out to be not only a swell contract bridge player but also the editor-in-chief of a mass-market paperback publisher called Curtis Books, a branch of Popular Library. Who knew? Well, of course, Dudley Perkins Fraiser knew, all along.

O'Connor called the next morning. He liked the title. After what seemed like forever he asked, "Get busy on a new one. I want to make a bit of a smash by doing your first two together. Get going."

Of course I did. I'd had such fun with the first, in which I'd written about the crooked streets, bars, and wild denizens of Greenwich Village.

I knew where I'd set my second book: somewhere like my hometown in Vermont. I'd call the place Bridgeton.

I had always thought I could only be happy on a stage. This was a brand-new me. I turned down several gigs to stay with my Royal. Blue loved having me there. I think he liked the hum of my machine and me banging away. I finished *Cat Got Your Tongue?* in less than a month.

A Bank Street neighbor and old pal, Paula Bauersmith, had a place out in Montauk, Long Island, and I'd drive out to visit from time to time. Her house, which had tennis courts and a pool, had been a U.S. lookout place during the war. She'd fixed it up nicely. We'd play games, including bridge, often with Edward Albee, a sweet guy and a terrific bridge-player. He lived close by. Paula's daughter Jennifer Warren (a super looker and later a super actress) often filled in as our fourth player.

Richard Barr knew that I was seriously writing now, and he called with some news for me. Had I heard about Albee's new venture? He filled me in on a longish tale about the suicide of Edward's longtime lover, the composer William Flanagan, and the writers' colony that Edward had opened in Montauk to honor him. Dick thought it would be a great place for me to write if I was interested, and he promised to call me when a bed opened up at the William Flanagan Memorial Creative Persons Center. The call came while I was still polishing *Cat Got Your Tongue?*

I grabbed a few clothes, then I parked Blue with my friend and press agent Alan Eichler, who lived on 14th Street. Jimmy Coco had recommended him to me. Off I headed to Montauk.

The Center was a two-story barnlike place deep in the woods, with four tiny bedrooms and a shower on the top story and a small but nice living room and dining room downstairs. You made your own breakfast and lunch. A neat gent cooked dinner. It was an ideal place for work, with no distractions. It seemed like Vermont. I felt at home at once.

After reading *Cat* from the top, I thought it was pretty tight. Off it went to O'Connor with a note asking him to add the following acknowledgment: "With my sincere thanks to the William Flanagan Center." I knew Albee would be pleased. I couldn't wait to get at the next story I had rumbling around in my head. I'd known the title for weeks, so it was fun to see *Gentle Jeopardy* typed on the page as I got to work on novel number three at the Center. I rose at seven, showered, had breakfast, then returned to my tiny room and desk. I never saw my three fellow writers (two gals and one guy) or heard anything from their rooms until about four or four-thirty; then I'd hear them on the porch directly below my window: "Carp! Take a break!" We'd grown used to having two drinks before dinner. The count rose as work progressed. They were all a thirsty group. Well, me too. I usually went down and joined them. We never discussed our work. I was very happy with that arrangement. Dinner, always terrific, was a bit before seven.

Dick Barr had a house in Montauk as well. He kept after me to visit. I told him repeatedly that I was here to work. He said I was an old poop and missing all the great parties he had almost every night. Idiot that I am, I finally trekked through the woods to his place. People were jammed into the house as though it were Studio 54 in New York. I saw many of the Warhol gang, stoned or coked or God knows what. People were ass-grabbing, pushing and shoving. I stayed as short a time as possible. Think of hell. Then think of something beyond that.

Gentle Jeopardy was racing along at my happy hole in the wall. I sent a copy off to Patrick. Three days later I got my first call at the Center. O'Connor was screaming at me. "You've got to do a whole series of this barber character! You've done a miracle!"

"You liked *Gentle*," I said. I think I actually smirked.

"No *Gentle*. We're calling it *Only Her Hairdresser Knew!*

Well, okay, I thought. But a whole series? I didn't think it was going to be much fun to use the same characters again. Besides, I mentioned, I'd started on a new book. That can wait, he said. Get your ass back here to the city. Your first two are selling like popcorn at a fair. They've already printed another hundred thousand of your first two.

Great gods, I thought. *Games* and *Cat* were huge hits. How does one celebrate? With a vodka (Popov) and Canada Dry Grapefruit Soda, I decided.

Back in Manhattan, I picked up Blue and raced to 28 Bank. My books were in racks everywhere, especially in the Village. There I was on the back cover with a tiny bio and (of course) "Aba Daba" spelled wrong, with extra b's. But those books looked good to me. The first time I saw somebody on the subway reading a copy, I had to try not to stare like an idiot. I felt as happy as a clam at high tide.

Patrick gushed about *Hairdresser*. He said it would be out shortly, before the Book Dealers Association's yearly meeting. The next one was in Los Angeles, and he wanted me to go to it and meet as many of the dealers as possible while having a good time. He offered me a choice: Curtis Books would pay for my round-trip airfare or pick up my tab at the plush hotel where the book dealers were staying.

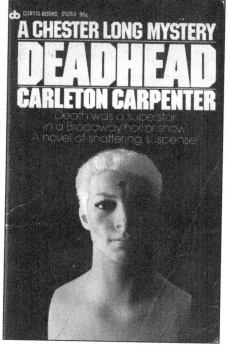

I told him to pick up the hotel tab. I'd get myself out there.

I headed west by Greyhound. They had a special deal: ninety-nine bucks round-trip to the coast and back. I jumped at it. I actually enjoyed the bus ride; it was a new adventure. It wasn't all that uncomfortable, and the rest stops were fun. I'd check the paperback racks. Spotting *Hairdresser*, I'd calmly ask how it was doing. I checked racks all across America.

Once I'd settled into the hotel in L.A., I started mingling. Every night there were many parties. Most rooms had a piano, so I'd head for it and sing a bunch of old favorites. The guys were singing along with me while they drank. Pat kept showing up. On his way out he'd lean over the piano and whisper: "You've just sold another thirty-thousand copies. Keep moving around, kid. Proud of you."

During the days, I'd invite a friend or two over for lunch. "Order whatever you want," I'd say. "It's on the house!" By the convention's close, my buddies and I had run up a huge bill. I never heard a peep out of Curtis Books. I guess they were happy that the first three mysteries were selling so well and that a fourth was on its way.

In all, I wrote six novels for Curtis and Popular Library. The final three were *Sleight of Hand*, *Deadhead*, and a gothic story called *Pinecastle*. The gothic genre demanded a female writer on the cover, so I became Ivy Manchester for that book.

Many gothics were written by men. I attended a "Gothic Get-Together" event that Murder Ink, the mystery bookstore in New York, held at a large room in the Steinway Building on 57th Street. There was a panel of nine authors and an avid, capacity crowd. One of the fans asked me if I was planning another book soon, because she had enjoyed *Pinecastle* so much. (I'd revealed that I was Ivy Manchester.)

There was rather a long pause before I answered from the stage.

"Probably not, ma'm." She looked astonished. "Why on earth not?"

"To be totally honest, Miss, I'm a mystery writer. I didn't much enjoy describing all that linen, wallpaper, silverware, jewelry, and knick-knacks!"

There was sudden laughter and applause, much of it coming from the stage. Eight of the nine authors were guys. The lady author was applauding the loudest.

Chapter 18

For several years I'd been going out on the odd weekend to a small village called Warwick in Orange County, New York. A good chum of mine, a stage manager, had a great house there with a pool. In time I got to know a whole new crew of people who lived or visited there, all fun folk who shared my love of games to the extreme. Those weekends were pure joy. Most of those friends are gone now. I have sweet, sweet memories of those magical years. If it weren't for my stage-manager friend, who was among the first to leave us, I never would have heard of Warwick.

I thought of it immediately when my nice landlord on the ground floor gave Blue and me a shock: Our rent was about to increase by twenty-five percent. Without hesitation, I called my stage-manager friend in Warwick and asked if he and my new friends there could look around for a house for me in that pretty, Vermont-like village. When a call came with news of a couple of places, I phoned a moving company in Warwick. Blue, that bright baby, knew that something was up, even before any packing or prep-work had begun.

I sent him back to Alan's to keep him away from all the hubbub at 28. That weekend I drove up to Warwick and decided on a house off a nice street, up a driveway that curved around trees like a big 9, all uphill. Exciting! Once I'd sealed the deal, my folks came down from Bennington to help get the place in shape. Wild creatures had been living in and outside the place, which was (I'll be gentle) a stinking mess. In a week or so we had the property hoed out, starting with the basement. It was exhausting, but we did it. That's where the piano would go when delivered.

My dad papered two of the bedrooms, and Dar had gotten everything else up to an almost liveable state. They went back to Vermont and I drove the Bug to New York to pick up Blue. Alan had given me the disturbing news that my roomie wasn't well. I was prepared. I'd checked the

With Alix Elias in *What Is Making Gilda So Gray?*, a two-person comedy written and directed by Tom Eyen and presented for two weeks at the Village Gate, New York, 1974. Photo by Zarko Kalmic.

Warwick telephone book and found a doctor fairly close to the house. I dropped Blue off as soon as we got to town.

I never saw Blue again. The doc called in the morning and said, "Your animal didn't make it. Sorry." Bang went the phone. Of course, I was a wreck. I couldn't stop crying. When I called Alan, he was almost as blunt as the doctor. He had a house full of cats. He kept trying to tell me about some new gig he'd lined up for me. I kept bawling. He kept yelling at me to pay attention. I finally got the gist of what he was saying.

He'd booked me for a run at a popular cabaret called Brothers and Sisters on West 46th Street. December 8-18, 1975. That was less than a month away.

"Are you listening to me, Carp? You can stay with me here for a couple of days. I need you to do some interviews and stuff. Okay?"

"Yeah, yeah. I got a commercial to do down there anyway."

"Good! I'll see ya. Oh, call your buddy Wallowitch and see if he'll play the date with you." John Wallowitch was a bespectacled, bald, professorial but wickedly smart and funny cabaret composer and pianist.

Above: At the New York premiere of *That's Entertainment!* with (L-R) June Allyson, Margaret O'Brien and Kay Armen; Ziegfeld Theatre, 1974.

Right: The publicity shot for my 1975 engagement at Brothers and Sisters, New York. Photo by Marc Raboy.

"Uh-huh," I said. I hung up, blew my nose and tried like hell not to cry.

It turned out that the doctor I took dear Blue to was listed as Animal Doctor. I should have asked what kind. Horse, pig, cow, you name it. Not dog or cat, that's for sure. And I was no saloon singer. Cabaret? I didn't even know how to spell it. Well, a gig's a gig."

Soon I was in New York with Alan and an interviewer. Alan beamed and smiled with more than his usual charm. That's a huge heap of charm. He was rattling on about my movies, my books, my voice. He never mentioned the other fellow's name. He seemed like a nice-enough guy. I figured he must have known something about me or he wouldn't have come out to interview me.

Alan finally paused to catch his breath, and the nice guy said, "How do you feel about Brothers and Sisters?" He was looking at me with a pleasant smile.

There was dead silence for about a full minute.

"Well," I said, "I honestly don't know why anybody would want to spend money to listen to a fifty-year old fruitfly singing 'Shine On, Harvest Moon,' sitting on a stool!"

The nice man shook with laughter.

Alan screamed: "You can't say something like that!" He was furious. "Why not?" said the nice guy, grabbing my hand and shaking it. "Great to hear a smidge of honesty. Good for you."

Here endeth the lesson.

*   *   *

I can't remember the product, but I sure remember the outcome of one commercial gig. I was in a small studio and there was a tight shot on my face. As soon as I mentioned the product's name, I was supposed to slip off the stool, disappearing from view. I followed directions.

"Perfect!" the director shouted. "Ouuchh," I yelled. I'd dropped full weight on my right foot or ankle. My shoe got caught up on some wires and I'd twisted it when my butt hit the floor. It felt like I'd busted something.

Getting back up to Warwick was not fun. I'd bought a cane after the incident and tried to keep the weight off my foot. The doctor thought my foot wasn't broken, but he bound it up carefully with some stretchy material and said to keep off of it as much as I could. When I told the doc I was opening in three days in New York, he said, "Then you'll need these, too."

He handed me a pair of crutches. "Take good care of them and they'll take good care of you." He looked and sounded like a Norman Rockwell *Saturday Evening Post* cover.

I stayed at the Hotel Edison on 46th. Just a simple, gimpy block's walk from Brothers and Sisters. Opening night was sold out. No surprise. The posters for the gig read, "Carleton Carpenter Brought Back Alive." I crutched down the center aisle to applause and laughter; most people thought it was a gag.

"John Wallowich," I said, introducing him. He gave me a hand getting up to the stool. I parked the crutches against the wall and we went directly into the opening song. I never said anything about the foot. I never said anything. I simply sang. Wallowitch could make anyone sound great. Business was okay through the 18th, but not boffo. A few days after closing, I had a long conversation with a bright old friend, Tracy Quinn. He convinced me to add some of my offbeat remarks at spots in the show; he said audiences would be interested in what I had to say as well as sing. He made a wonderful suggestion about maybe including something from *Hello, Dolly!* I agreed, and told him that the scene that takes place in court would be perfect, and would lead into "It Only Takes a Moment." I could picture Wallowitch (in the part of the judge) throwing me the cue. Tracy and I had a great afternoon together, and I could hardly wait for the foot to heal so I could get back to fixing the act.

I stayed in Manhattan for a while. One morning I was having coffee at a shop on Eighth Avenue. A young kid came over to me and asked, very politely, if I would do him a favor. He was a fan, a sweet, gentle one, with a slightly odd way of speaking. I said I would if I could. He wanted me to sign something he had at home. I told him to bring it tomorrow at this same time and I'd be happy to sign it.

He returned the next day with a record—either the RCA Red Seal LP of *Lady in the Dark* or "Aba Daba." I signed it for him. He kept smiling, and we talked for a while. He was mad for Broadway shows and anything to do with theater. Over the next week or two, he showed up at the coffee shop and we'd talk and laugh. His name was Kevin Brofsky. He was such a happy person, and I was always glad to see him. He told me he longed to be a writer. One day he brought a couple of pages of a play he was working on. It was about a young couple who marry and move to Queens to run a deli. They're poor and have to rent a place. The play spans a period of forty years, with the couple hoping all that time to finally own their own building. It never happens.

I was intrigued, and told him it might make a good musical. Kevin nearly jumped out of his skin. "Would you ... could you maybe help me?" I laughed. I couldn't help but say, "Maybe. We'll see." He literally jumped up and down. I told him I would be leaving town for a tour with Nanette Fabray the next week. But his idea about a striving couple had struck a chord. In a couple of weeks, the doctor in Warwick unwrapped the foot and pronounced it A-okay. "Just don't start doing Ray Bolger-type splits!" he warned. He was a hoot.

I returned to New York and to John Wallowitch. We kept most of the numbers, but added a couple of songs I'd written, along with "Row, Row, Row" and "Aba Daba Honeymoon," which I'd avoided at Brothers and Sisters. He loved the *Dolly* bit. I was anxious to try everything out. John was busy for the next month, but thereafter he'd be mine again.

Overeager to test the new act, I booked a gig in a huge room in Albany with a pianist I didn't know. I helped to fill it by sending word to dozens of cousins, aunts, uncles and other family members spread across the region. We were jammed. The kid at the keyboard was less than okay, but I laughed a lot, gabbed a lot and everybody had a good time.

Once more I went back to Manhattan, where I managed to get shots at three more clubs, smaller and not well known, that were hidden in the Village. It was like being on the road with a play, and it kept me busy until Wallowitch was free for our biggest and best engagement yet: a week at the hottest cabaret at that time, Reno Sweeney, on West 13th Street.

Alan had worked out an interesting arrangement: I did the early shows and Geraldine Fitzgerald, another client of his, performed at midnight. I got rave reviews. The *New York Times* one was the best. Alan was finally happy with me.

Soon I was on the road with Nanette Fabray. Her show was called *Oscar Ladies*. Nanette had commissioned it, and she toured it often. It consisted of three short two-person plays. In the middle she played opposite an old actor friend. The first and third were allotted to me. She directed me as to exactly how she wanted me to play both gents, who were very different types.

We toured a group of dinner theaters in central Ohio. Dinner theater was very popular then. Typically, the audience was all around you. I'd never played them before, but I quickly learned how to keep moving and block out as few diners as possible. During that time, a call came from John Kenley, the foremost theatrical impresario in Ohio. His "Kenley Players," as he called them, had included countless stars who toured the state in his productions, playing the theaters he owned. He wanted me to come up to one of them in northern Ohio. He said he had a business deal to discuss.

This was the first time I'd met him. Kenley was wild as a teenager and old and wise as the hills. He wanted to hire me to assist him with a new revue: write, rewrite, make suggestions, whatever. The money was great and the fun began to roll after I'd finished my gig with Fabray and moved up to his theater. The finished product was called *Greenwich Village Scandals of 1923*. The cast included Cyd Charisse, Rip Taylor, Imogene Coca, Phil Ford, Lee Meredith and me. We toured the Kenley Players circuit for most of the season. I loved doing sketches with Imogene. What an incredible talent!

I had hardly settled in back in Warwick when I got a four-month booking—March through June of 1982—at the Goodspeed Opera House in East Haddam, Connecticut. Once more I'd be appearing in *Lock Up Your Daughters*—but this time I had Cyril Ritchard's role, Justice Squeezum, the lead. Before I left, I needed a couple of weeks to have an old rupture sewn up. I went to our small hospital in Warwick. I saw one of its two surgeons, Dr. Momin. I stripped off my trousers, and his face brightened as he looked at the scar on my stomach. "Forty-eight street hospital," he said, to my amazement. He then proceeded to name the doctor who'd performed the surgery on me in 1949. I was dumbfounded. He must have been a student studying at that hospital all those years ago.

"Well, Doctor," I said as he was running his finger over the long scar, "You've won the hernia gig!"

"I remember you were an actor," he said, smiling. "Were you auditioning me?"

"Well, there was another surgeon there besides you. It was my great luck I picked you. I can hardly believe it."

Doc Momin became my physician and friend for the rest of his life. When he passed, he was head surgeon at a much bigger Warwick Hospital and beloved by everyone. I still miss him and his wife and kids.

* * *

For me, the Goodspeed Opera House was something magical to behold. Sitting on the bank of the Connecticut River, it seemed to call out: "Come in, come in, you'll love this wonderful theater! Hurry in. We're here to entertain and enchant you!"

Sounds a bit much, huh? Well, that's the way I felt about it. Read on. I'll calm down in a while.

An enthusiastic lady greeted me and took me to the big old house where I'd be living for the next four months. It had a piano and a kingsize bed. I was all set. I unpacked the electric frying pan and eating utensils with which I traveled to gigs. On the road I like to cook in whenever possible.

Since, in my eagerness, I'd arrived way early, I'd meet the rest of the cast a couple of hours later at the theater. I tried the piano and got a huge surprise: It was in tune. I sprawled on the bed and read over the mass of papers and songs I'd been working on. I had written some songs for Kevin Brofsky, the aspiring young playwright whom I'd befriended in the Eighth Avenue diner. I had called and sung them to him. He was thrilled.

Kevin had been calling our show *Northern Boulevard*. I figured I could get a lot of work done in my four months at Goodspeed, and I began right then to do a bit of rewriting.

The next thing I knew, I heard a voice: "Hey Carpenter! Where are you? Everybody's waiting for you!" I'd drifted off. "Right there," I yelled.

At a sing-through, everyone in the cast was super—a great cluster of wonderful voices. The guy at the piano was like a magician at the keyboard, and nice away from the keys, too. He looked maybe twelve. His name was Glen Kelly, and he went on to become one of the most sought-after musical arrangers on Broadway. (His credits include *Beauty and the Beast*, *Spamalot*, *The Drowsy Chaperone*, and *The Book of Mormon*.) During our run at Goodspeed he took the time to help me with my music for *Northern Boulevard*, bringing over singers he felt were right for my score. I ended up with some really great demos on my tape recorder. What a sweetheart!

Since we played only an early matinee on Sunday and didn't perform again until Monday night, I drove home almost every other week to check up on my house in Warwick. It was only a two-and-a-half or three-hour trip, and it felt nice to sleep in my own bed on Sunday nights. But one Monday morning I awoke to see about four inches of snow outside, and more coming down. This was late *May*, for heaven's sake! I got in the Bug early and headed back to work slowly and carefully. Traffic was all over the place. I edged along almost inch by inch.

I had arrived at the theater by six-thirty p.m., very pleased with myself. I'd made it in time for the show, even though it was still coming down.

Then one of the kids came over to my place and said, with a happy grin, that for the first time ever they were canceling that night's performance! We bought a couple or more six-packs of Bud and had a great evening playing charades.

Sometime after midnight, the snow decided we'd had enough of it. We'd also had enough of charades. We called it a happy goodnight, and everyone scattered to their various domains. The next night's performance was fantastic. So was the rest of the run.

All the while, I could hardly wait to see what Kevin had been doing with his script. We'd been in touch only by phone for nearly a half a year. He was pleased with the songs I'd only sung to him in snaches. We both loved the demos, so wonderfully sung and played by the talents at Goodspeed.

But my first duty was to my publisher, Curtis Books. My latest novels needed plugging. We turned to Joe Franklin, with his invaluable late-night TV talk show. He'd promoted my first three books relentlessly, bless him. Alan Eichler called him the minute I was back and got me rebooked. I had been asked to join the Mystery Writers of America, and soon I found myself elected to treasurer of the board. Mary Higgins Clark was president. Dear Higgy-baby is still hitting homers with every new novel.

Those were fun years. I met so many terrific authors at the annual awards dinner. I had the honor for many years of presenting the best Movie Mystery Script.

Once more, gigs piled up. The Dramatists Guild of America asked me to direct and star in *The Rainmaker*—in South Dakota, in the dead of winter. Well, I love that play and had done it several times, so I said sure. They had rounded up a pretty good cast and were eager for direction. The gal who played the spinster farm woman Lizzie was very much a plain Jane. But in the barn scene, when she succumbs to a smooth-talking con man, she became truly beautiful. It was amazing. For me that scene alone was worth the long trip and the high snow drifts between theater and hotel. I directed other productions of *The Rainmaker*, but I never saw another Lizzie like the one in South Dakota.

Finally *Northern Boulevard* was complete. Kevin and I made twenty copies of the script, complete with his book and my music and lyrics, all bound in a bright red cover. I gathered some performer friends to record the demo. Bobo Lewis "sang-acted" the part of the mother; Steve Ross, the wonderful cabaret singer-pianist, had recommended a student of his who he thought would be just right to sing another song, and she was. John Wallowitch and I filled in the rest.

It dawned on me that maybe I should call Rosetta LeNoire, the great black actress, who had been on and off Broadway since 1939. I didn't know her, but I knew she ran the AMAS Repertory Theatre Company in Spanish Harlem and that it specialized in multi-racial casting. The four or five landladies in the story might tickle her fancy, I thought. At the time Ms. LeNoire was on Broadway in a revival of Moss Hart and George S. Kaufman's *You Can't Take It with You*. I left a script for her at the theater.

She was on the phone to me the following day. Not only did she love the book and songs, she said, but she wanted to be the show! She would produce the thing and, for the first time ever, act in one of her productions. Rosetta wanted to play all the landladies using various accents. What a great gimmick! We'd never thought of it.

But this was the mid-'80s, and Rosetta was quite an in-demand actress. She was missing a lot of rehearsal time as she flew back and forth between the coasts. My friend Shepard Coleman, who had won a Tony for his vocal arrangements in *Hello, Dolly!*, had helped me find a bright young guy to lead at the piano, as well as a drummer and a reed player. I called up Dennis Dennehy, who with his wife Margie had cofounded the highly respected Dennehy School of Irish Dance, to do the choreography for four male and four female dancers; it would help define the changes in what was hot over forty years. The actors were as good as we could get for off-Broadway. What little set we had worked well, and the guy who did the lights was a genius. Rosetta ended up playing just the last landlady. (We hired two gals to play the others.) She got to do the showstopping number in the tag of the show.

Opening night was great. Kevin's mom and my Dar met and were thrilled with their sons. *Northern Boulevard* got more newspaper coverage than I'd expected, and it was kinder than we really deserved. The *New York Times* said that the score was "in the mode of Irving Berlin and Jerry Herman." I couldn't knock that company. And there were kind words for William Martin's direction. *Northern Boulevard* had its four-week run, and we were happy to get on with something new.

In my case, I got on with something old, when I joined the cast of a revival of the Rodgers & Hart musical *Babes in Arms* at the music Hall in Tarrytown. At the age of seventy-four, Ginger Rogers was making her debut as a director. But the very talented choreographer Randy Skinner did most of the actual direction, as well as staging the great dances. The best thing about the experience, for me, was meeting the show's young costar,

Karen Ziemba, and falling in love with her and her singing. In a few years I'd be on the road with her.

But first I had a few shows to do in Manhattan. The Jewish Repertory Theatre in New York staged a revival of Moss Hart's *Light Up the Sky*, a backstage comedy I'd done in summer stock years before. Now, instead of playing the show's young, idealistic playwright, I played the weepy director whose hotly anticipated smash is a bomb. The company was strong; it included the character actor Stephen Pearlman, an original member of the Second City comedy troupe in Chicago. The play opened with my recording of a sweet song about actors; I'd written it for the occasion.

When *Light Up the Sky* closed I moved down to the East Village to appear along with Quentin Crisp in *Murder at Rutherford House*. It was a whodunit in which viewers voted on who they thought the killer was. Months later, I got a call from Tom Chiodo and Peter DePietro, the show's writers. They were taking their play to Singapore and needed a "name." So I got a two-week working vacation and good pay.

After I'd returned, I got a call from Patrick O'Connor. He told me that CBS was closing out its literary branch. No surprise there. We had both seen it coming long before. What that wonderful guy did was incredible. He signed the rights for all my books over to me. That's how my own company, Black Walnut Books, was born.

I had started a new mystery not more than two weeks earlier, a story based on a theater like Goodspeed. Hell, it *was* Goodspeed; I just gave it a new name. I loved the theater, the river, all the wonderful people that worked there, the whole staff and local helpers and cast. Everything was so perfect, so clean and neat and proper. It was maybe the best four-month gig I ever had. In my story I turned it all upside-down and inside-out, making it the opposite of decent. What fun!

By the time I had finished the new book, Black Walnut was going strong, I called my new novel *The Peabody Experience*. I had discarded the old gothic theme—that wasn't so popular anymore—and put my own name on it, although I sort of missed my former nom de plume of Ivy Manchester. The book's title became *Stumped*. Soon I had new paperback editions of all seven of my books, with good paper that didn't turn yellow and crumbly after a few readings. And a new price: $3.25 a copy. They took off, selling very well for the first couple of years.

I'd been driving my pick-up down to the city, giving personal deliveries. But shops devoted to mysteries began closing up. Regular bookshops started closing as well. Then, horrors of horrors, the distributors folded.

All those thousands of copies of my mysteries landed at my driveway in Warwick. Thirty or more heavy boxes with God-knows how many books in each box. Two delivery men and yours truly lugged all those mysteries up my hill, down a lot of stairs and into (thank heavens) my giant basement. Over time they've thinned out a bit but there are still a lot. I'm perspiring as I type this. So let's move on.

Chapter 19

I was home in Warwick, and the phone rang. It was my old agent Bill Schill, who hated work as much as I adored it. He commanded me to get my ass into New York the next day: "You've got an audition at one-thirty!"

"Where do they want me and what's the gig?"

"It's at the Shubert. At one-thirty!" You already told me the time, I thought.

"What's the show?

"It's called *Crazy for You*. I think it's an all-Gershwin score."

After a lovely bath in my big tub and a long night's happy sleep, I was ready to get back into the ring and fight the battle of all auditioners. The Bug and I headed south again.

I auditioned for the part of Mr. Walker, the leading lady's father. It's nice typing that word, father. I'd played younger than I was for too long. I'd been aching to play older guys. I sang my audition song, probably "I Love a Piano." I got a callback for the following day at four. It went well. I was told I'd hear from them.

I waited and waited. Finally I decided I hadn't won the role. Then I got the word that they had two of us on their minds, and I'd know in a few days who was in.

It turned out to be the other guy, but they said the road company gig would be mine. That turned out to be terrific for me. I'll tell you why later.

Crazy for You opened on Broadway in February 1992. It earned nine Tony nominations and three wins, for Best Musical, Best Choreography (Susan Stroman), and Best Costume Design (William Ivey Long). Almost immediately, the producers launched a road company with me in it. On the first day of rehearsal, Susan asked me if I'd mind doing a bit of dancing. I was thrilled. She kept adding bits for me as we went along, including

285

a section of "I Got Rhythm," to be performed with my "daughter," Karen Ziemba, at the end of Act I. I was in Seventh Heaven.

Because of Susan, I ended up with a wonderful part to play. When we opened in Dallas, I was applauded on my first entrance. The same thing happened at every performance for the next two years. Then came the crowning thrill. I got a call on the road from Ronn Carroll, who was played Mr. Walker in the Broadway production. Ronn was leaving to appear in a new play. "They're bringing you to New York," he said. They called. I went.

For the first five weeks I did the role as Ronn had. Then Karen joined the New York company, and Stro put back all of my stage business from the road version. The cast loved it. A couple of fun facts: I opened at the Shubert on March 2, 1994, exactly fifty years after the opening night of my Broadway debut in *Bright Boy*. I had a quiet drink at Sardi's in celebration, alone. On July 10, my birthday, Vincent Sardi threw a party for me and the cast and dozens of others on the second floor. There was music, food, and a presentation of my caricature, which still hangs on the wall there today.

A wild thing happened during the run. Several guys wanted to play my part. Roger Horchow, the main producer, won out. When I went on a two-week vacation, he invited a batch of critics to see him. Oops! The press screamed, "Bring back Carleton Carpenter!" He did the part for one week, having the time of his life. Then, cutting my vacation short, I came home to the role—and got an extra three weeks' pay as a bonus. Roger was a sweet guy, but not too hot an actor.

After the show had finally closed, Ziemba and I looked forward to reprising our roles in a revival at the Paper Mill Playhouse. PBS had made plans to tape and broadcast it. But by the time the Paper Mill version was set to open, Karen had signed on for four months of *Chicago* at the Shubert, and I was in San José, appearing in a revue called *Legacy*. We both love working steadily. But you knew that already.

When *Legacy* closed I did join the Paper Mill company for a few one-week tour dates, starting in Atlanta. But my knees were getting very sore, and I interrupted my touring to return to Warwick. I asked a neighbor if she could suggest a good knee specialist. She gave me the name of a doctor I knew, Martin Alchek. "He's a wonderful orthopedic surgeon," she said.

Off I went to his office in Middletown, New York. He was happy to see me, and sat me up on a high bed. I told him my knees were killing me. He sent me into the next room to have some X-rays taken.

Back in the doctor's office, I watched as he shoved a couple of shots up on his wall and stood back. "Look at these," he said. "Those are your knees, and they're not not your problem. Of course you are probably aware that your skinny body is jam-packed with arthritis." I smiled. That I certainly knew.

He pulled the knee X-rays down and pushed up the two others. "Those are your hips," he said. I saw big black holes.

"Where are they?"

"That's your problem. They aren't there." All my dancing in *Crazy for You* had destroyed them. I needed new ones.

I was shown an instructional tape that pointed out all the things that can go wrong in this procedure, including death. I signed a consent form, set the date, thanked Dr. Alchek, and asked him to give my love to his wife. He had two sons. One was the official doctor for the New York Mets; the other was also a doctor.

I started with one hip replacement. Eight weeks later, I had the other hip done. So as not to waste any time in between, I worked piano gigs (seated on a pillow) at the Landmark Inn in Warwick and at the West Town Inn in—you got it—West Town, New York.

Obviously, taking it easy isn't easy for me. I had barely mended from the second hip replacement when the phone rang. "What do you know about Athol Fugard?" said an unfamiliar voice.

"Who's this?"

"Tom Ehas." An unfamiliar name. "I'm directing a play of his," he said, "and I want you in it."

"Is it *The Road to Mecca*?" I asked.

"Good guess. It is. You know it?"

"I've read it. It's a mother-grabber!" The one male character, Marius Byleveld, is a pastor who tries to convince a frail, elderly artist, Helen Martins, to move into his church's rest home. "He never shuts up," I told Tom Ehas.

"Only in Act Two," he said.

"That's the one he's in."

Tom laughed. "It's for Creative Theatre Group," he explained, "at the Paramount Theatre in Middletown. Are you available, or will you be in a couple of weeks or so? I haven't cast the two ladies yet."

I paused, smiling to myself. "Well?" he said.

"Okay, uh, what's your name again?"

"Tom."

"Okay, Tom. Can't say no."

Now (happily), I was in for a ton of work. So much dialogue to learn, such a challenge to master the South African dialect needed for it. All the while, I knew it wasn't an equity job. That meant no pay. Only three performances, two on a Saturday and a matinee on Sunday.

But the joy for me was in the work. I loved it. The tougher, the better. And my legs were becoming stronger all the time. No gimpy walk. Onstage, the two ladies played along with me in close harmony. Great gig.

*   *   *

I returned to a Monday-night piano spot I'd held for years, even when I was in a show. The place was Ten Railroad Avenue, a restaurant in Warwick. It was easy and fun to play there—except for the New Year's Eve when they hired a bass player from the city to accompany me. It was expensive, but I thought it would be great having someone to thump along with me. I was dressed for the occasion with tux and all the trimmings, and topped off—or rather, bottomed off—with my famous saddle shoes. Everybody got a kick out of that. Unfortunately the bassist wore a sport shirt, untucked. And he didn't know any of the old standards and show tunes I was playing. He disappeared on a smoking break. As midnight arrived, he was nowhere to be found. No one, especially me, missed him or cared. I was happy to sing out the old and embrace the new.

One Monday morning I awoke to find that my entire left arm was three or four times its regular size. It didn't hurt, but naturally I was concerned. My wonderful Dr. Momin had passed away, so a friend gave me his doctor's name and address. I drove my pickup over to his office. A gal there said he was on vacation, but she called the Warwick Hospital and told them to expect me.

As I lay in bed, a procession of medical "experts" filed in and out. I kept telling them I had to be in Vermont a week from tomorrow. I had to start rehearsals for a new musical based on the Mark Twain story "The Man That Corrupted Hadleyburg." I'd heard a run-thru a few weeks ago. This was at the wonderful Oldcastle Theatre Company in Bennington. I'd been doing shows with them for several years. It was an Equity company, so we always had professional cast, and consequently we received mostly glowing receptions from the press in New York State and Massachusetts. My work at the Oldcastle was a homecoming.

But the parade of doctors didn't seem impressed. Finally a dear one came to my bed and said: "It's Lyme disease. We'll fix you up, but you're not going to any rehearsal next week. Or the week after."

This gentle gent, Mayank Shah, became my doctor. He still is. As for Oldcastle, I was back in a show there in less than a month. For over twenty years I'd been doing plays at least once or twice a season (sometimes as many as five). I won't go into all of them now, but later I'll include a list of the titles. You'll be surprised at the number of shows I fitted into my schedule while doing TV, commercials, and one-nighters.

In 2009 I got a call from Scott Siegel, a concert and cabaret producer from New York. He was presenting a three-day series of shows called the Broadway Cabaret Festival at Town Hall, the enormous theater on 43rd Street. He wanted me for a show of songs from musicals produced by David Merrick, and asked if I would stop by to set a key for whatever number I cared to do. I said I could get there the following day if that would be okay. Of course, he said.

I took the bus down on a pouring, windy day. Umbrella in hand, I met him at the theater, and we headed off to a rehearsal space. We walked three blocks up Sixth Avenue with me holding the umbrella over both of us. He was quite short. We arrived at a building and walked up three flights to a tiny room. A nice guy sat at the keyboard. We found the key for "It Only Takes a Moment." I asked if I could use a stool, and Mr. Siegel said yes, of course.

A second rehearsal was scheduled for a Saturday; the Merrick show was on Sunday—I thought. I arrived in New York on Friday night, having made plans to sleep at a friend's house. Soon I learned that the show was on Saturday night. I was wearing an old shirt and pants that had seen way too much wear. There was no time to go back home and change. I told Siegel, "What you see is what you get." He didn't seem to care.

When I showed up for the rehearsal, Siegel handed me a long sheet of paper containing the intro he planned to give me. I read it through. It was very long, practically my life story. I asked if he could just introduce me, then I would come on and explain how Merrick and I had met. He agreed. I was assigned a dressing room two floors up with eight other guys, all big Broadway names. They all seemed to know one another, and chatted and joked and, thank God, ignored me. I huddled up in a far corner and listened to them all. I learned that up one more flight you could watch the stage from an unseen spot. I wasn't in Act I, and I took advantage of that spot while most of them were down in the wings, watching or waiting.

There was a huge orchestra and about two dozen dancing gals and guys. The place was jammed to the brim. Suddenly, it seemed, Act Two was going strong. I was in the wing at stage left. I heard my name, and I was on.

A stool awaited with a mic sitting on it. I pulled the stool farther downstage and sat on it. Then I told everyone about how, in a 1944 Broadway show called *Bright Boy*, coproducer Merrick—a young lawyer from St. Louis—and a seventeen-year-old kid from Vermont met and fell in love (I paused) with the theater. I glanced over at the wonderful piano player and quietly sang "It Only Takes A Moment." It's a short number with no repeat, so when I got to the last phrase, "a whole life long," I dropped my chin down and then there was this terrible loud noise. It scared me, and I quickly put back the stool, left the mic on it and ran off stage. I had never heard such a noise in my life. It just would not stop. Across the stage cast members were cheering, too. I was pushed back on by the people at stage left—twice. Siegel called me back one last time.

I guess you could truly say I stopped the show. Well, I slowed it down for a while, anyway.

After the show, everyone in the cast was called downstairs. Siegel said loudly, "Anyone not going to the party, pick up your check." Not only did I not know about a party, I didn't realize I was getting paid. I grabbed my jacket from the upstairs dressing room. People from the audience were breaking through to get to the actors. I pushed my way out into the alley and raced to catch the eleven o'clock bus back to Warwick.

* * *

My reaction to the Town Hall show calls for some self-reflection. I raced away from the theater as soon as my work was done. That's typical of me. After every performance in a long-running show, I'm out of makeup and out the stage door so fast I could be one of the stagehands.

I am not a celebrity. I am not famous. I'm unable to be that. It's not in my bones. I'm a professional and love to work. That's my joy. I can't hang around with the other actors in the theater crowd—unless it's opening night, when I'm expected to show up at a cast party after the show. That's part of my work. So I go. Then I split as soon as I can. I've never learned the games other actors seem to play, climbing up some invisible ladder, higher and higher toward … what? Fame, maybe. If I tried that I'd slip off the first rung.

Enough analysis. You must know me by now. Maybe even better than I. Cary Grant, anyone?

Okay, okay. On September 2, 2012, I did receive a Career Achievement Award at Cinecon 48, the 48th annual five-day celebration held by Cinecon (originally the Society for Cinephiles). It takes place in Hollywood, and I must admit I had a fun time. What made it extra-special was the appearance of my old "Aba Daba" partner, Debbie Reynolds. That was a surprise! She presented my award to me during the closing Sunday-night gala. It now sits on the shelf over the fireplace here in Warwick.

Not all of my recent surprises have been so pleasant. In 2009, not too long after I'd acquired my new hips, I had a routine exam for prostate cancer. I know, I know—here we go with another story about a hospital visit. Sorry about that, but I'm awfully glad I made this one. The test came back positive. Luckily it was caught at the very beginning, and the doctor began a series of treatments. They weren't helping, and after several weeks I was referred to a hospital in Middletown. Two very nice doctors decided upon radiation. I was put on a bed that had a clay-like mattress. Above me were camera-like instruments that were concentrated on the area in question. Afterward I was lifted carefully off the mold I'd made and cleaned up. Throughout all this, both doctors kept smiling and comforting me. They assured me that everything was going to be fine.

I was told to return at a certain time every day except Sunday for five weeks.

I'd arrive, wait my turn, and strip. They would place me carefully into that mold; then I couldn't move for a couple of minutes while the latest technology was (supposedly) killing the cancer.

I felt terrific. No pain. Then, on the fifth day of my first week, something terrible happened. I got a phone call. It was Roger Horchow, the lead producer of *Crazy for You*. Would I come join the cast of a Broadway revival of *Guys and Dolls*? The guy who was playing Arvide Abernathy, the grandfather of beautiful missionary head Sarah Brown, was leaving. The job was mine, said Roger. Just say yes. I was perfect for the part. He wished I'd been doing it all along. And I'd get to sing "More I Cannot Wish You."

It nearly killed me to tell him I couldn't. I'd lost a great gig on Broadway. *That* was pain.

I finished my weeks of radiation. Then learned I had to have an operation—a big one. They gave me a shot in the arm and told me to count backwards from a hundred. I have no idea how long I was out, but when I awoke the two doctors were standing on either side of me. I felt pain, but somewhat muted. They asked me to stay still and to try and relax for as long as I could. I asked how I'd done.

"We cleaned out the last of the cancer," said one of them. "But to ensure that you'll never have to worry again, we took out the whole kit and caboodle." I looked from one doctor to the other, trying to imagine exactly what they meant. Finally I said, "You mean I'll never be a papa?"

"You're right. You won't make babies, but you'll be alive and strong for the rest of your life, and you'll be cancer-free."

After a long pause, I asked what time it was. Just relax, they said. Dinner would be sent up to me. I asked when I could go home. In a couple of days, they said. They would both see me later.

Now I was alone with my thoughts. The first thing that sprang to mind was a song I had heard years ago at a supper club in the Village. It was called "Unique Martin from Martinique." I started to laugh, thinking how funny it would be if I altered it just a bit now to suit me after my operation. I could be "Eunuch Martin From Martinque!"

I giggled myself into a nap. When a nurse woke me up with a tray of dinner, she said, "What are you smiling about?" I thanked her for bringing the food, and told her I had just remembered an old joke.

So that's how my sex life ended. With a smile. I had certainly enjoyed every bit of it while my equipment was still in place.

* * *

Long ago in California, I met the playwright Ernest Thompson at CBS. He told me I should do a play of his, *On Golden Pond*. It's about an elderly couple who spend every summer of their later years in a home on a lake. *On Golden Pond* ran on Broadway in 1979, but it was much more successful on the screen, when Henry Fonda and Katharine Hepburn played the couple and Jane Fonda was their daughter.

After our initial meeting, Ernest and I kept running into each other in New York, usually backstage at a theater as we waited to see someone after a show. We'd end up walking together a couple of blocks and he'd say "When are you going to do my play?" He didn't have to sell me on the idea. I would have loved to play that role.

In 2007, when I was eighty, the Oldcastle Theatre Company told me they were doing *Pond*. They wanted me for the Fonda role. I was thrilled. Eighty was the age of Norman, my character. I had been playing younger for what seemed like forever. I was so happy doing the rehearsals. I loved the role and the gal who played my wife, the wonderful Sheila Childs. I got so carried away with the joy of playing someone my own age, I forgot my birthday. But the cast and producer didn't. Three days later, on July 13, we opened. I'd turned eighty-one. So in a way, I was still playing younger.

Thompson showed up that night, as he often did wherever his play opened.

It went well, and the audience was huge. Ernest came up on stage, hugged me, and whispered in my ear, "You'll get even better." I did. Audiences flowed in for the entire run. We broke all attendance records at Oldcastle.

Chapter 20 ─────────────

E ven at my very ripe old age I still take care of myself, cook, clean, drive, shop and root for my Mets. I see Dr. Shah every three months and have my teeth scrubbed every six. I really love living alone. But I'm not a loner. I have so many friends and great neighbors. I love visiting and having people in.

The *New York Times* is delivered every day around six a.m. It's wrapped to protect it from the weather. I'm an early riser, so I most often go down the driveway (which is shaped like a 9, as I mentioned) and fetch it by six-thirty. I make breakfast and read the paper happily to start my day. Well, I haven't been so happy lately with the obits. So many friends I knew, loved and worked with have passed.

In April 2015 I lost my darling Julie Wilson, whom I had met in 1946. She joined *Three to Make Ready* when Meg Mundy left, and for one fun number she became my dancing partner. Meg was a tiny thing; Julie was a statuesque beauty. I'd remind her to please bend her knees a bit before I heisted her up to my shoulder. We'd both giggle. She was anything but heavy.

Soon after she'd arrived, Julie and I both left to do the show in Chicago. We stayed close buddies, and for years saw each other frequently in New York. In December 2014, I was in the city to see the singer Richard Hol-brook at Don't Tell Mama, a cabaret on 46th Street. Richard has been sing-ing my song "Christmas Eve" beautifully for five or six years now. I went to another cabaret, 54 Below, to see Marilyn Maye. I was by myself. Marilyn introduced a couple of other guests. One was Julie. I turned to where Maye had pointed. Julie was waving for me to come to her booth in the back. I raced over and she grabbed me in an embrace with lips locked. As always, we were so happy to see each other that we had tears running down our cheeks. She was holding me tightly with both arms from across her booth. What a welcome!

When your caricature is on the wall of Sardi's, you've really made it.

I did *Love Letters* at Oldcastle with Betsy Palmer, and it was a honey. She was pure experience onstage. She had done that A.R. Gurney play with dozens of other guys but there was something special about our outing. We'd never met before, and I think I surprised her when we first ran through it in rehearsal. At the end of the engagement, she hugged me and said she thought I was the absolute best ever. Maybe she had said that to all the others, but I didn't mind. We were special together. Betsy left us in 2015 at the age of eighty-nine.

Then there was Ronnie Gilbert, the gal in the Weavers. Ronnie and I met in 1999, late in her career, at the San José Repertory Theater. I was there for a four-month run in the revue *Legacy*. The show was based on Studs Terkel's *Coming of Age*, a volume of interviews with activist elders, mostly of the Weavers' era. Ronnie had written the lyrics and coauthored the book with the playwright Jon Marans.

There were five of us in the cast: Yolande Bavan, Joan Roberts, David Rogers, Ronnie, and me. We all played many different roles and sexes. It was great fun portraying all those odd people, singing, dancing, emoting. The five of us spent worked, ate, and played together, but I was the tightest with Ronnie. It turned out that she was a fan of mine, and I most certainly became an instant admiring fan of hers. We did everything together except sleep. Those were four wonderful months.

Ronnie died in 2015 at eighty-eight.

I first met Monica Lewis when I arrived at MGM. That beautiful, dimpled gal was so well-known as the voice of Chiquita Banana, but she also had a glorious singing voice. We got to know each other when we went upstate during the Korean War to perform for the young guys in the hospital. Those young kids were fresh from the front with too many wounds. Monica and I would go up most Sundays (our only day off from the studio) and talk to the guys in the ward, then give them a full show in the evening. Monica was always such a hit. We'd hang out together at the studio from time to time, and when I got permission from MGM to do a play in Laguna, I asked Monica to join me. She'd never done a stage play before, but she eagerly agreed. We went to a playhouse and did a comedy called *Remains to Be Seen* for a couple of weeks. God, I miss her. She too passed away in 2015. Monica was 93.

* * *

Since enlisting in the U.S. Navy at seventeen, I've lived happily alone. Back in my earlier years, my old buddy Shel would pop in on me whenever he was in the city. I always enjoyed that, but he returned to Chicago ages ago and has been married for years. We stay in touch by phone a couple of times a year.

Having lived in so many apartments and houses, how good it feels to have a home! Even though I'm away from it for long stretches to work, knowing that my woods await me is so comforting. Even at my very ripe old age I love doing things for others and taking care of stuff here at home. Fixing things that get broken, keeping the grounds in good shape. I planted the lawn and nursed it along until it was green. I loved mowing it for years—

then my hips were done. Now Chris, a dear guy, takes care of it for me and for a ton of other customers. He started with me when he was in high school. He's married now with two kids. He has a night job as well with UPS.

Here in Warwick, we're in the thrall of the wonderful, huge Albert Wisner Public Library. In 2014, I got a call from a staff member. The library would be showing *Two Weeks with Love* the following Monday at one p.m. Could I possibly attend and talk to the audience after? I told her I'd be delighted. It would be fun for the mostly older bunch, myself included. I explained to the audience that the film had originally been called *The Tender Hours*—I've always thought that was such a nice title—then renamed *Kiss Me in the Catskills*, until it was finally released as *Two Weeks with Love*. They wanted to know all about "Aba Daba," of course, so I told them about the ruse I'd employed to get it in. I went on to host screenings of *Lost Boundaries*, *Sky Full of Moon*, and *Fearless Fagan*.

Fifteen years ago, when I started this thing you're reading, it was a hell of a lot easier to remember details. Friends helped by reminding me of things I'd forgotten. There are lots of appearances I've left out. A few have come to mind, notably *A Tribute to George White's Scandals* at Town Hall in 1985. I joined a fabulous cast—Terry Burrell, Peggy Cass, Connie Coit, Dolly Dawn, Mia Dillon, Katherine Kendall, Paula Laurence, Jeanne Lehman, Patrice Munsel, Marge Redmond, John Remee, Charles Repole, Randy Skinner and a bevy of dancing beauties—to perform the songs that DeSylva, Brown and Henderson had written for that legendary Broadway revue series of 1919-1939.

Then there was *Fans*, a celebration of Sally Rand's 100th birthday, done at Town Hall in 2004. Written by Deborah Grace Winer, the show was a benefit for Animal Haven, a pet adoption service. My colleagues onstage included Rex Reed, Julie Wilson, Bebe Neuwirth, Patrice Munsel and Karen Mason. Thirty or forty dancers were onstage as I sang "The Most Beautiful Dog in the World" (new lyrics by Winer) while eight pretty gals paraded across the stage with dogs on leashes.

I also loved appearing in a tribute to Woody Guthrie, the composer of "This Land Is Your Land" and countless other classic folk songs. I got to sing his last song. He had sung it just before his death into a tape recorder. It had no title. I listened to the tape and could hardly hear it; still I managed to write out a lead sheet for the music conductor. Sitting on a stool and dressed in denim and a checked shirt with a handkerchief around my neck, I was honored to sing the world premiere of a song I called "Forever."

I'll leave you with a list of some of the other plays I did for the Old-castle Theatre Company:

> *An American Daughter* (Wendy Wasserstein)
> *Spinning into Butter* (Rebecca Gilman)
> *Night and Her Stars* (Richard Greenberg)
> *Travels with My Aunt* (Giles Havergal)
> *Crossed Wires* (Jesse Kellerman)
> *You're a Good Man, Charlie Brown* (Clark Gesner)
> *Morning's at Seven* (Paul Osborn)
> *The Apple Tree* (Jerry Bock, Sheldon Harnick)
> *Alphabetical Order* (Michael Frayn)
> *The Mule and the Milky Way* (Susan Kander)
> *Your Own Thing* (Hal Hester, Danny Apolinar, Donald Driver)
> *Kiss Me, Kate* (Cole Porter, Samuel and Bella Spewack)
> … and many more.

As I close, I'm eighty-nine, and am off in two weeks for yet another gig up in Keene, New Hampshire. So long for now. Hope you had fun. I'm still having it.

Filmography

Lost Boundaries (1949)

Father of the Bride (1950)

Three Little Words (1950)

Summer Stock (1950)

Two Weeks with Love (1950)

Vengeance Valley (1951)

The Whistle at Eaton Falls (1951)

Fearless Fagan (1951)

Sky Full of Moon (1952)

Take the High Ground! (1953)

Up Periscope! (1959)

Cauliflower Cupids (1970)

Some of My Best Friends Are ... (1971)

The Prowler (1981)

The American Snitch (1983)

Acknowledgments ―――――

For a long time, no one knew I was writing an autobiography. I'd done the seven mysteries and a bunch of short pieces for the two publications edited by Eleanor Sullivan, *Ellery Queen* and *Alfred Hitchcock's Mystery Magazine*. Writing for Eleanor was fun, and she and I became close buddies. She even sneaked me onto a cover to surprise me. Great dame! A love!

Now it was just me and the Royal typewriter. Difficult. I'd get going great-guns for four or five pages, then I'd get a call for a gig. I'd replace the Royal's lid and off I'd go. That's how it went. Job. Type. Long job. Type. After months of this off-and-on typing (I can't call it writing because I was just sort of talking to the Royal and remembering and reliving stuff) I piled up eighty or ninety pages. I decided I'd better get someone to look at it.

So I drove to Florida, where my old friend Tom Hougland now lived. We'd met years ago across a contract bridge table in a semi-posh apartment building in the East 50s. In those days he worked at the *New York Times* and did book editing on the side for some well-known writers I'll not name. Tom was always very happy to see me. I visited him often in various apartments in various parts of the state. The state of Tom's health varied, too. When he and I reunited, Tom was no longer driving, and his once-strong, Ohio-bred, World War II-fit-and-fighting body had new crippling things to deal with.

But his smile and wit were intact. Our routine on visits rarely changed. He'd settle me into his other bedroom, then we'd have a drink accompanied by jokes and gossip. Then the backgammon board would appear for three or four games. He always won. He had managed to make a marvelous meal. Tom was a wonder. This time as we ate he said, "Well, are you going to have the gumption to ask me if I'll read whatever it is?"

It's scary how bright he is. Those bright eyes would be the first to see the thing. The next morning over coffee he looked at me sternly. "After you eat I'm throwing you out. Get your ass in the Ford and get home. Get it in gear, kid. You've got something terrific going and I don't want you stopping for anything. I'm hooked. Get back to it and don't let up." Tom always called me kid. Well, he was three years older. And it was all a positive rant, which I liked.

As I got into the pickup he was leaning in the doorway, beaming. "You old son of a bitch!" he said. "Call me on a break."

Alan Eichler should have been "number one" in these thank-yous. Without dear Alan there would never have been a book. He's put up with my odd ways of doing things ever since Jimmy Coco got us together ages ago. He quietly goes about his business except when he's screaming at me for okaying billing smaller than he thought I deserved. He's always right. He even tended my cats when I was on the road. I think he is the kindest human being I've ever met. Even as I wound toward the ending of the book he was pulling changes out of me over the phone. When my health was a bit off he'd buoy me up, sending notes to my tablet: "Keep the pages coming. I'm loving it!" LOL. You are so special, I flat-out love you, my darling friend.

James Gavin. Wow, how lucky can a guy get to have you handy to correct my bad typing and odd English use and to make sense of expressions known only by Vermonters and the U.S. Navy? You fix! I looked at our meetings as treats I didn't deserve. Too short and too few. I can only hope they're the beginning of a long friendship. You're such a joy to be with. Thank you for your wonderful work. You're a beautiful man and I'm thrilled you like the book.

The monkey gives the chimp-half of "Aba Daba" his thanks for her nice note. Deb, you're a doll. That was very sweet of you. Happy April 1 all year 'round.

Of course, enormous thanks go to Ben Ohmart of BearManor Media for accepting my book and allowing me to put my story out into the world.

– Carleton Carpenter, Warwick, New York, 2016

Made in the USA
Monee, IL
22 July 2025

21640499R00174